Agile Strat
for the 21st Century

Agile Strategies for the 21st Century:

The Need for Speed

By

Herbert Nold

Cambridge Scholars Publishing

Agile Strategies for the 21st Century: The Need for Speed

By Herbert Nold

This book first published 2022. The present binding first published 2022.

Cambridge Scholars Publishing

Lady Stephenson Library, Newcastle upon Tyne, NE6 2PA, UK

British Library Cataloguing in Publication Data
A catalogue record for this book is available from the British Library

ISBN (10): 1-5275-8921-8
ISBN (13): 978-1-5275-8921-6

TABLE OF CONTENTS

ACKNOWLEDGEMENTS

Few, if any, projects are successful with just one person working on them. This book is no different. I must thank my wife, Addie, for her patience and encouragement to keep me focused on the end objective. The Continuous Loop Management Model emerged from my doctoral research and was refined with reflections of my 30+ year career in business and experiences after entering academia at the relatively advanced age of 61. Dr. Kelly Conrad with the University of Phoenix, School of Advanced Studies was instrumental in encouraging me to refine my research and to publish my findings after earning a doctorate in organizational leadership. Without Dr. Conrad's encouragement and advice, none of what has happened since 2011 would have been possible. The second half of this book is dedicated to delving into the elements of the Performance Triangle which was developed and refined by my friend and colleague, Lukas Michel of Agility Insights SA. Lukas graciously supported this project and helped to edit portions to be sure that the final product properly and clearly adhered to the vision of designing agile organizations that we both share. Special thanks are extended to another friend and colleague, Dr. Johanna Anzengruber with the Upper Austria University of Applied Sciences, Linz, who was instrumental in organizing the effort to test the validity and reliability of the Performance Triangle diagnostic instrument. Without her deep knowledge of statistical methodologies and insistence on precision, we would not have been able to test the diagnostic instrument and demonstrate that it is reliable and that decisions made based on the results from the diagnostic are valid. Many thanks also go out to Barry Caponi and Bruce Wyse who kindly volunteered their time and expertise to read, edit, and offer constructive feedback to make the final product worthy of publication.

INTRODUCTION

In 1979, I entered the business world as a manufacturing engineer at Texas Instruments in Dallas, Texas, building infrared sensor systems for tanks and missiles. With a master's degree in education and six years of teaching and coaching experience, I knew absolutely nothing about manufacturing or engineering or tanks and missiles or business. My parents were both teachers and coaches, and I grew up surrounded by educators and leaders in sports. Issues related to manufacturing, engineering, or business were not topics of dinner conversation. Over the next few years, I took a few courses on manufacturing engineering so that I could do my job effectively. Along the way, I decided that I did not want to be an engineer when I grew up so I returned to school taking accounting and finance classes to qualify for the CPA exam, which I passed in 1983.

With several years of experience in manufacturing and now an educational foundation in accounting and finance, I was reassigned to the business side of running the business at TI. Here, I discovered that my experience and education combined with earlier education and experience in education working with emotionally disturbed or learning-disabled teenagers gave me a distinct advantage over anyone else in the "administrative" functions. My unique combination of experience and education in multiple settings in which problem-solving was highly valued helped me to become recognized as the primary "trouble shooter" in the business unit. One of the primary issues that hurt our business at this time was the length of time it took to make decisions and implement them.

After leaving Texas Instruments, I worked for several companies over the years in executive roles as controller or chief financial officer where I discovered and developed a talent for guiding companies through periods of rapid change. Again, I observed burdensome decision-making processes that were detrimental to these companies. Executives debated on possible decisions for so long that it was too late to either respond to an emerging threat or take advantage of an opportunity. The results were always bad for the company. I always found this behavior somewhat of a mystery after being brought up in a sports environment where the coach must evaluate and analyze a situation, make a decision, and issue commands in a space of a 60-second timeout.

In 2007, I returned to school to earn a doctorate in organizational leadership, while at the same time serving as vice-president of finance and operations at a large company. My initial academic inquiry focused on the decision-making process that had mystified me for decades. Researching the decision-making process led me to conclude that the way to accelerate the decision-making process was dependent on accelerating the rate of knowledge creation. Essentially, executives and managers had to get smarter and faster, in order to make an informed decision quickly. Three and a half years of research and study resulted in the emergence of the Continuous Loop Management Model that combines elements of Eastern culture with elements of Western culture to describe an accelerated decision-making process. The effectiveness of accelerating knowledge creation and the environment that was necessary for the model to function was demonstrated in my doctoral research. I also successfully applied these theories in practice before exiting the business world and joining academia.

Shortly after receiving my doctorate in 2011 and publishing my research in 2012, I was approached by Lukas Michel in Switzerland who had been developing a model and tool to help executives assess the ability of their organizations to adapt to change…. quickly. The key to effective management in the 21st century was to design an organization that was agile and could sense and respond to rapid changes quickly. Accelerating the decision-making process was an essential part of an agile organization. I had found a kindred spirit. It turned out that my work on knowledge creation and organizational culture helped to connect some of the dots to fill out the *Performance Triangle* and develop a diagnostic tool to evaluate underlying unseen and unspoken elements of the culture that inhibit change or agility. Years of collaboration with Lukas and other practitioners and academics in Austria and Germany resulted in work that statistically confirmed the validity and reliability of both the *Performance Triangle* model and the diagnostic instrument that Lukas had developed.

After retiring from business in 2011, after earning my doctorate, I entered academia and continued my research that was expanded to include knowledge creation, organizational culture, and now organizational agility. All were inextricably connected. I began sharing the research papers, several of which received "best paper" awards, with students. Some students actually read them. I worked these new and emerging concepts into my classes on strategy, leadership, and operations when I realized that few of the undergraduate students who read the papers could actually understand them because the published papers are intended for master's or PhD level readers. However, those few students who "got" what I was saying began to apply these novel concepts in their careers, and I began receiving feedback that they were being successful. Applying these new and novel ideas in practice was giving my students a competitive edge in the workforce.

Therefore, I resolved to write *Agile Strategies for the 21st Century: The Need for Speed* as a way to convert academic language into a form that normal people can understand and hopefully apply. Several chapters contain brief descriptions of traditional management techniques to establish a baseline for readers to compare with my emergent ideas on knowledge creation, culture, and organizational agility. While traditional methodologies remain relevant, the rapid pace of change demands that effective managers and leaders design organizations that are built for speed. The way to do this is by developing a people-centric culture that enables knowledge sharing at all levels and a structure with processes that encourage people to share their ideas so that they can be acted on… quickly. *Agile Strategies for the 21st Century: The Need for Speed* is a handbook of traditional methodologies and a roadmap for effective and agile management in the new world.

CHAPTER 1

THE VUCA WORLD

Few executives or academics would argue that the 21st century world in which we live is not Volatile, Uncertain, Complex, and Ambiguous hence the acronym, VUCA. The term, VUCA, was first introduced by the United States Army at the US Army War College in Carlisle, Pennsylvania, to describe the military environment after the fall of the former Soviet Union and the end of the Cold War. The concept of a VUCA environment has since been expanded to describe other environments, including business, in a rapidly changing world. The VUCA vision of the world emphasizes the unpredictable and rapidly changing nature that exists and affects virtually every aspect of personal and business life. Information, both true and false, is transmitted around the globe at nearly light speed via social media over the internet, and developments spread worldwide at a previously unimagined speed. The worldwide spread of Covid-19 and the resulting pandemic is an excellent example. Military doctrine prior to the end of the Cold War was primarily based on the concept of uniformed opponents lining up, then fighting it out along an identifiable line of combat. The "good guys" and the 'bad guys" are easily identifiable and fight it out with well-known, common, rules of engagement. In a VUCA environment, the "good guys" and the "bad guys" may not necessarily be easily identified and can attack from any direction using new and never anticipated weapons. A basic understanding of VUCA helps leaders gain greater insight into how and why systems, people, and organizations either fail or succeed in today's global world that is shaped by rapid technological developments.

- V = Volatility refers to the nature and dynamics of change, and the nature and speed of forces that drive change as well as the catalysts which accelerate the rate of change.
- U = Uncertainty refers to the lack of predictability and the probability of unanticipated surprises, and emphasizes the need for a heightened sense of awareness and understanding of issues and events that shape the environment and decisions.
- C = Complexity refers to the intertwined interactions of many forces surrounding an organization, the confounding of multiple

issues, with no apparent cause-and-effect chain of reactions that confuse and befuddle leaders.

- A = Ambiguity refers to the haziness of reality, the potential to misinterpret information or events, and the mixed meanings of conditions leading to confusion about cause and effect.

These elements describe the environment in which organizations must view their current and future state in the 21st century. A clear appreciation for a VUCA environment helps leaders appreciate both the importance and limitations of planning and policy making. Acknowledgement and recognition of these elements can help leaders sharpen their ability to look ahead, plan ahead and move ahead by making rapid decisions to adapt to whatever the VUCA world throws at the organization. An appreciation for VUCA sets the stage for managing and leading. In general, the underlying premises of VUCA tend to help shape an organization's ability to:

1. Anticipate the issues that are shaped by internal or external forces,
2. Understand the intended or unintended consequences of issues and actions,
3. Simultaneously appreciate the interdependence of a multitude of variables,
4. Prepare for alternative outcomes and challenges, and
5. Interpret and respond quickly and effectively to relevant opportunities or threats.

For virtually all 21st century organizations – business, the military, education, government, and others – VUCA becomes a practical philosophy that promotes awareness, anticipation, and readiness along with rapid evolution and action.

When I describe growing up in the 1960s to my students ... no calculators, just pencil and paper.... libraries with books and the card catalogue ... rotary phones ... black and white television, air conditioning in houses and cars, color television, and air travel being advantages that only the wealthy or most privileged had, they just stare and cannot imagine such a world. Textbooks were used for years and worn out long before they became out of date. Powered by seemingly endless technological advances in virtually every aspect of modern life, the pace of play continues to accelerate as information is distributed and shared at light speed throughout the globe. In the 1980s, Buckminster Fuller calculated that until 1900 human knowledge doubled approximately every 100 years, and Fuller created the "Knowledge Doubling Curve" to illustrate the rate of change and predict the future rate of knowledge creation. By the end of World War II, the total amount of knowledge in the world was doubling every 25 years (longer than the life span of a textbook). By 2013, David Shilling observed that the world had become more complex and that different types of knowledge grew at different rates. Knowledge in the field of nanotechnology, for example, is doubling every two years while clinical knowledge is doubling every 18 months. On average, the total body of human knowledge was doubling every 13 months in 2013. IBM at the time predicted that the "internet of things" will result in the doubling of human knowledge every 12 HOURS![1] Even the most superficial observer can have no reason to question IBM's reasoning that the rate of knowledge creation is accelerating and will most likely continue to do so in the foreseeable future.

But how does the "knowledge doubling curve" concept translate into practice and influence strategy or business performance? While examples are many, the evolution of the smart phone is a good example of how some companies respond to rapid change while others suffer from the inability to react quickly. Figure 1 illustrates the rapid change in worldwide smart phones market.

At the end of 2006, Nokia, Research in Motion (RIM), Motorola, Palm, and Sony Ericsson commanded 75% of the worldwide smart mobile device market. Nokia alone commanded 50%. However, even by the end of 2006, Figure 1.1 shows that Nokia's market share was declining and being taken by RIM and Motorola.[2] The total worldwide market for smart mobile devices increased by 30% between 2005 and 2006, but Nokia's share was being taken away by RIM and Motorola. Nokia had been the dominant market player for years after having been instrumental for popularizing cell phones in society in the 1990s. All of these companies had developed sound strategies, management designs, and practices that worked well and helped make them very successful. The loss of market share by Nokia from 54% to 50% was probably discussed by Nokia executives but overshadowed by the increased profit generated by an increase in total shipments of units sold. Shareholders are happy, executives at all of these companies get their bonuses so they are happy, and executives build an organization that maximizes efficiency to squeeze the most from their resources. Apple was not on anyone's radar in 2005.

Figure 1.1 – Worldwide Market Share for Mobile Devices

Worldwide Market Share for Mobile Devices

Vendor	Q4 2005	Q4 2006	3 Years	Q4 2009	Q4 2018
Nokia	54.3%	50.2%		38.6%	
RIM	7.0%	8.3%		19.9%	
Motorola	4.6%	6.6%			
Palm	9.2%	5.5%			
Sony Ericsson	0.6%	5.1%			
Samsung				3.3%	18.7%
Apple				16.1%	18.2%
HTC				4.5%	
Huawei					16.1%
Xiaomi					7.6%
Oppo					7.8%
Others.	24.3%	24.3%		17.6%	31.6%

Sources: canalys.com ltd (2006-2007) and IDC.com
Smart mobile device market: handhelds, wireless handhelds, smart phones

"I think there is a world market of maybe five computers" – **Thomas Watson, CEO of IBM, 1948**

Then, in January 2007 the CEO of Apple, Steve Jobs, unveiled the iPhone which he claimed is "a revolutionary and magical product that is literally five years ahead of any other mobile phone". Nokia, RIM, Motorola, Palm, Sony Ericsson, and other executives responded with a collective "cool, but not a threat." The response at the time was like that of Thomas Watson, CEO of IBM who in 1948 stated that "I think there is a world market of maybe five computers," or Ken Olsen, the founder and CEO of Digital Equipment Corporation (DEC), who in 1977 said, "There is no reason for any individual to have a computer in his home." In retrospect, we struggle and laugh when we ask, "How could these gifted and intelligent individuals have been so wrong?" and maybe more importantly, why didn't people around them push back? We are not privy to the internal discussion that may have occurred at the time in either case, but the fact is that IBM did not dive into computers until decades after Watson's death and DEC died quietly in the 1990s. The rapid sequence of events that highlight the evolution of smartphones illustrates how quickly knowledge is disseminated and opportunities or threats materialize forcing both executive thinking and organizational designs to be more flexible and agile than in the prior century.[3]

- January 2007 – Steve Jobs, CEO of Apple, introduced the iPhone, but Steve Ballmer, CEO of Microsoft calls the iPhone "the most expensive phone in the world."
- April 2007 – Gartner, the technology research company, said that in the first quarter of 2007 Microsoft's Windows Mobile commanded 18% of the smartphone market then totaling 17 million handsets.
- November 2007 – Google announced it will offer the Android mobile operating system for FREE. Android is an open system so that anyone can use or change it, and by default it uses Google services for search, email, and video. Andy Rubin, Google's head of Android, when asked if there will be Google phones stated that "There will be thousands of Google phones – some you like, some you don't." In response to Google, Microsoft's Steve Ballmer arrogantly said, "We'll have to see what Google does. Right now, they have a press release, we have many, many millions of customers, great software, many hardware devices, and they're welcome in our world!"
- October 2008 – Apple announced it sold 4.7 million iPhones in the summer quarter capturing nearly 13% of the smartphone market.
- November 2008 – Less than two years after launch of the iPhone, the first Android phone, the G1, was launched with a slide-out keyboard and limited touchscreen capability.
- December 2008 – Just a year after welcoming Google "in our world" Steve Ballmer announced that Microsoft was killing off Windows Mobile because it cannot compete with the iPhone and Android. Microsoft's new strategy would be to develop a completely new mobile operating system, Windows Phone.
- Autumn 2009 – Gartner data indicated that Nokia's Symbian and RIM continue to command the smartphone market with 44% and 20% respectively.
- January 2010 – Apple launched the iPad, a 10-inch tablet.
- February 2010 – Android phones with full touchscreen interaction like the iPhone began to appear. Jobs' five-year advantage over the competition was just three years.

- March 2010 – The fun began with fights over intellectual property powering smartphones as Apple fought back. Steve Jobs met Eric Schmidt, CEO of Google, and threatened him over copying iPhone features in Android phones. Apple sued Taiwan's HTC over its Android based touchscreen phone.
- April 2010 – Google's Android took nearly 10% market share in just three months. Competition in the smartphone market was getting crowded and heating up.
- September 2010 – Samsung launched the Galaxy Tab, a 7-inch tablet.
- October 2010 – After nearly two years of development Microsoft launched the first phones running Windows Phone but sales were low. Development took too long, and the market, driven by consumer expectations, had already moved beyond Microsoft.
- January 2011 – The researchers at Gartner and IDC announced that sales of smartphones exceeded PCs worldwide for the first time during the fourth quarter of 2010. The world was changing very quickly now.
- February 2011 – The CEOs of Nokia and Microsoft made a joint announcement with great fanfare that Nokia would use Microsoft's Windows Phone software for future smartphones.
- April 2011 – In a little over four years Apple had become the largest smartphone vendor in the world by number of units sold and revenue with 18.6 million units. Samsung was second with 17.5 million units in the first quarter of 2011. Android became the best-selling smartphone platform with a 36.6% market share, ahead of Symbian's 27%. Apple sued Samsung in the US over the Galaxy Tab tablet, and legal cases sprung up around the world.
- July 2011 – Android commanded 43% of the smartphone market, according to Gartner.
- October 2011 – Samsung became the world's largest smartphone vendor. Jobs' five-year lead over the competition was completely gone. Nokia introduced the Lumina 800, its first Windows Phone device which was too little, too late.
- December 2011 – RIM took a $485 million charge for an estimated 1.2 million unsold Playbooks sitting in warehouses. The end was near for RIM.
- January 2012 – Jim Balsillie and Mike Lazaridis resigned as co-CEOs and co-chairmen of RIM to be replaced by Thorsten

Heins and Barbara Stymiest, who have been with the company for several years.

I suggest that these failures, that are almost laughable today in hindsight, are not the fault of Watson or Olsen or Ballmer but rather the result of management philosophies, methods, and training that were developed and worked in the last century but are now unable to cope with the accelerating rate of change that defines the 21st century. Knowledge and expertise flow to all parts of the globe at near light speed thanks to the internet and other digital highways. Figure 1 illustrates the changes in the smart mobile device market that have shifted since Steve Jobs introduced the iPhone to the world in January 2007. Once-dominant players like Nokia, RIM, Motorola, Palm, and Sony Ericsson who initially defined the market either no longer exist or were minor players by the end of 2018. Knowledge and expertise have clearly moved from North America and Europe to Asia, and tech companies are in a constant and fierce struggle to introduce improved features and services.

Companies with long histories like Nokia (est. 1865) and Motorola (est. 1928) developed management structures and cultures that emphasize efficiency and performance using management principles developed at a time when knowledge creation was much slower than today. Even relatively new companies like Research in Motion/Blackberry (est. 1996) and Palm (est. 1992) were managed and built by leaders who applied management principles or strategies developed in the industrial age. Senior leaders of even these relatively new companies would have completed their college education and MBAs in the 1980s so were indoctrinated with management principles that are woefully inadequate for the pace of change in the 21st century.

Executives of these corporations were schooled and drilled on the benefits and the processes needed to analyze and evaluate the technical aspects of their organizations using one or more of many structured activities like the SWOT (Strengths, Weaknesses, Opportunities, and Threats) and PEST (Political, Economic, Social-cultural, and Technical) analyses that were promoted and used for thousands of years by luminaries like Sun Tzu and Carl von Clausewitz and more recently Gary Hamel and Henry Mintzberg. While clearly being useful processes to help leaders and executives focus their attention on the critical factors needed to be successful, whether in a military campaign or running a company, they essentially represent a snapshot of conditions at one moment in time. While virtually all the champions of these processes suggest that the SWOT or

PEST analysis establishes a baseline that is best used when compared to a later analysis to identify changes, the reality is that most organizations have an offsite strategy session to develop a SWOT or PEST analysis then never, or rarely, repeat the process and compare the results. Executives enjoy the weekend and congratulate themselves on the development of an insightful document to help plan the way forward, then file the document away in a filing cabinet… never to be seen again. In a world where knowledge was doubling every 100 years, it did not matter. One may argue that in the military context, situations change much more rapidly, which is true. In the military context the battle or campaign is over quickly in a life-or-death struggle, and the issue is resolved. In the business world, the issue is never, or rarely, resolved in such a manner so that the need to continuously reevaluate the situation becomes a necessary evil, which is rarely addressed.

Michael Porter's five-forces model of industry analysis was first proposed in the *Harvard Business Review* in 1979 and is arguably the most studied and promoted process for strategy development in the modern world. Porter's five-forces and value chain models are included in virtually every textbook used in business schools since the 1980s. Like the SWOT and PEST analysis processes, the mental gymnastics needed to evaluate the various forces helps to bring the focus on key success factors to executive decision-makers at one point in time. These processes establish a baseline that could and should be revisited regularly to help leaders sense changes and then take action. Unfortunately, too often, the results are filed away and forgotten which for practical purposes makes the effort and expense expended in the analysis a waste of time and money in many if not most organizations.

"Culture eats strategy for breakfast" – **Peter Drucker**

Massive corporations were built using a wide variety of methods after months and sometimes years of analysis and debate among executives. Important decisions that drive critical actions are based, justified, and supported by mountains of data, data, and more data that ostensibly give decision-makers a thorough picture of the impact, risks, and potential outcomes in almost any scenario. The underlying implication of such a process is that thorough analysis of the data increases the likelihood of making a good decision and reduces risk. Data-driven decision-making has been pounded into executives through years of academic indoctrination or demands from bankers, investors, and myriads of stakeholders. The development of "meta data" or "big data" technologies has further reinforced the dependence on and belief that more is better. The increasingly popular technologies that enable the collection of every keystroke, website, or transaction that individuals execute combined with algorithms that collate, track, and categorize every activity in theory, provide increased insight into the needs, wants, and preferences of users worldwide. Traditional strategic initiatives like mergers, acquisitions, strategic alliances, reorganizations, and other techniques undergo intense analysis before being adopted after, sometimes, years of indecision or legal wrangling.

Yet research shows that despite mountains of data supporting the analysis and decisions, many strategic initiatives fail for reasons that are not quantifiable such as differences in organizational culture. Edgar Schein, one of the world's leading researchers on organizational cultures, described culture as a set of beliefs, values, and assumptions that is shared by a group of people which shapes behaviors and decisions.[4] Culture exists in the minds and experiences of people and has proven be an elusive organizational dimension to quantify and measure yet it is widely recognized as a critical success factor for success. Yet, despite the wide recognition of culture as critical to the success of strategic initiatives many, if not most, executives avoid the issue.[5] The result is that the failure rate of foreign mergers might be as high as 83%.[6] Cultural incompetence in global partnerships is a primary contributor to the high failure rate of foreign mergers. Culture, values, work ethics, and authority all play crucial roles in new business ventures and the success or failure of a partnership.[7] The merger of Daimler and Chrysler illustrated the potentially dramatic effects of national and business cultures in a merger.[8] Leaders of the two, seemingly equal companies failed to examine national and business cultures during the due diligence process or take effective steps to blend the cultures until it was too late. Executives frequently discover that many unseen, unconscious, and rarely discussed barriers can negatively affect operational efficiency even when members of the two entities communicate with the same basic language and share common business concepts. The ability of two organizations or even departments in the same company to function effectively suffers because performance expectations and management styles do not translate into the language and culture of the two organizations.[9] Senior executives know that organizational culture is a key to success yet they ignore the issue. I believe that the business school and business environment emphasis on data-driven decision-making combined with a seemingly human nature to avoid things we do not understand or cannot touch and feel contributes to this inconsistent behavior.

"Success in war depends upon the golden rule of war, speed – simplicity – boldness" – **Inscribed in Gen. George Patton's field notebook**

Demands for efficiency and productivity along with command and control have resulted in the evolution of many rationalized organizational designs. Management techniques based on the classical bureaucratic structure outlined by Max Weber in the last century have proven to be inflexible in environments of rapid change and increased turbulence and complexity.[10,11] Traditional management structures and practices that emphasize command, control, and uniformity are essentially anti-change.[11] That is, the culture and structure of traditional organizations are such that adapting to rapid changes is inherently difficult and slow. If management focus is on, as Katz and Kahn wrote; "reducing the variability and instability of human actions to uniform and dependable patterns" (p. 28),[12] then creating an organization that adapts quickly to turbulence and complexity will be difficult indeed. Over time, organizations of all types develop processes, systems, and structures that become "hard wired" into the fabric of the organization both structurally and culturally. How many times have you heard "the system won't allow that" which means that the system is not flexible enough to serve the needs of the current client or customer. Consider too the reaction of a manager or executive who has spent 10, 15, or 20 years climbing the corporate ladder to occupy the corner office when some consultant says, "you need to change how you do business" or "change how you are organized." The reaction that I have seen too many times is "thank you for your observations." Then the manager or executive does nothing to jeopardize his or her hard-fought position, salary, and perks as soon as the door closes. All of these structural and human conditions contribute to making it difficult for organizations to adapt strategies in response to changes in the business environment. Consider that Sears, once an icon of American business, may soon be going the way of the dinosaur because of competition from internet-based retailers like Amazon and eBay due to a combination of all the factors that I have mentioned. Senior executives may be aware of emerging threats or opportunities but are handcuffed by their organizational design and lack insight into unseen and rarely discussed elements of the organizational culture.

What have we learned and where do we go from here?

In a VUCA world these widely accepted processes for strategy development must, or should, be repeated periodically, probably quarterly, in an environment that results in decisive decision-making. The rate of change in the 21st century is so rapid that three months may be a lifetime in some industries. Just look back at the timeline for the smart phone or consider the affects due to the Covid-19 pandemic. Steve Jobs did not have a five-year advantage on the competition, and Motorola, Palm, and Sony Ericsson had even less to sense and adapt the changing technologies and socio-cultural changes. The Covid-19 pandemic emerged worldwide seemingly overnight and crushed the hospitality industry but was a boon for Zoom, Amazon, and other internet-based service providers. What was a strength, became a weakness in short order as new threats emerged and opportunities disappeared before executives at these companies recognized what was happening! Conversely, vast opportunities emerged for companies equipped to respond quickly. Forces exerted by customers and competitors as well as the availability of substitutes and barriers to entry for new competitors changed at a pace never before experienced. One can argue that the iPhone fundamentally changed society at a rate never seen before making the tried-and-true methods of strategy development, knowledge sharing, and organizational design and management ineffective if not obsolete. The iPhone is just one of many examples of the need for new strategies, ways of thinking, and organizational designs that harness the power of the culture and accumulated knowledge of the people quickly and efficiently. Consider too, the Covid-19 pandemic of 2020 that infected and killed millions worldwide, forced the shutdown of entire national economies, and forced companies large and small to identify and implement new ways of doing business. Many companies will never be the same, and some may not survive.

The ability of an organization to design an agile internal environment that senses changes in its environment and then create new knowledge to take rapid and decisive action is what is needed for success in the VUCA world of the 21st century. Chapter two will be a brief review of 20th century strategies that are widely discussed in management textbooks and dominate boardrooms and management thinking through many if not most companies. The remaining chapters will discuss strategies and managerial designs that will help organizations to be successful in the global 21st century.

Thinking exercises

1. Identify a recent emergent and disruptive innovation enabled by technology like internet retail sales or electric vehicles, then build a timeline with major developments and the emergence of competitors. Reflect on how and why the major developments propelled the emergence of competition.
2. Are the early adopters identified in your timeline in #1 still operating today? Explain how and why, whether the answer is yes or no.
3. Review the timeline of the Apple iPhone and the emergence of smart phones. What is the moral of this story? Is there anything that Steve Jobs might have done to extend Apple's competitive advantage in response to the quick reaction by competitors? Explain your reasoning.
4. Consider Gen. Patton's observation "Success in war depends upon the golden rule of war, speed – simplicity – boldness." Is this line of thinking applicable in a business setting? Why or why not? Explain your reasoning.
5. Take a close look at the organization that you work for or one that you know well. Map its history and reflect on how the organization has reacted to changes that affected its success or failure. What actions or inaction might have been taken to improve outcomes? Explain your logic.

Suggested Reading

Bennis, W., & B. Nanus. *Leaders: The Strategies for Taking Charge.* New York, NY: Harper-Row, 1985.

Johansen, R. *Strategic Planning, Leadership, Business Forecasting, Decision Making.* San Francisco, CA: Berrett-Koehler Publishers, 2007.

CHAPTER 2

TRADITIONAL STRATEGIES THAT WORK....
IN A NON-VUCA WORLD

Roots of Strategy

The oldest treatise on military strategy in the world is *The Art of War* written by Sun Tzu in China around 500 BC.[1] While modern militaries no longer use chariots to ride into battle or spears as weapons, the fundamental principles contained in these 13 chapters remain as relevant today as they were 2,500 years ago. *The Art of War* is studied at military colleges worldwide today, and Sun Tzu's principles have influenced military strategists as well as others in non-military strategic contexts. Many Japanese companies require the book to be read by executives. *The Art of War* is popular in many western university business school reading lists, and many successful sports coaches, like Bill Belichick in the National Football League, have applied the principles effectively. With just a little imagination, one can visualize how Sun Tzu's 13 brief chapters can apply to modern business strategy. For example, in chapter one "Laying Plans" Sun Tzu contends that success in war, or in our case business, is governed by five primary factors. Figure 2.1 illustrates how Sun Tzu's factors might be applied to modern businesses.

Even the most casual reader should be able to see the connection between Sun Tzu's philosophy for military success and success in business and similar nuggets of wisdom abound throughout *The Art of War*. For example, in chapter six Sun Tzu wrote that whoever is first in the field and awaits the coming of the enemy has a distinct advantage by being fresh for the fight and whoever is second to the field must hurry to battle and will arrive exhausted. In the business context, whoever is the first to market with a unique or new product has a distinct advantage, at least for some window of opportunity. The five dangerous faults of a general that can lead to ruin listed in chapter eight are as relevant today in business as they were two and half millennia ago; (1) recklessness, (2) cowardice, (3) a hasty temper, (4) a delicacy of honor that is sensitive to shame, and (5) over-solicitude for his men which exposes him to worry and trouble. An overarching theme throughout *The Art of War* that is many times overlooked is that the general (business executive) must be flexible and adaptable and make speedy adjustments as conditions change. Over the centuries, military and business leaders have forgotten this principle and employed methods or designed organizations that resist change or adaptation. The following sections are brief descriptions of common strategic planning processes, tactical approaches to executing the strategy, and common organizational designs that evolved during the last century. These sections were compiled from several widely used textbooks on strategic management.[2,3,4,5,6]

Figure 2.1 – How Sun Tzu's factors translate into business strategy.

Factor	Sun Tzu's Explanation	Business Application
The Moral Law	People must be in complete accord with the ruler or general and will follow the leader regardless of danger or possible death	People buy into a common purpose or cause then become engaged to go above and beyond minimum expectations
Heaven	Uncontrolable conditions like night and day, cold and heat, times and seasons	Quarterly or annual reports, economic developments in other countries, natural disasters
Earth	Decisions made by generals on distances (great or small), security, choosing open ground or narrow passes, and evaluating the chances of life or death	Decisions by executives on product development and introduction, whether to compete on cost or quality, evaluating the possible success or failure of initiatives
The Commander	The commander must demonstrate the virtues of widsom, sincerity, benevolence, courage, and strictness	Business executives must demonstrate the same virtues to inspire followers and be transformational
Method and Discipline	The army must be organized into proper subdivisions, commanded by various ranks of officers, logistic systems put in place to supply and maintain the army, and control expenditures	Companies must be organized to fit the business and environment, lead by trained and competent managers, with effective supply and logistics systems with proper control and governance

Common Strategic Planning Processes

Heaven and Earth

Clearly, Sun Tzu put a great deal of thought into developing his timeless strategies that emphasized speed and maneuver. He advised against direct battle until the conditions are favorable for victory. Favorable conditions are achieved indirectly through careful planning and swift execution that take advantage of all opportunities to weaken the enemy BEFORE engaging the enemy directly in battle. Sun Tzu said that "All men can see the tactics whereby I conquer, but what none can see is the strategy out of which victory is evolved." In the modern business context, there are many tools that can help executives identify opportunities or ways to weaken competitors. In addition, there are innumerable tactics that executives can employ to create favorable conditions for victory. C-suite executives will retire to some off-campus location for several days of analysis, dialogue, and strategy formulation using a multitude of widely accepted processes facilitated by a highly paid consultant and then congratulate each other on the fine document they created. Unfortunately, too many executives seem to forget Sun Tzu's emphasis on speed and maneuver because in too many companies the strategy documents that were created with the help of consultants or the internal "priesthood" of strategy specialists are locked in a safe, never to be shared or looked at again until next year. Heraclitus, a Greek philosopher, is quoted as saying, "Change is the only constant in life," which has also been translated to "the only constant is change." In a VUCA world, conditions that are favorable for victory today may reverse very quickly due to the high rate of change. So, while executives should employ the basic tools and process that encourage reflection and analysis of the conditions in order to develop an effective indirect strategic plan, they must be mindful of Heraclitus and routinely and frequently repeat the process because the common tools create a snapshot of the current situation which will change rapidly.

SWOT

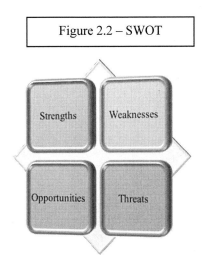

Figure 2.2 – SWOT

One of the most basic tools to promote introspective dialogue is an analysis of the strengths, weaknesses, opportunities, and threats that exist at one moment in time in the internal and external environment. Identification and recognition of strengths and weaknesses may provide insight into internal conditions that may be leveraged to gain an advantage or weaknesses to be strengthened before engaging in battle with a tough competitor. Dialogue on potential opportunities may uncover a worthwhile target of opportunity while recognition of the potential threats from competitors or other external sources like government regulation or general economic conditions can help the development of contingency plans. In over 30 years at senior levels with multiple companies I participated in many SWOT exercises but not one time, ever, did the management team revisit the resulting decisions made from the exercise to evaluate how the conditions had changed. Not once did the executive teams go back, pull out the SWOT analysis and ask, "what worked?", "what did not work?", and most importantly, WHY and what changed? The SWOT analysis can be a valuable exercise ONLY if revisited routinely, regularly, and objectively in a VUCA world. Executives must fight natural human nature to interpret why and what through preconceived biased beliefs or positions and importantly…. ego. Only by being objective and sometimes brutally honest can executives interpret why and what changed and then make adjustments targeting future performance.

General Environmental Analysis

It is absolutely essential for executives to be sensitive to and develop a deep understanding of the general environment in which the business operates. Most of the conditions that represent powerful forces are not controllable or can only be affected indirectly. Sun Tzu would classify general environmental conditions as "heaven." The general (business leader) must be cognizant of these conditions and be prepared to change strategic objectives quickly as the heavens change. The PEST (Political, Economic, Social-cultural, and Technical) model is widely used to provide a framework for executive discussion. However, in a VUCA world that has become globally interconnected, where social events and trends are transmitted globally via Facebook, Instagram, Twitter, and other social media platforms, PEST must be expanded and, most importantly, be constantly monitored as the environment changes.

- **Political/Legal conditions** – The P in PEST for political should be expanded to include legal issues and changes. Clearly governmental regulations that regulate or deregulate industries, taxes at federal, state, and local levels, and legislation like the Americans with Disabilities Act (ADA) or the Affordable Health Care Act (Obamacare) must be factored into any strategic decision. In addition, court rulings on cases directly affect many aspects of strategies. Issues like tort reform and compensatory or punitive awards for damages have a direct impact on decision-making. Executives must always consider risk versus reward as judged by the judges and juries who are profoundly influenced by changes in societal norms or expectations. The Covid-19 experience introduced additional potential legal risks from executive orders or decrees from state and local officials.
- **Economic conditions** – General economic conditions have a strong influence on all companies. Interest rates, the unemployment rate, inflation rate, and consumer price index can be significant forces that can benefit or hurt the best strategic plan. Increases in personal income or changes in stock market valuations directly affect the behavior of consumers and corporate executives.
- **Socio-cultural conditions** – Socio-cultural conditions both reflect and influence the values, beliefs, and lifestyles of people in a society. Long-term trends like an increasing number of women in the workforce, an increase in dual-income families, and the postponement of marriage and having children must be considered. More recently, emerging trends like an increasing concern for healthy diets and physical fitness or increasing levels of obesity or environmental issues drive consumer behaviors. Of course, I would be remiss if I did not mention the affect that social media have had on the social structure and personal interactions in society, not all of which has been positive.

- **Demographic conditions** – I believe that demographics are important enough to be a separate group. Changes within the makeup of a population have a significant influence on consumer attitudes and behaviors. Populations continue to age and are being replaced by millennials who have a very different life experience and worldview as well as needs and expectations. The geographic distribution, and ethnic, religious, and lifestyle composition of populations continue to change on both national and local levels. Certainly, disparities in income levels are a great determinant of needs and wants in a specific geographic area.

- **Technological advancements** – Advancements in technology and the constant and rapid expansion of new technologies for purposes undreamt of a few short years ago present new opportunities and create new threats at a dizzying pace. The internet, social media, wireless technology, genetic engineering, nanotechnology, artificial intelligence, and so many more areas offer an unending string of possible applications to help or hurt (in the opinion of some) humanity and change our world.

- **Global conditions** – I suggest that awareness and appreciation for global conditions must also be a separate category. In a world where people and goods can travel around the globe in hours and information, data, and news are transmitted almost instantaneously around the globe, conditions and events anywhere can have a significant effect on any other business. Companies operate on a global scale. The economies of nations are intertwined, and the continued emergence of economies in nations that were minor players in the world economy in the past century like the BRIC (Brazil, Russia, India, and China) nations must be considered. Trade agreements among regional blocs of nations as well as risks from global terrorism must be contended with and planned for.

Porter's Five-Forces

Another common exercise to assist executives in identifying favorable conditions for battle is Michael Porter's five-forces model of Industry Competition (now expanded with a sixth force) which is illustrated in Figure 2.3. Similar to the SWOT analysis, Porter's forces model promotes introspective dialogue on industry conditions at one moment in time. A deep understanding of the underlying forces that drive profitability is essential to help executives identify opportunities and set reasonable expectations. The

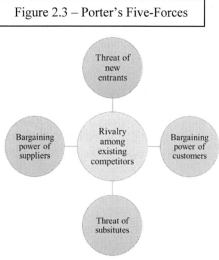

Figure 2.3 – Porter's Five-Forces

primary objective of Porter's methodology is to help executives identify a product or service that will give the company a competitive advantage over key competitors. The focus is primarily on the product or service with the struggle to gain an advantage over competitors as a war. It is critically important to recognize that the forces driving industry profitability in the 21st century are very different from those that existed in the 20th century, and they will likely change dramatically in many industries in a few years or even months in some industries. Internet-based companies like Amazon, eBay, Craigslist, and many others have changed the retail industry to such an extent that iconic institutions like Sears or J.C. Penney will likely go the way of the dodo bird. The evolution of the smart phone/devices demonstrates the speed at which technology can change and have a dramatic effect on the underlying forces in an industry as well as change society as a whole. I frequently use the chicken or egg conundrum by asking students which came first. Did Apple use technology to meet the changing expectations of society or did the iPhone change society?

Sun Tzu might equate the process of evaluating Porter's five-force's industry competition model to assessing heaven and earth conditions to evaluate the chances of success. The questions that the model forces executives to consider are:

- Threat of new entrants – What is the possibility of new competitors entering the market? Some industries like energy generation have high barriers to entry while internet-based businesses can have very low barriers to entry.
- Threat of substitutes – What is the possibility of customers turning to alternative methods to fulfil their needs? For example, when shipping products customers may prefer transportation by air, but railroads, trucks, and ships are alternatives. These alternatives act as a force to hold prices in check.
- Bargaining power of suppliers – If suppliers raise their prices, will that affect our profitability? In many cases, the answer is a clear yes. If the cost of raw materials rises, then the alternative is to absorb the cost and the resulting reduction in profit or pass the increases along to customers with price increases which may cause issues with customers. Unions, in many cases play a significant role in labor costs which should also be considered.
- Bargaining power of customers – If we raise prices will we lose customers or increase profits? This force prevents a company from overcharging but creates a definite friction with the power of suppliers.
- Rivalry among existing competitors – If we take an action, what will be the response from our competitors? Newton's first law says that for every action there is an equal and opposite reaction. Of course, competitors in the same industry are subject to many of the same forces, but the competitive response to any action must be anticipated and planned for.

Value Chain Analysis

Another of Michael Porter's important contributions to strategic thinking is the value chain which he first suggested in 1985 in *Competitive Advantage: Creating a Sustaining Superior Performance*.[7] The value-chain concept encourages executives to look closely at the internal workings of their company to understand what capabilities can be leveraged to gain a competitive advantage. While the five-forces framework provides a vehicle to help executives visualize the industry-wide forces that influence profitability, the value-chain framework focuses attention on the internal capabilities of the company that convert material or intellectual inputs into a product or service that brings value to customers. The trick to gaining a competitive advantage, according to Porter, is to manage the costs needed to create or provide value to generate healthy profit margins. Simply put, reducing costs and expenses is a competitive advantage that increases profit margins…. Pretty basic.

Porter broke down the activities of an organization into two broad categories: primary activities and support activities.

Support activities shown in Figure 2.4 are those that typically exist at a corporate level and provide services to the entire organization. They add value by coordinating essential activities and gaining efficiencies through scale.

Figure 2.4 – Porter's Value Chain

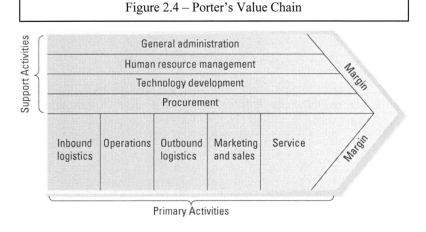

Source: Adapted from Stevenson, W. (2012). *Operations Management* (11th. Ed.), New York, NY: McGraw-Hill Publishing

- **General and administrative (G&A)** activities include functions like general management, planning, finance, accounting, legal, public relations, and governmental affairs. Information technology needed to integrate all parts of the organization and share essential information throughout all the value-creating activities falls into G&A.
- **Human resources management (HR)** activities include functions like recruiting, hiring, training, leadership development, payroll, labor negotiations, and more. Human resources include tasks like developing and maintaining good relations with labor unions and developing and managing reward or incentive programs intended to motivate employees.

- **Technology development** includes a broad range of activities like developing and maintaining the technological tools that are used in virtually every part of the organization. Research and development (R&D) activities are part of technology development and include the development of positive relationships with R&D and other parts of the company.
- **Procurement** refers to the purchasing of items used throughout the value chain, by all units and functional departments and includes items used by the units or departments in the primary activity organizations. The procurement function also purchases material, consumable supplies, and equipment used in direct production and other primary activities. A primary responsibility of procurement is to aggregate orders to gain economies of scale and develop collaborative win-win relationships with suppliers.

Primary activities are those functions that are directly involved in creating and delivering products or services to the company's target market. All companies, even services, have these activities in one form or another.

- **Inbound logistics** activities deal with receiving, storing, and distributing the materials used to produce the company's product or service. Inbound logistics include functions like material handling, warehousing, inventory control, vehicle scheduling, and returns to suppliers. Trucks transporting raw materials to a plant for processing are one element of inbound logistics.
- **Operations** activities are focused on transforming materials or other inputs from inbound logistics activities into a final product. Operations include functions like machining, packaging, assembly, testing, the purchasing of direct materials, and facility operations.
- **Outbound logistics** activities are responsible for safeguarding finished goods, warehousing, material handling, delivery vehicle operations, order processing, and scheduling. The Walmart or Amazon Prime trucks that you see daily on the interstate highways delivering items to stores are part of the outbound logistics category.
- **Marketing and sales** activities focus on attracting customers and trying to induce people to purchase the product or service. Marketing and sales include advertising, product promotion, branding, managing a sales force, product quotations or pricing, sales channel selection and strategy, and developing and maintaining healthy channel relationships.
- **Service** activities include all the functions needed to provide service to customers after the product is initially delivered. Service tasks include

product installation, repair, training, parts supply, and product adjustments or customization.

In general, Porter's five forces and value-chain framework are fairly simple. Business leaders need to identify an industry where they can be successful, and then aggressively manage their internal operations to gain a competitive advantage over the competition. Applying Porter's strategy successfully means that executives should identify a target or niche market within an industry, and then develop and deliver products or services aimed specifically at the selected customer group. The secret then is to deliver the product or services more efficiently than the competition and gain market share. Porter and Sun Tzu would have been friends because both see the objective as gaining a sustainable competitive advantage over adversaries and then defeating or obliterating them. Gaining as close to a monopoly as possible would be the ideal result in Porter's world of business and economic warfare.

The Resource-based View

While Porter's model focuses on industries and markets for opportunities, the resource-based view (RBV) suggests that opportunities can be identified and exploited by taking advantage of a company's resources and capabilities. It is from the RBV, which is summarized in Figure 2.5, that the strategy of developing products or services that are valuable, rare, hard to imitate, and difficult to substitute comes. Proponents of the resource-based strategy see the objective as gaining a competitive advantage over competitors by developing and effectively utilizing resources and capabilities that are owned or controlled exclusively by the company. In the RBV model, there are three general categories of resources and capabilities: tangible resources, intangible resources, and organizational capabilities. Each of these general categories can be broken down into several sub-categories. Figure 2.5 shows a partial list along with some examples of each sub-category. In this way, firms will exploit unique core competencies to achieve superior performance over rivals.

In 1990, C.K. Prahalad and Gary Hamel popularized the resource-based strategy and expanded on the concept of developing core competencies as a source of competitive advantage.[8] Prahalad and Hamel outlined three main strategies in their paper.

1. Core competencies are fundamental capabilities found in management's ability to consolidate and leverage company-wide

production skills and technologies that enable the business to adapt quickly to emerging opportunities or threats.

Figure 2.5 – Resources-based View: Resources and Capabilities	
Resource-Based View	**Examples**
Tangible Resources	
Financial	Cash and cash equivalents
	Capacity to increase investor equity
	Capacity to borrow money
Physical	Plants and facilities
	Advantageous location of manufacturing facilities
	Modern machinery and equipment
Technological	Trade secrets
	Innovative production or processing methods
	Patents, copyrights, trademarks
Organizational	Effective strategic planning processes
	Effective evaluation and control systems
Intangible Resources	
Human	Experience and knowledge of employees
	High level of trust
	Effective managerial skills
	Unique company-specific practices and procedures
Innovation and creativity	Technological and scientific skills and experience
	Capacity to innovate
Reputation	Brand name recognition
	Reputation for quality and reliability
	Reputation with suppliers for fairness and reasonableness
Organizational Capabilities	
Production skills	Superior customer service
	Efficient production and delivery processes
Integration skills	Ability to combine tangible and intangible resources
	Innovative products or services
	Capability to hire, motivate, and retain people

Source: Adapted from Dess, G., McNamara, G., Eisner, A., & Lee, S. (2019). *Strategic Management: text and cases* (9th ed.), New York, NY: McGraw-Hill.

2. Business leaders should dedicate a significant amount of effort creating a corporate design that enables the development of core competencies.

3. From core competencies emerge unanticipated opportunities, and the competitive advantage emerges from the company's ability to bring the new product or service to market more quickly and less expensively than competitors.

The winning strategic formula, according to Prahalad and Hamel, becomes simple:

- Develop and leverage unique core competencies that are inherent if the resources and capabilities of the company are unique, valuable, and internally controlled,
- Block the ability of competitors to imitate or substitute the product or service to make the competitive advantage sustainable for a longer period of time,
- Implement and execute operations efficiently so that the cost to leverage the advantage does not outweigh the benefits.

By developing products for specific market segments and controlling the resources needed, companies can make the product or service difficult to substitute or imitate. Similar to Porter's strategies, the idea is to gain as much of a monopoly in a market as possible and eliminate the competition. The difference is that practitioners of the RBV strategic approach will focus on internal capabilities and resources to leverage core competencies and gain a competitive advantage.

As with the SWOT analysis, Porter's models, and the RBV approach, many executives go through the mental exercise of checking the forces with "this one is strong" or "this one is weak", identify core resources and capabilities to leverage, make a strategic decision, then file the analysis in a file cabinet. They do not appreciate that in a VUCA world, there could be a paradigm shift at any moment and that shift may not happen in a way that slaps them in the face but rather emerges relatively slowly in a way that does not trigger alarm bells. In order to avoid waking one morning and saying, "What has happened?" executives should routinely and frequently revisit their analysis after establishing an initial baseline.

Textbooks and hundreds or maybe thousands of research studies suggest that strategic planning is a process, and if one follows the process, one will end up with an effective three- or five-year plan. Unfortunately, this is not necessarily true. Conditions may change so rapidly that a very good plan may become a death knell if conditions change, or the culture sabotages the plan, or if the organization does not have the capabilities to execute the strategy and maintain control while being agile. I have been intrigued by the well-known story of the origination of the digital camera and Kodak which clearly illustrates the unseen power of organizational culture in the strategy development process.

The first hand-held digital camera was invented in 1975 by Steven Sasson, an engineer at Eastman Kodak. The prototype camera that Sasson built was a technical exercise, not intended for production. When presented to the senior executives to secure funding for further development and production, the executives scoffed at the idea of photography without chemicals. They did so despite the fact that Kodak had the resources, capabilities, and corporate architecture (core competencies) needed to develop this new technology into products that would be unique, valuable, and difficult to imitate. The senior decision-makers had many years of experience in photography and shared the assumption (the culture) that "real" photography had to use traditional processes that could not be improved upon by electronic technology. They were slow to support and fund digital photography technology, that was invented at Kodak. The executives at Kodak failed to recognize the possibilities of Sasson's digital camera because of the culture at Kodak. The first commercially available digital camera was introduced in 1981... by Sony. It was years before Kodak executives recognized their mistake, but it was too late to make up ground in the digital photograph market that by then was dominated by Sony, Canon, and others.[9] Kodak, once an icon of American business, filed for chapter 11 bankruptcy in 2012. Sadly, the Kodak story is not unique. The list of once great companies that had all of the needed resources and capabilities but squandered their competitive advantages is long: Smith Corona, Sears, Radio Shack, Bethlehem Steel, DEC, and so many more.

Strategic Positioning

By far the most common and widely accepted approach to achieving a strategic advantage over rivals is developing, promoting, and selling a product or service that is best positioned to attract customers because of its superior qualities compared to the competition. This concept essentially boils down to two choices: low cost and differentiation. Clearly, there are many excellent companies that have used these strategies to dominate their markets. Southwest Airlines, McDonalds, and Costco have been very successful with the low-cost strategy while BMW, Rolls-Royce, and Rolex have carved out unique niches in their markets by differentiating their products when compared to Delta Airlines or Ford. These well-known exceptions suggest that the basic strategy remains relevant and is justified. It is important to recognize that these general strategies are not mutually exclusive. Many companies, like Walmart, blend the two into an effective strategy. Walmart differentiates itself from the competition by offering virtually anything that a common person can need in one location (one-stop-shopping) at a low price. One does not go to Walmart to purchase a Rolex or a designer wedding dress, but the stores are filled with items that everyday people use every day. Each strategy has its advantages and disadvantages. Figure 2.6 summarizes some of the major advantages and disadvantages of each basic strategy.

Figure 2.6 – Basic Strategic Positioning Strategies

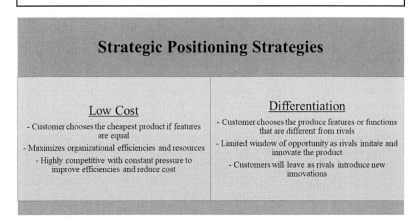

The low-cost approach attracts customers who are cost sensitive. If all else is equal, the customer will choose this option to save money. Many terrific companies have been successful with this strategy. However, there can only be ONE lowest cost provider. Competitors are constantly working to improve their value chain and use of resources to reduce cost and improve profit margins. Therefore, there is great pressure on management to focus on internal operations to improve efficiencies at the exclusion of other potential or emergent threats.

The differentiation approach attracts customers to some unique or unusual feature or characteristic of the product that is different from the competition. In this strategic approach, price may or may not become an issue. Consumers are ready and willing to pay a premium for quality, uniqueness, style, or any of the countless differentiation attributes of the product. The problem in this strategy is that unique attributes may be copied and improved upon through innovation by competitors. Therefore, a differentiation competitive position may be short-lived as rivals respond. The example of the iPhone in Chapter One is one such example. Apple's unchallenged window was not five years as Steve Jobs predicted but only 18 months.

"You can analyze the past, but you have to design the future" – **Edward de Bono**

Evaluating Past Performance and Projecting Future Performance

No analysis to help formulate a strategic plan would be complete without evaluating vast amounts of data. Established companies have years of historical data that can expose trends, reactions to key events, comparison to competitors, comparison to industry norms, and much more. Analysts will use historical data to help estimate future results if the emerging strategy is successful to help executives in making the "right" decision. Many financial ratios and key non-financial metrics have become established as key indicators of performance. Cash is king, so both short- and long-term liquidity evaluations using metrics like the current ratio and debt-equity ratio are common starting points. The effective utilization of assets and managing liabilities and debt are key metrics that include ratios like inventory turnover, accounts receivable turnover, total asset turnover, and debt to equity. Of course, the "bottom line" is what draws the attention of most investors so projections on profit margins, return on assets, and return on equity become important data points in the decision-making process. The price-earnings ratio is another closely watched measure by stock market analysts. In today's world where knowledge drives success I contend that the market capitalization-to-book value ratio is important because it represents an estimation of how much investors value the intellectual capital and knowledge creation capabilities in a company.

Other non-financial data points are also relevant, many of which are specific or unique, to a certain industry. Measures like same store sales (for restaurants and retailers), click through (for internet companies), subscribers (for online services), and market share (for just about any company) are all important and should be forecasted and tracked. While using data to help with making informed decisions is important, an over reliance on data can lead to "paralysis by analysis." I have seen company executives become so consumed with analyzing vast amounts of data under multiple scenarios or data that is conflicting that they hesitate in making decisions for so long that they miss an opportunity or fail to respond to an emerging threat or act on an opportunity… until it is too late.

Methods and Discipline

Sun Tzu identified the method of executing a strategic plan, the need to organize the army into effective units, and the need for discipline as one of his five key factors for success on the battlefield (see Figure 2.1). In the business world there are many strategic and tactical approaches to take to execute a strategic plan, and the need for effective command and control is well established. The challenge in a VUCA world is to remain agile in order to adjust the strategy and tactics to rapid changes in conditions then find the right balance between command and control. It becomes essential to give employees adequate freedom to respond quickly to customers' or clients' requests. I will touch briefly on some of the most common and widely employed tactical approaches that emerged during the last century because they are still relevant and can be effective if executed with speed and designed to be agile if conditions change.

General Strategies

Most companies identify early in their lives a general strategic direction and may evolve using one or a blended combination of these general approaches. Some companies decide to gain a competitive advantage by being a low-cost provider of goods or services. Walmart and McDonald's would be examples of companies seeking a competitive advantage through low cost. You would not go to Walmart to buy a Rolex watch or wash a filet mignon steak down with a bottle of fine wine. Another well-known general strategy would be to find a market niche and offer a product or service that is so unique or superior that the target potential customers are relatively limited to some special demographic or part of society. Rolex watches and Rolls-Royce use this general strategy. Developing a product that has characteristics that differentiate it from the competition is another general strategy. Companies develop products for existing markets, but their product is different enough in some characteristic that consumers value, to attract a portion of the total market. We as consumers make value judgments daily as we seek a product or service that meets our needs at the best value. We do this unconsciously as we decide what brand of ham to buy at the grocery store or what restaurant to go to for dinner or whether to buy an Apple iPhone or Samsung Galaxy. Consumers evaluate the various features and the price, then decide which one differentiates itself enough to gain their business. But business executives must make a conscious decision on each of these strategies, or some combination, in order to develop the "right" product for the "right" market.

Mergers and Acquisitions

The tactics that probably get the most media attention are mergers and acquisition. Billion-dollar transactions get a lot of media attention. Companies merge or acquire all or some part of another company for a host of reasons: economies of scale, diversification, acquiring new technologies, focusing on primary business segments, and many other reasons. Mergers and acquisitions are different things and can take many forms. Generally, mergers occur when two roughly equal companies combine resources to make one larger company. Acquisitions occur when one company gains control of all or a part of another company. Conversely, companies may divest part of a company by selling it to another company or spin it off to become an independent company. Again, there are many reasons for divestitures such as unlocking value for shareholders, shedding underperforming segments, focusing on main products or services, and many more. The tricks for executing successful mergers or acquisitions are speed, blending operations, and integrating two cultures. As Chrysler and Daimler-Benz so famously learned, cultural differences can, many times, determine the success or failure of the venture.

Strategic Alliances

Strategic alliances are created when two or more independent companies agree to work together for some common good or objective. The companies may agree to work together to develop new products, manufacture products, or sell products or services in multiple ways. Non-equity alliances are created when companies agree to cooperate and are bound by licensing agreements, supply agreements, or distribution agreements. Equity alliances happen when companies add strength to other contracts by acquiring some equity (ownership) in one or more partners. A joint venture is a legal entity (new company) formed by two or more companies with profits shared in proportion to the ownership percentages in the venture. All of these forms of alliances can be very complex and take years to form, and in many cases, they are very difficult to cancel or withdraw from if conditions change or do not emerge as expected.

Internal research and development and entrepreneurship

Many companies can, and do, develop new products and services internally rather than acquire another company. Formalized research and development (R&D) departments are standard practice in most technology, medical, and other companies whose products require extensive research into new or emerging technologies. When we think of an entrepreneur, we generally picture an individual starting a new business down the street on a shoestring budget. While this would be an accurate picture, large companies also encourage entrepreneurship in order to facilitate innovation and new products.

3M is a good example of entrepreneurship in a large company. A corporate requirement that at least 25% of sales must be generated by products that did not exist five years ago has led to the development of a culture that encourages experimentation and a tolerance for failure. The 15% rule allows employees in engineering and R&D to spend roughly 15% of their time experimenting on pet ideas and inventions. Once a potential invention has been identified, 3M provides the resources necessary to develop the invention and bring it to production. Some of the principles at 3M that encourage autonomy and entrepreneurship include the following:

- avoid over planning,
- minimize paperwork,
- accept mistakes and failures as normal,
- allow and encourage employees to cross organizational boundaries,
- encourage individual initiative,
- minimum interference from upper management,
- a small and flat organizational structure.

Inventions such as Scotch Tape by Dick Drew and Post-it Notes by Art Fry are the results of applying these principles. Art Fry used adhesive from a failed effort by Spencer Silver to develop a super strong adhesive, to create peel-off stickers marking pages in the church choir hymnal. Fry built a crude machine to apply the adhesive to pieces of paper in his basement and then distributed samples of his invention to people within 3M after the "experts" in marketing had determined there was no potential market. The marketing "experts" had used traditional strategic planning methods to come to this conclusion. However, the people at 3M who used the stick notes raved about the new invention and… the rest is history.[10] Organizations large and small of any type must encourage risk-taking and knowledge-sharing. Stories like Art Fry's are repeated and told throughout 3M to continue that culture of innovation and experimentation.

Organizational design and structure

Owners and upper-level managers have a definite need to know what is going on and to control processes and people to maximize efficiency and ultimately profits. In the 20th century, this led to the development of many structures with top-down management styles. We are all familiar with many of the structures in the form of organizational charts.... CEO >>> vice-presidents >>> directors >>> managers >>> supervisors >>> and finally workers. The idea is to control the behavior and results of the organization from top to bottom. In order to do this, management implements volumes of standard operating procedures, work instructions, and rules, and then employs tactics like a balanced scorecard or management by objectives (MBO) intended to shape actions in ways that reinforces company strategies. I have found that the traditional structures and methods intended to shape behaviors are strong forces against change. In many cases well-intentioned numerical goals or "stretch" goals have unintended consequences and actually result in behaviors that are detrimental to the organization. They become counterproductive. While it would be difficult to argue that 21st century companies should not have hierarchal structures, I suggest that the organizations should be more flexible and that balanced scorecards and MBO must be critically evaluated to see if they are actually doing what they are intended to do. In most companies, lower-level workers, supervisors, and managers do not share their observations with senior executives so upper-level executives lack the insight needed to make changes to improve the organization. A culture must be nurtured that enables knowledge to flow up and down and across the organization.

Improving operational effectiveness

As the last century progressed, business executives found an increasing number of ways to apply the "scientific management" principles popularized by Fredrick Winslow Taylor early in the 1900s. Breaking tasks down to their most basic elements, then measuring the time or units needed to produce a given product became an obsessive science for business leaders. Preaching data-driven decision-making became the sermon of choice at universities in the United States and abroad. The thinking was simple, break down a task to its most simple elements then hold people accountable to production standards developed many times by some engineer who had never actually performed the task more than one or two times. Tom Peters' well known "What gets measured gets done" became the primary motto in many companies. We who teach operations management preach that data, then more data, are needed to make rational decisions in virtually every area of the business: forecasting, inventory, quality, marketing, budgeting, logistics, project management, and many more. Perfecting the performance of these internal functions is the core component of Porter's value chain and resourced-based view of strategic development and execution. What happens in too many companies is that productivity increases throughout the decades assisted by an endless procession of improved tools and technology. People are trained to do specific jobs with little variation, which is a good thing if executives want a consistent product with high productivity and low cost. On the other hand, people become so good at one specific task that they become unable to adapt when conditions change. This also applies to senior executives as well as front line employees who become conditioned to focus almost exclusively on maintaining the status quo and improving internal efficiencies.

Increased productivity leads to increased profits which can be used for multiple purposes including reinvesting in the company's future, but history clearly shows that no company ever cost cut itself out of trouble. When conditions change, the first thought in many executive teams is "cut costs" which makes sense since good times tend to mask inefficiencies and bloated administrative organizations, in particular. Typically, "cut costs" means reorganizations and a reduction in staff. However, costs can only be cut so far until the reductions begin to hurt product quality or customer service at which time the company goes into a self-destructive spiral. Many times, reorganizations just move the problem around and mask the underlying causes of the problems. We have seen this scenario play out in many companies and entire industries. Successful strategy and tactics in response to changes in conditions must address BOTH the top and bottom lines that are affected by productivity.

What have we learned and where do we go from here?

The processes, philosophies, and tactics developed over the last 2,500 years remain relevant and useful. In this chapter, I discussed some of the most basic and long-established methods to develop and execute a strategic plan. But the rate of change in technology, demographics, and social/economic structure in the 21st century demands that many of the strategies and tactics that were so effective in the 20th century must be adapted to new conditions both in the marketplace and workforce. Analysis must be performed more frequently, and organizational structures must become more flexible. Sun Tzu advised that the effective general (business leader) makes a thorough analysis of heaven and earth but employs methods that are flexible in order to adapt to whatever the enemy does or if conditions change. So where do the ideas come from that give executives in large and complex organizations the answer on how to adapt and change... quickly? What is today a competitive advantage regardless of the strategy may become an albatross tomorrow'. Executives must find a way to access the bank of knowledge of contained in employees and design organizations that are agile. Are there new models for strategic thinking that are more effective in the 21st century? I suggest that adopting more relevant ways of strategic thinking and accelerating the rate of creating new knowledge and organizational agility are the keys to superior performance in the VUCA 21st century.

Thinking Exercises

1. Are traditional strategic methodologies and strategic approaches still relevant in the VUCA 21st century? Why or why not? Explain your reasoning.
2. Select a well-known public company and identify its strengths, weaknesses, opportunities, and threats. Then using the resource-based view of the company, identify its core competencies. Explain your reasoning for the core competencies.
3. Using the company you selected in #2, identify and discuss some of the forces for change that might drive strategic decisions. Explain your reasoning.
4. Using the organization that you work for or one that you know well, discuss the strategic methods that were used to build the organization. What methods do you think should be used in the future, and why?

Suggested Reading

Hammer, M. *The Agenda: What Every Business Must Do to Dominate the Decade*. New York, NY: Crown Business, 2001.

Phillips, T., ed. *Roots of Strategy: The 5 Greatest Military Classics of All Time*. Harrisburg, PA: Stackpole Books, 1985.

CHAPTER 3

NEW THINKING ....
THE CHANGING MINDSET
IN A VUCA WORLD

Strategic planning and management evolved in the 20th century with an emphasis on logical and analytical processes using deductive or inductive thinking. Strategic decisions were based on existing data that are easily quantifiable. Data-driven decision-making was based on the Fredrick Taylor scientific management principles like the "experience curve effect" developed by the Boston Consulting Group or the profit impact of marketing strategy (PIMS) developed at General Electric in the 1960 dominated boardrooms.[1] Porter's theories and the resource-based view shaped the strategic thinking of an entire generation of business leaders who graduated from business schools worldwide. The focus of thinking was on ways to develop and leverage corporate capabilities and products or services to gain a competitive advantage over rivals. Omitted from much of the thought process and university curriculum were questions like "What does the customer really want?" or "How will the customer behave?" Also, largely overlooked were questions like "How do we adjust or adapt when new technologies emerge or demographics change?" or "How can we take advantage of core competencies to adapt to changes?" Human factors that are difficult to quantify like values and experience were largely ignored in the formal decision-making processes. Peter Drucker who coined the phrases "knowledge work" and "knowledge workers" around 1960[2] was largely ignored by business executives for many years. Drucker, who continued developing and refining his theories, suggested in 1993 that the world is entering a "knowledge society" and that the most important challenge for organizations in the emerging "knowledge society" is to develop practices that allow the organization to be self-transformational.[3] Successful organizations in this new knowledge world must continuously question the value of existing knowledge and abandon knowledge that has become obsolete. Leaders must then learn to create new knowledge by nurturing a culture and institutionalizing processes for continuous improvement and innovation in all activities to identify and develop new applications that emerge from improvements and innovation.[3] Of course, the question becomes "How can this be done?" In a world where we don't know what we don't know and we certainly do not know how the world will change next year, next month, or, in some cases, tomorrow, business leaders need new ways of thinking about strategy and how to tap into the vast reservoir of knowledge inside and outside of their organizations. Knowledge is the key to success in the 21st century, but knowledge for the sake of knowledge does not create a sustainable competitive advantage any more than having core competencies and market leadership helped Sears, or DEC, or Blockbuster. In this chapter, we will explore sources of knowledge as well new ways of thinking to apply that knowledge in a VUCA world.

"Knowledge is power" – **Sir Francis Bacon, 1597**

What is knowledge?

The concept that knowledge is a powerful force and possession of special knowledge gives one a strategic advantage is not new. However, finding ways to institutionalize processes that harness the collective knowledge of a group of people are relatively new…. and difficult to implement. Doing so requires an understanding of what knowledge is and where it is stored. Scholars and philosophers have debated this question for centuries.

Data

Data are a set of facts or figures compiled from events that can be measured and quantified. Standing alone, data has little relevance, meaning, or purpose. Proponents of data-driven decision-making argue that if you gather enough data, then correct decisions will naturally emerge through deductive reasoning. I contend that this is a false assumption, particularly with the emergence of massive data sets that capture every keystroke, transaction, or movement that people do virtually anywhere in the world. There is simply too much data to be able to sort through to find what is relevant and meaningful to whatever question is at hand. The creation of "big data" sets has led to the development of data mining techniques and artificial intelligence to assist but we have a long way to go before these technological tools can make a significant difference. Data is important, but it is just the basic raw material for information.[4]

Information

Data becomes information when the user adds context either through combination with other pieces of data or information on who, what, and when the data was collected and what is being compared to it. The example I use in class to illustrate this point is to write "42" on the white board and ask the class what it means. For those who have seen the movie *Hitchhiker's Guide to the Galaxy* this is the ultimate answer to everything… which always gets a chuckle…. Then they see that "42" tells us nothing as it is. Then I give "42" some context by saying that this is the number of hits a baseball player has gotten and ask if the hitter is good or not. Immediately someone reminds us that it depends on how many times the hitter was at bat. 1,000 at-bats and this player needs to find another sport but if the hitter has 100 at-bats, I want him on my team. We added both context and data to give "42" meaning and it becomes information. The ability of the receiver to understand the context is another factor in converting data to information. My baseball analogy would have little meaning in a country where baseball is not played.

Knowledge

Again, the question "What is knowledge?" has perplexed philosophers for centuries, but we are not philosophers. We are practical business professionals. We need a practical and pragmatic working definition. Davenport and Pruzak offered just such a definition:

> Knowledge is a fluid mix of framed experience, values, and contextual information, and expert insight that provides a framework for evaluating and incorporating new experiences and information. It originates and is applied in the minds of knowers. In organizations, it often becomes embedded not only in documents or repositories but also in organizational routines, processes, practices, and norms.[5]

We get information from a wide range of sources: media, data bases, books, and documents, and through person-to-person interactions. However, the conversion of information to knowledge requires humans to do virtually all the work.[6] Both the sender and receiver must understand the underlying context and meaning of the shared information for new knowledge to be created.

"*Any fool can know. The point is to understand*" – Albert Einstein

Actionable Knowledge

Chris Argyris and Donald Schön coined the term "actionable knowledge" to make the point that knowledge without action is essentially worthless for practical purposes.[7] The purpose of converting data to knowledge is to generate new insight or new meaning on some topic and then take ACTION (see Figure 3.1). The example I use with students is that I "know" that the moon is 240,000 miles from the earth, but unless I work for NASA or am on *Jeopardy* when the question comes up, it has no value. Knowledge without action has no value to the organization. The whole purpose of spending billions on information systems that collect and tabulate mountains of raw data is in the hope that some small nugget of information might emerge to assist decision-makers in making rational and informed decisions. Yet, at the end of the day, despite the expenditures of untold billions of dollars, humans, with all their inhibitions, biases, and cultural filters, must interpret the information and then have the leadership traits to take decisive action. Also, in a VUCA world decisions must be made quickly … time is not the friend of executives. The slow, steady, and deliberate approach that worked fine in the 20th century may be a handicap in the 21st century. As with the scientific development of strategy and tactics, at the end of the day a human being must correctly and quickly interpret the available information, then make a decision and have the fortitude to defend that position. Sun Tzu describes nine situations where the general (business executive) must make decisions on the ground on which to fight. Generals and business executives must evaluate all available information and then make decisions on what action to take to fight on (1) Dispersive ground; (2) facile ground; (3) contentious ground; (4) open ground; (5) ground of intersecting highways; (6) serious ground; (7) difficult ground; (8) hemmed-in ground; and (9) desperate ground.[8] Any action has inherent risk, but the successful leader is able to evaluate those risks with the available information even if incomplete, then take action to determine the ground that will give the organization a competitive advantage.

Figure 3.1 – Actionable Knowledge

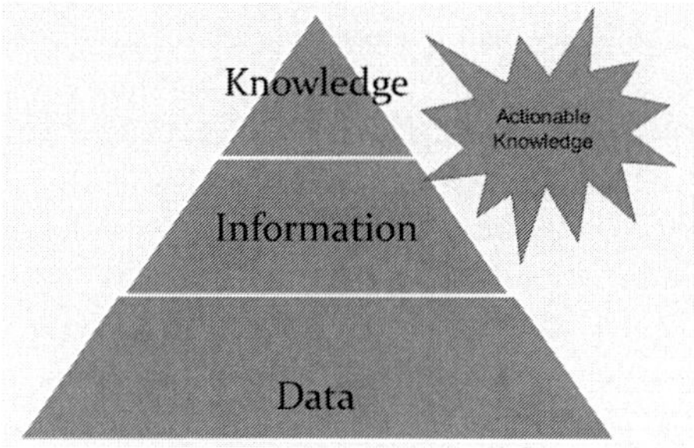

Knowledge

Actionable Knowledge

Information

Data

Dimensions of Knowledge

Michael Polyani (1966) advanced the now widely accepted concept that knowledge has two dimensions. Polyani grouped knowledge into explicit and tacit knowledge to describe the mechanism whereby knowledge is transferred within an organization.[9] Figure 3.2 summarizes the main differences between explicit and tacit knowledge. Knowledge can only be created by humans, and the resulting information is transferred in a flow of messages using a variety of formal and informal means. Explicit knowledge is codified in such a way that it and the resulting information may be easily transmitted in formal, systematic, and understandable language. Organizations worldwide spend billions of dollars on information systems that collect, archive, and make data and information available to anyone who needs them. Explicit knowledge and information can also be distributed using a wide variety of modes such as emails, memoranda, social media, standard operating procedures, work instructions, and many other means. Indeed, the bulk of research on "knowledge management" has focused on the technological needs of and impact on organizations. The interpretation of transmitted information and the resulting creation of new knowledge are shaped and formed through the lenses of the receiver's values, beliefs, and assumptions. This is where the various dimensions of

Figure 3.2 – Tacit versus Explicit Knowledge	
Tacit Knowledge	**Explicit Knowledge**
Personal knowledge embedded in the mind and body of an individual	Based on facts and data that are verifiable and widely distributed
Personal experience shaped by intangibles like personal beliefs, values, assumptions, and perspectives	Recorded in databases, documents, memoranda, standard operating procedures, work instructions, emails, etc. in form that is easily shared
Informal and observed through actions of the knower: attitudes, point of view, competencies, and skills	Formalized using language the is understandable and formatted in conformance with rules, norms and social acceptance
Many times unconscious "know-how", "know-why", "know-what", "know-when", "know-who"	Limited to what can be seen, touched, measured, or easily verbalized by documentation
The 80% to 90% of the body of knowledge in an organization	Captures only 10% to 20% of the total body of knowledge in an organization
The real key to getting things done	Helpful in getting things done but sometimes a detriment

culture are most influential, and can support or destroy the best strategic plan. Just because data or information is widely available, there is no guarantee that the receivers of the data or information will understand its meaning, effectively interpret it or assimilate it in a way that results in something new. In the 1989 film *Field of Dreams,* Ray Kinsella (Kevin Costner) is told by a voice "If you build it, they will come" referring to the construction of a baseball field in a cornfield in Iowa.[10] I contend that executives, encouraged by IT experts and technology companies, have a similar mindset "if you make it available, people will use it." In the movie, Ray builds the baseball field and indeed the deceased players come for a final historic baseball game, but in the real world, availability does not necessarily result in people making the best use of the IT tools, data, or information at their fingertips. History is replete with examples of key individuals failing to correctly interpret data or information which resulted in disaster: McClellan at Antietam in the Civil War, the US military before Pearl Harbor, or Kodak executives who did not recognize the potential of digital photography.[11] People are the weakness of the effective use of explicit knowledge since we must depend on proper recognition and interpretation of the information and knowledge.

Polyani suggested that all knowledge has a tacit dimension where knowledge is contained in insight, intuition, or physical skills acquired through time by individuals who may not even realize that they possess special knowledge. Tacit knowledge is unique and personal to each individual, specific to a certain context or situation, and therefore difficult to formalize and share with others. Tacit knowledge has both cognitive and technical components. The cognitive component refers to when people create things or new ideas and are influenced by mental models of the world through which people filter incoming data and information. Mental models contain perspectives, beliefs, viewpoints, and yes, bias through which people filter and interpret incoming data and information. The technical component of tacit knowledge consists of unconscious, learned, know-how, crafts, and skills acquired through time and experience.[1] We can all relate to the tacit knowledge that is accumulated when doing a task that takes 10 minutes to complete on the first attempt. But, after doing the same task 100 times, it may only take 2 minutes. That is the technical component of tacit knowledge. Morina Rennie described the technical component as six "knows": "know-why" (knowledge of scientific principles and laws of nature), "know-how" (learned skills or capabilities), "know-where" (ability to find the "right" information at the "right" time), "know-what" (accumulation of relevant facts), "know-when" (sense of timing), and "know-who" (who knows what).[12] Most people would find it difficult to write down the steps in the 2-minute process in a form that others could follow which is what makes the transference of tacit knowledge so very difficult. They simply "know" how to do it. Similarly, all organizations have a person who "knows" why, how, where, what, when, and who that may not show up on an organization chart yet whose insight is or should be sought out during the decision-making process. The same applies for the cognitive component of tacit knowledge; it is virtually impossible for two people to share the same mental model.

"To know that we know what we know, and to know that we do not know what we do not know, that is true knowledge" – **Nicolaus Copernicus**

The Delta Model

While generating new actionable knowledge is essential for superior performance, interpreting it and applying what you know in different ways are the key for success in the VUCA 21st century. Porter's approaches and the resourced-based view approach popularized in the last century led business leaders to focus on products and competitors. This product/competitor mentality led business leaders to view strategy as rivalry with the objective as defeating a rival. Missing from this mindset are customers. In 2001, Arnoldo Hax and Dean Wilde, from MIT, introduced a different way of viewing strategy that, I suggest, is a better fit for the 21st century business environment called "The Delta Project".[13] Arnoldo Hax expanded on the original theory in 2010 in *The Delta Model: Reinventing Your Business Strategy* to provide a strategy roadmap that focuses on the customer with the final objective to achieve market dominance.[14] Achieving market dominance is similar to defeating rivals, but HOW you get there is very different and better suited for using the technological advances that we have witnessed over the past few decades. Applying these new enabling technologies and strategies to meet customers' needs and wants is the key to achieving market dominance, according to Hax.

The Delta Model offers an alternative mental model for executives that goes far beyond the classic low-cost/differentiation strategies that can be enabled with technology and complementors. The Delta Model, summarized in Figure 3.3, provides food for thought to help leaders chart a strategic path from the traditional "best product" approach to provide "total customer solutions" to achieving market dominance through "system lock-in." The primary strategic objective is to form an unbreakable bond with customers using technology and complementors. Complementors are external companies who develop features that complement or add to the functionality of a base product. iPhone app developers and Microsoft Excel add-in developers are examples of complementors who develop features that meet specific customer needs and thereby solidify reliance on the base product. The customer bonding mindset challenges the classically trained executives who have been conditioned to focus on product-centric strategies. Figure 3.3 illustrates fundamental changes needed to the strategic mindset and the various strategic positions that companies can target along the way to system lock-in and market dominance.

Best Product Strategies

The best product (BP) strategies are essentially the application of traditional low-cost and differentiation solutions. Each approach has pros and cons that have been applied successfully in many superior companies. However, each of these strategies has limitations that may become detrimental in a rapidly changing world that is dominated by technological advances. Low-cost providers attract customers seeking a bargain who can quickly change providers if a lower cost provider emerges. There is little customer loyalty if the purchase decision is based primarily on cost. Similarly, the differentiation strategy has a limited lifespan as competitors copy a new feature or product and offer it in a better package or with better features. The history of the smart phone discussed in Chapter One illustrates this phenomenon. Another easily recognizable example could be Sony. Sony introduced the first flat panel television with side speakers in 1998 which significantly differentiated the Wega Television from the competition. However, that advantage did not last long as competitors adopted the new technology and improved on it. By 2006, plasma TVs and improved LCD technology allowed the introduction of increasingly larger and larger and thinner and thinner flat screen units offered by a host of competitors. By 2020, flat screen TVs up to 85 inches in size were being offered by both Sony and Samsung.

Total Customer Solutions

The total customer solutions (TCS) strategy goes far beyond the best product strategy that essentially commoditizes products for specific groups of potential customers. Instead of developing and offering standardized products that target groups of customers, the total customer solutions approach encourages the formation of close and trusting relationships with specific customers. In forming these intimate relationships, executives are able to gain a deep understanding of the customer's needs and value propositions. These relationships allow the execution of a strategy that seeks to provide a coherent range of products or services that enhance the customer's ability to expand his or her own value propositions. Instead of focusing on what the competitors are doing or your own internal capabilities, the TCS strategy encourages collaboration to find ways that integrate all of the customer's corporate capabilities. This process may include engaging other external third parties, like complementors, who enhance the product offerings of both companies. Providing products or services that help customers to leverage their own resources becomes a win-win, mutually beneficial, relationship forming a bond that becomes difficult to break. Hax offered three strategic actions to facilitate the TCS strategy: redefining the customer experience, customer integration, and horizontal breadth.

Redefining the customer experience means that companies should abandon the traditional sales force approach to dealing with high-priority customers and replace it with establishing a close relationship. Establishing cross-functional relationships, ideally, beginning at the CEO level to the first line service people allows both companies to gain a comprehensive and deep appreciation for each other's value propositions. The resulting dialogue results in the development of customized ways that add value to both organizations and establishes a long-term bond that is difficult for a competitor to break.

Figure 3.3 – Mindset and Strategic Positions of the Delta Model

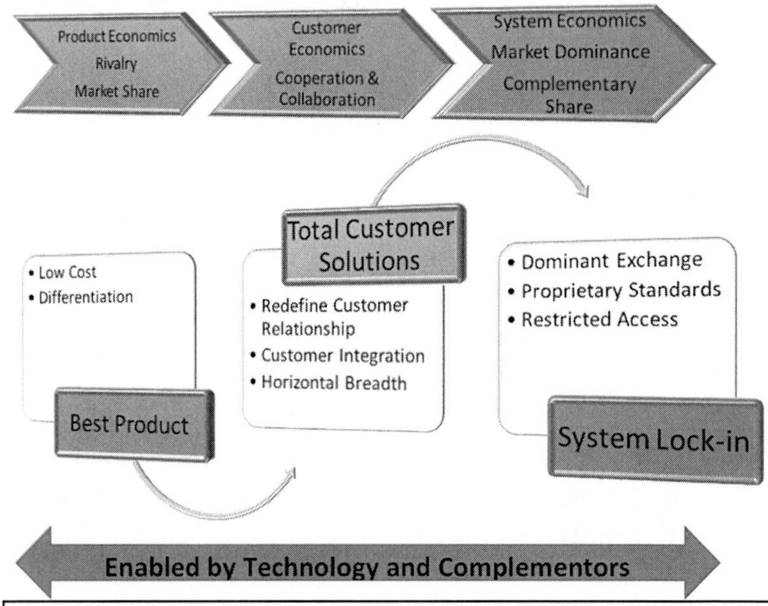

Source: Adapted from Hax, A. (2010). The Delta Model: Reinventing Your Business Strategy, New York, NY: Springer. Pg. 16

In order to execute the *customer integration* actions, companies must first make a major shift in their mental models by moving away from the mindset of developing, manufacturing, and delivering products or services. Through the established relationships, you must let customers know that your company has unique capabilities, knowledge, and experience to help them in many ways. Executives must visualize their organizations, not as a simple deliverer of products, but a bundle of capabilities and unique knowledge that can be shared with the customer for mutual benefit. Companies like Paychex have the ability not only to process payroll but to assume most other sticky human resources functions like hiring and onboarding, compliance, time and attendance, and benefits which reduces expenses and risk for the client company. Dell would be another example of what has successfully worked to integrate its competencies with its corporate clients for the benefit of both companies.

While customer integration is essentially the process of working with a customer to bundle various products to satisfy the customer's needs, *horizontal breadth* goes beyond bundling. Horizontal breadth is a strategy of integrating and customizing products or services in a way that is better than if each component were purchased separately. In this strategy, there is one point of contact (and invoice) where the contact has both the knowledge and authority to engage all the capabilities of an organization to benefit the customer. This single point of contact may also engage external complementors to supplement the services when their organization does not have sufficient capabilities. With a single point of contact, it becomes possible to coordinate and integrate all the products or services to achieve a synergy whereby the results are greater than the sum of the parts. The bonds between the two companies become even stronger than customer integration.

While adopting a total customer solutions approach results in a win-win situation, it may not be appropriate for every opportunity. In many cases, the traditional best product approach remains effective and satisfies the needs of both companies. Interestingly, for large companies with highly developed internal organizations, particularly in the support activities, the best product approach may be the most beneficial. On the other hand, small or mid-sized companies might be better targets to offer total customer solutions because they may lack the capabilities or knowledge in one or more key functional areas.

System Lock-In

The system lock-in (SLI) strategic approach is the most desirable and offers the greatest benefits for the greatest number of participants. SLI is also the most difficult to achieve because it requires active engagement with the *extended enterprise* which includes the company, customers, suppliers, and complementors. At this level, technology becomes critically important to link all the players together for the benefit of the entire extended enterprise. Complementors, which may be internal or external to the company, become an essential component of the SLI strategy. Complementors develop and provide products or services that enhance your offerings with products that expand the core capabilities to meet the specific needs of customers. The apps developed for the Apple iPhone or Samsung Android smart phones are good examples of how external complementors contribute to adding value to a base product.

Microsoft may be the most highly visible and best example of a company achieving system lock-in. With something like a 90% share of the personal computing market and 80% of the complementors, Microsoft products link the extended enterprise worldwide. People chose to purchase Microsoft products because of their widespread compatibility with each other and the availability of a wide range of complementing software applications or add-ins that greatly expand the functionality of the core product. Complementors design applications because they can reach the widest number of potential customers for their products through integration with the core Microsoft product. This becomes a quadruple, win-win-win-win, situation for Microsoft, its customers, the customers' suppliers and their customers, and, of course, the complementors. System lock-in is the ultimate strategic goal, and Hax suggests three ways to get there: proprietary standards, dominant exchange, and restricted access.

The ultimate way to achieve system lock-in is to develop a product or service that becomes an industry standard. *Proprietary standards* establish the product or service as the essential interface among users worldwide. As a result, the product becomes the natural choice and necessary choice for users and attracts complementors to develop expansive applications for uses that may have not even been considered at the outset. Consider Microsoft's MSDOS operating system that powers millions of personal computers worldwide and Windows operating systems that allow users to integrate with the internet. While there are competing systems like Apple's Macintosh and more recently Google Chrome or Firefox, Windows and now Microsoft Edge remain the most common and extensively used systems. If you want to reach the most potential customers, the quickest and most effective way is to develop applications that integrate with Windows or Edge. However, be careful because developing a proprietary standard does not necessarily lead to system lock-in. Consider the case of JVC which developed VHS that became accepted as the standard format for video recording systems in the 1980s. Because VHS was not proprietary, it was adopted by all manufacturers and gave JVC no particular advantage.

Another strategic action to attain system lock-in is to achieve a *dominant exchange* position. Companies like eBay and Amazon have achieved a dominant exchange position by establishing or hosting systems that quickly and efficiently connect potential buyers with potential sellers of a wide variety of goods or services from many providers. In this case, achieving a critical mass of users and suppliers becomes the important deciding factor for success. As the number of buyers and sellers increases, the number of both continues to expand. This is similar to the natural phenomenon of gravity, which is that gravity increases as the mass of an object increases so that the larger an object becomes, the stronger gravity becomes and attracts more and more matter so that both mass and gravity continue to increase. Increasing the number of users and sellers on eBay and Amazon attracts more and more of both in a cycle that becomes very difficult to break.

The third strategic action is to achieve *restricted access* that prevents competitors from gaining access to key markets. Restricting access to potential markets can be achieved if the market or the distribution channels needed to gain access to customers contain bottlenecks that restrict capacity. Similar to the military strategy of controlling key locations to disrupt or stop the flow of the enemy's material, gaining control of key points in the distribution system effectively locks out competitors. Walmart was able to achieve this by establishing stores in rural communities, then by building a highly effective and efficient logistics system to support locations in widely disbursed rural communities. The Walmart logistics system became so large and efficient that it effectively locked out potential competitors to become the largest and most powerful retailer in the world.

Hax, however, points out that while system lock-in may be the most desirable strategic approach, it may not be feasible for many companies for several reasons. First, standards may not be practical or allowed in many industries, and in those that do have standards, they may already be claimed by another competitor. Second, few business segments or industries are conducive to building a dominant exchange or may even allow it. Lastly, restrictive access is not only strongly resisted by competitors but may raise regulatory issues for the restraint of trade. While these barriers may be challenging to overcome, strategic minded business leaders should not rule out SLI as a possibility. If the business can engineer a mutually beneficial relationship based on a unique and valuable value proposition, it may be possible to bond in a way that makes it unthinkable to break the bond and nearly impossible for competitors to break the bond.

*"The greatest danger in times of turbulence is not the turbulence; it is to act with yesterday's logic" – **Peter Drucker***

Ambidexterity

Charles O'Reilly III and Michael Tushman introduced the concept of ambidexterity in their 2016 book, *Lead and Disrupt: How to solve the innovator's dilemma.*[15] In Chapter One, I used the example of the iPhone and the rapid emergence of smartphones that displaced established mobile communications in just a few short years. The technology and society changed faster than the executives at Motorola or Erickson could process new knowledge and adapt to the new realities. O'Reilly and Tushman provided additional evidence that these conditions and results are not limited to just one industry or industry segment. One study of companies founded in 1976 discovered that only 10% of the original 1976 group were still in existence in 1986.[16] Another research study found that of the companies founded in the United States, less than 0.1% make it to forty years in existence.[17] Think about that. The average life expectancy in the United States is nearly 80 so the chances are good that you will outlive the company you work for by a long shot. To reinforce the point that most organizations have a limited life span, Richard Foster and Sarah Kaplan, with McKinsey, charted the performance of 1,008 large companies over a forty-year period. Of the sample of 1,008 companies in 1962, only 160 survived to 1998.[18] Out of the companies listed in the Fortune 500 in 1970, one-third did not survive until 1983.[16] The obvious question is "Why and how does this happen?" How is it that highly developed organizations commanding significant positions in their industry with highly developed capabilities in their value-chains stumble and fall?

O'Reilly and Tushman trace the histories of numerous companies and compare many that evolved and adapted over time as new, disruptive, technologies emerged along with society today as healthy businesses with companies that were industry and societal leaders at one time but stumbled and fell into oblivion. Among the most striking examples of companies that changed and adapted over time are the following

- BF Goodrich was founded in 1870 producing fire hoses and rubber conveyer belts. Goodrich then built on its expertise and capabilities in producing rubber products to transition into automobile and aircraft tires and then again into high-performance materials. By 1986, the company was one of the largest manufacturers of tires in the world. However, in 1988 Goodrich sold the tire business and leveraged special capabilities to transition into defense and aerospace systems generating $6 billion in sales by 2000. In 2012, Goodrich's evolved defense and aerospace company was purchased by United Technologies for over $18 billion and absorbed into the United Technologies conglomerate.

- IBM was established in 1913 producing mechanical tabulating machines. IBM transitioned over the decades into mainframe computers and personal computers and then again into a software and services company. By 2020, IBM was generating nearly $80 billion in sales with over 350,000 employees servicing clients worldwide in areas like cloud computing and artificial intelligence which did not exist fifty years ago.

- Consider the history of the lesser-known GKN which is a British aerospace company. GKN that was founded in 1759.... 144 years BEFORE the Wright brothers made their first flight. GKN initially mined coal, then transitioned into producing iron ore and by 1815 was the largest iron ore producer in Great Britain. Then GKN leveraged expertise in metal working into producing nails, screws, and bolts to become the world's largest producer of metal fasteners in the world by 1902. With the emergence of airlines and flight, GKN again leveraged expertise in metal working to manufacture parts for the emerging aircraft industry. In the 1990s, the company sold the fastener business to focus on providing products and services to aircraft manufacturers. Today, GKN supplies metal components to Lockheed-Martin, Boeing, Airbus, and others with tens of thousands of employees in 48 countries.

While these companies represent the relative few that have been able to thrive over time, O'Reilly and Tushman contrast them with the histories of others like Sears, RCA, Kodak, and many others that squandered their industry and societal leading position. The Sears story is typical of many examples:

- Founded in 1886 by Richard Sears selling gold pocket watches by mail, within a few decades the company expanded to sell all kinds of products by mail. People could order nearly anything they needed from the Sears catalogue and have it delivered by mail. Sears became the Amazon of its time by making items available to virtually anyone at a price that was cheaper than others could offer similar items. By 1910, Sears had become a retailing empire. In the 1920s, Sears executives recognized that the mobility enabled by the emergence of the automobile would transform American society and so began expansion into stores. By 1932, store sales exceeded sales from the catalogue business. Over the next few decades, Sears expanded their stores and offering in the stores to include home appliances, automobile parts and services, and car and life insurances, and offered credit to people who could not pay the full price right away. By 1972, Sears had become a colossus of retailing employing over 400,000 people in multiple countries. Then, American society began to change, and by 1978 the cost of running Sears with its bloated bureaucracy exceeded revenues.

  The response by Sears senior executives was to essentially hunker down and play defense by taking advantage of their size and name, and by increasing efficiencies in the traditional businesses. Sears already owned Allstate insurance and tried to leverage off this service to diversify into multiple services by buying the Dean Witter securities brokerage and Coldwell Banker in real estate. The grand strategic thinking was that Sears customers could buy a house from Coldwell Banker, finance it with a mortgage from Dean Witter, furnish it with goods from Sears stores, and insure the whole lot with insurance from Allstate. With all these additions, Sears became the largest retailer in the world, the second largest property insurance company, the largest residential and commercial real estate brokerage, and the seventh largest securities brokerage firm. Despite all of this and many efforts to cut costs and improve efficiencies combined with numerous attempts at incremental improvements with ventures like Western Auto, Sears Homelife, and Sears Essentials, the losses continued to mount at an ever-increasing rate. In 2005, Sears was bought by the hedge fund manager, Eddie Lampert, who has licensed key Sears brands like Kenmore appliances, Craftsman tools, and Diehard batteries so that Sears is worth little more today than the liquidation value of the real estate properties it owns, between $15 and $20 billion.

O'Reilly and Tushman document and contrast many other examples of both survivors and dinosaurs and then explore in depth the rise of the powerhouse Amazon to become dominant in many businesses. The emergent question becomes, why do some firms rise to prominence and then adapt to a changing world to remain successful, while other prominent firms go the way of the dinosaurs? The difference according to O'Reilly and Tushman is in how senior executives think, which guides their actions to changes in technology or demographics. Again, we see that simply having knowledge does not lead to effective action. Leaders at flourishing companies have the ability to think ambidextrously…they use two parts of their brain to mentally operate both in the past and the future. Conversely, managers in extinct or going extinct companies focus on past history to navigate the present and overlook opportunities for the future. Leaders must learn to exploit the capabilities inherent in their old-line businesses to continue looking for internal opportunities for increased efficiencies and incremental innovation while at the same time looking for opportunities to explore inherent core capabilities to open up new businesses and opportunities. Senior leaders in a VUCA world must be able to both exploit and explore at the same time.

Aristotle is supposed to have said, "Whom the gods want to destroy, they send forty years of success." Aristotle may well have been talking about modern day managers because the natural tendency when companies have been successful seems to make managers highly risk-averse, conservative, and internally focused. The thinking becomes not "What and how can we use our capabilities to innovate new products or services?" but "What and how can we protect and not lose what we have?" Companies are in grave danger as soon as the senior executives begin thinking like great managers instead of leaders. The well-known expert in organizational leadership, Warren Bennis observed, "Failing organizations are usually over-managed and under-led."[19] Mental ambidexterity, therefore, means that corporate executives must be *both* great managers *and* great visionary leaders. Figure 3.4 illustrates the ambidextrous thinking or mental gymnastics that are needed to reinvent a mature company as technology, demographics, and the business environment in general change through time.

Exploitation

As companies grow and expand, they are typically led by visionary leaders who drive the company forward through their innovative insight and courage to take risks. Trying something new always involves risk so innovation is inherently risky. At some point in the life cycle of most organizations there becomes a need to get organized to be efficient and effective in all the activities of the company. Here is where traditionally trained managers take over the many functional activities of the value chain outlined by Michael Porter. Focusing attention and efforts to squeeze maximum output from the various activities becomes particularly important as competitors appear to challenge your product positioning. It is a natural,

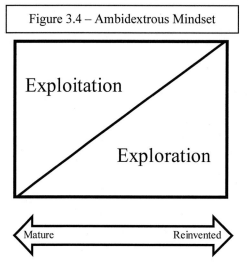

Figure 3.4 – Ambidextrous Mindset

Exploitation

Exploration

Mature   Reinvented

and necessary, tendency for managers of successful enterprises to focus on internal processes while simultaneously, unconsciously, becoming assimilated into the culture of the organization. That is, managers and employees begin to unconsciously accept a common set of beliefs and values that shapes the decision-making process. Combining cultural assimilation with the focus on internal capabilities produces a strategic mindset at the highest levels of the company focused on deploying the company's capabilities for low-risk, incremental innovations. The manager class making executive decisions restrict their thinking to limited innovations that fit the current organizational design. Since one of the classic objectives of strategy is alignment, then too many classically trained managers have limited innovative horizons that are bounded by the current organizational design and capabilities. They focus on exploiting the current capabilities rather than leveraging those capabilities to develop new and previously unimagined opportunities which are inherently risky. The end result, as O'Reilly and Tushman point out, is that too many great companies become anchored in the past and fail to adapt to changing demographics or adopt emerging new technologies. The result in many cases is that the company goes the way of the dinosaur.

Exploration

At some point, new emergent technologies and changing demographics present a threat to the status quo of all companies. This is what happened to Sears. However, Sears is not unique. Consider the life cycle of Blockbuster that made a fortune by exploring the possibilities presented by VHS and video discs to make movies accessible to the masses at a low cost but overlooked the threat from internet streaming. Blockbuster was replaced by Netflix and a host of other streaming companies that not only make Hollywood movies available but produce their own unique content. In the VUCA 21st century, it is critically important for managers to also be visionary leaders that seek to leverage existing capabilities to explore entirely new possibilities, not just make minor improvements or changes to existing operations or products. Exploration inherently involves risk, so it takes an entirely new mindset both in the executive suites and with stockholders. This requires leadership in addition to sophisticated management skills. It also requires patience from stockholders, employees, and all other stakeholders who must accept risk and the fact that some innovations fail. The reality is that not all ideas work out. O'Reilly and Tushman present numerous examples of companies where executives explored entirely new business opportunities by leveraging their existing capabilities. The meteoric rise of Amazon from humble beginnings selling books out of Jeff Bezos' garage over the internet to the retail and services behemoth it is today is an example for aspiring business owners and executives to follow.

Ambidextrous Mindset

The key to a successful long-term strategy, according to O'Reilly and Tushman, is for senior managers to also think like senior leaders, not only on what has worked in the past but how they can take advantage of the company's core capabilities to explore new opportunities that propel the company into the future. Successful business leaders must think with two mindsets: how to exploit current capabilities and at the same time how to explore new opportunities. This dichotomy is not natural for most people and is especially challenging for classically trained managers who have been conditioned to focus on efficiencies and productivity which typically defines a good manager. Mental ambidexterity… thinking with both sides of your brain in both the past and the future… is not an easy task for most people but becoming aware of the difference is the first step.

Implications …. What have we learned?

Today's organizations have become so large and complex that the relevant knowledge necessary for change and ultimate success is distributed throughout the organization and contained in the minds of individuals at different levels with different biographies, skill sets, and mental models. Individuals within the organization represent various educational backgrounds, diverse experiences, and abilities relevant to contribute toward creating actionable knowledge needed to solve a problem, improve processes, add value, or innovate. Knowledge for knowledge's sake may not necessarily be valuable. Therefore, knowledge contained in the collective must be actionable and generated through the social interaction of numerous individuals with diverse biographies. [1,20,21,22] It then becomes imperative for managers to also be leaders who create conditions that facilitate tacit knowledge-sharing throughout the organization. Knowledge and information must be shared vertically and horizontally within an organization quickly and in such a way that receivers (leaders) are able to sort through the irrelevant, then make actionable decisions from relevant information and create new knowledge. The need for speed becomes a key element in the strategic decision-making process. Leaders who are successful in quickly bringing multiple biographies together benefit from leveraging individual abilities that contribute fresh insight and experiences to a problem-solving situation or to innovate.[15] Front-line employees who are dealing with customers or vendors or making products on the shop floor intrinsically know what is going on and what needs to be changed. They are trying to get a better deal from suppliers or customers or be more productive every day, and the body of tacit knowledge of these individuals is immense. Research shows that between 80% and 90% of the total body of knowledge in an organization is tacit in nature.[23,24] So, if a company can access just a small percentage of this vast body of knowledge, the emergent ideas and innovation give the organization a strategic and tactical competitive advantage. If an organization can access this massive body of knowledge not only more effectively but faster than the competition, will they have a competitive advantage? …. Definitely, YES! I contend that if organizations can access this reservoir of tacit knowledge more effectively and faster than competitors, they will effectively "get smarter, faster" than the competition.

In a VUCA world, the ability to sense changes in the environment both internally and externally, and then innovate and adapt faster than the competition is a distinct competitive advantage. This capability is, in fact, necessary for survival in the 21st century. If "yes" is the answer, then the question becomes, HOW is it done? How do executives tap into the inherent body of tacit knowledge within their organizations to accelerate the decision-making and strategy development process to innovate, adapt, and change?

What Hax, along with O'Reilly and Tushman, illustrate is HOW senior executives need to think is drastically different from the last century. Gaining access to the vast reservoir of tacit knowledge in an organization is just the first step. Interpreting it, then channeling what is learned quickly and effectively into strategic action is a very different process in the VUCA world. Successful 21st century executives must expand the view of their role from traditional manager to innovative leader. As Arnaldo Hax proposes, innovative leaders must expand their mindset and strategic toolbox to focus on forming unbreakable bonds with customers rather than ways to gain an advantage to defeat a competitor. Strategic actions should incorporate the possibilities provided by new technologies and complementors to cement the bond with customers. O'Reilly and Tushman reinforce the point that leaders must think with ambidexterity, in both the past and the future. In a VUCA world, the mental agility to exploit existing capabilities while simultaneously exploring new and different opportunities that leverage core capabilities is a necessary skill for long-term survivability. As the rate of change accelerates, it becomes increasingly critical for senior executives to shift focus from products/competitors to customer bonding by taking advantage of core capabilities in new and, sometimes risky, ways. Processing vast quantities of information quickly, assimilating it, and taking rapid and proactive action to take advantage of past capabilities and adapt core competencies to fit the present are essential mental skills for longevity in the 21st century.

Thinking Exercises

1.   Research and select a company that is over 100 years old and then create a timeline that identifies key decisions or moments in the company's evolution. Then discuss the effectiveness of key management decisions on your timeline. In retrospect, were the decisions beneficial? If not, what alternative decision might have been made that would have

been better? Try to consider only information that might have been available at the time, then explain your reasoning.

2. Look closely at the history of Amazon. Then identify six examples where Amazon and Jeff Bezos leveraged existing core competencies to innovate and enter new markets or businesses. Explain how and why?

3. In what ways are the Delta Model and ambidextrous thinking approaches to strategy different from the Porter and resource-based view of strategy? What are the advantages and disadvantages of the different approaches? Explain your reasoning.

4. How might executives who visualize Delta Model type strategies or demonstrate ambidextrous type strategic thinking be able to develop and execute agile strategies in the VUCA 21st century? Explain your reasoning.

5. Discuss how executives who demonstrate ambidextrous thinking to develop strategies might use this mental model to adapt to changing environments.

6. Select the organization that you work for or one that you know well. Are the senior executives primarily exploiting organizational capabilities or are they displaying ambidextrous thinking and also exploring new opportunities? Explain your reasoning.

Suggested Reading

Davenport, T., & L. Prusak. *Working Knowledge: How Organizations Manage What They Know*. Boston, MA: Harvard Business School Press, 1998.

Hax, A. *The Delta Model: Reinventing your Business Strategy*. New York, NY: Springer, 2010.

Nonaka, I., & H. Takeuchi. *The Knowledge-creating Company: How Japanese Companies Create the Dynamics of Innovation*. New York: Oxford University Press, 1995.

O'Reilly, C., & M. Tushman. *Lead and Disrupt: How to Solve the Innovator's Dilemma*. Stanford, CA: Stanford University Press, 2016.

CHAPTER 4

ACCELERATING NEW KNOWLEDGE CREATION
.... CONTINUOUS LOOP MANAGEMENT

The concept of organizational learning, with the ability of organizations to create new knowledge, is relatively new but has become widely recognized as a key element of organizational success over the past 25 years or so. It has become widely and generally recognized that an organization's ability to learn, adapt, and change faster than competitors can be a significant competitive advantage in today's VUCA world. In fact, Arie de Geus in 1988 suggested that a company's ability to learn faster than its competitors may be the only sustainable competitive advantage of a company.[1] In complex 21st century organizations, organizational learning means engaging multiple individuals across multiple boundaries. Peter Senge gave meaning to what a learning organization looks like in 1990 with his influential book, *The Fifth Discipline: The Art and Practice of the Learning Organization.*[2] Then, beginning in 1994, Ikujiro Nonaka and his associates provided a workable model for converting the vast tacit knowledge base in an organization to explicit knowledge so it can be shared and combined to generate innovation and help organizations adapt and change quickly.[3,4,5,6,7,8,9,10] The emergent SECI model (Socialization, Externalization, Combination, Internalization) for the tacit-explicit knowledge conversion cycle describes a dynamic and continuous process whereby tacit knowledge is gathered and disseminated vertically and horizontally, throughout an organization in a way that allows various bits of tacit knowledge to be combined to generate new knowledge in the form of innovation and ideas for improvement. Nonaka applied attributes of Eastern culture to develop the SECI model that begins with socialization; creating an environment where people talk to each other and share what they know.

Virtually every CEO includes statements in their talking points or corporate mission statements along the lines of "our employees are our most valuable asset". Yet, few actually actively and purposefully engage their supposedly most valuable asset or design structures or foster a culture that taps into the "most valuable asset." While learning and knowledge are helpful, knowledge for the sake of knowledge may not necessarily yield benefits. Companies must focus knowledge resources on tasks and activities that add or create value for the organization. Leadership of organizations must develop and use systems and processes that work synergistically to yield actionable knowledge rather than give lip service to their "most valuable asset."[2]

While some of these concepts have begun to be included in organizational behavior textbooks and college curricula, precious little has been included in textbooks on strategy. Textbooks that are many hundreds of pages long include little more than a couple of paragraphs or maybe a few pages on the benefits of a learning organization, and none, that I have found, include a model or propose a clear method to nurture a learning organization in anything other than general terms. Textbooks include vague descriptions of social networks or encourage employee engagement or the development of knowledge management systems in an attempt to cover the topic but fail to offer specifics on HOW to develop or manage learning organizations. Are there any processes that can be institutionalized to access the vast body of tacit knowledge and accelerate the creation of new knowledge to create a learning organization and add value to the company in the form of accelerated decision-making, innovation, and the emergence of new ideas? Some companies have unknowingly or unintentionally developed effective learning organizations, and investors reward these companies handsomely. In the 20th century it was common when negotiating the sale of a company to begin with the book value of the company and then negotiate a premium to determine the sale price. The premium would be recorded in the accounting records as goodwill. The difference between the book value and the sale price may be interpreted to be the value of inherent intangibles with the ability for the company to innovate being a primary consideration in determining the premium. Since innovation and new ideas emerge from the body of tacit knowledge contained in people, the premium represents the value of tacit knowledge in the organization as perceived by investors. In the 21st century knowledge economy, much of the market value or capitalization of a public company derives from investors' perception of the ability of the company to access tacit knowledge and innovate. The portion of market capitalization as determined by the ratio of stock price to book value represents a reasonable valuation of the company's ability to access its inherent intangible tacit knowledge base as perceived by investors. By comparing the ratio between of stock price to book value for companies shown in Figure 4.1 like Apple vs. Hewlett-Packard or Sears and Kohl's to Amazon or Google and Facebook to Twitter we can gain a sense of how investors perceive the value of intellectual assets of these companies.

Figure 4.1 – Perceived Value of Intellectual Assets

Ratio of Market Cap to Book Value					9/12/2021
Company	Stock Symbol	Industry	Market Cap* ($ Billions)	Price to Book Value ** (P/B)	Industry Average P/B (MRQ)
Southwest Airlines	LUV	Airlines	28.3	3.0	1.7
Delta Airlines	DAL	Airlines	25.2	19.7	1.7
United Continental Airlines	UAL	Airlines	15.2	2.9	1.7
Apple, Inc.	AAPL	Computers/Peripherals	2,462.5	38.3	8.3
Hewlett-Packard	HPE	Computers/Peripherals	20.2	1.1	8.3
Dell Technologies	Dell	Computers/Peripherals	73.9	8.4	8.3
Sears Holdings Corporation	SHLDQ	Retail Dept. Stores	15.9	-0.01	3.1
Kohl's	KSS	Retail Dept. Stores	8.4	1.5	3.1
Nordstrom	JWN	Retail Dept. Stores	7.8	1.5	3.1
Walmart	WMT	Retail Supermarket	408.8	4.7	1.5
Costco	COST	Retail Discount Stores	205.6	12.2	1.5
Target	TGT	Retail Discount Stores	124.3	8.2	1.5
Alphabet (Google)	GOOG	Internet Services	1,892.3	8.0	2.8
Facebook	FB	Internet Services	1,065.8	7.7	2.8
Twitter	TWTR	Internet Services	49.8	6.4	2.8
Amazon, Inc.	AMZN	Internet Commerce	1,756.9	15.3	4.8
Alibaba	BABA	Internet Commerce	454.8	2.7	4.8
Ebay, Inc.	EBAY	Internet Commerce	49.5	3.8	4.8

* Calculated by multipying the current stock price by the number of shares outstanding.

** The Price to Book ratio or P/B is calculated as market capitalization divided by its book value. (Book value is defined as total assets minus liabilities, preferred stocks, and intangible assets.) In short, this is how much a company is worth. Investors use this metric to determine how a company's stock price stacks up to its intrinsic value.

Source: Zacks Investment Research Center 9/12/2021

The companies with high market cap valuations and price to book value ratios compared to competitors or their industry average seem to have stumbled onto ways to create new knowledge at least in the early stages of their life cycles. But what processes can be institutionalized to continue the flow of innovation and promote rapid change as these companies grow and mature?

"Knowledge has to be improved, challenged, and increased constantly, or it vanishes" – **Peter Drucker**

Knowledge Processes

The process of developing intellectual knowledge assets may be generally grouped into three categories: knowledge management, organizational learning, and knowledge creation. I call these knowledge processes.[11] The concepts and processes supporting knowledge management practices have been around and been developing since the early 1970s.

Knowledge management practices have been widely researched, and organizations worldwide spend billions and billions of dollars on materials, software, and increasingly sophisticated artificial intelligence routines. However, while research shows that organizations enjoy improvements in productivity and efficiencies, additional research suggests that organizations are not benefiting as much as they could be. Executives tend to cling to old ways and metrics that may or may not be relevant in the current business environment.[12] We have seen companies gather key metrics that are needed to help identify and take action to solve some issue. But, 10 years later, executives are still using the same metrics to make decisions even though the original problem has long since been resolved. The data is no longer valid or meaningful. Therefore, decisions based on the obsolete data are inherently flawed. In contrast, efforts to facilitate the practical application of organizational learning and knowledge management theory have been modest despite the evidence that an organization's ability to tap into inherent intellectual assets delivers superior value compared to competitors.

Knowledge management

Knowledge management theories and practice have historically focused on and been centered on the use of technology to facilitate the transference and sharing of information throughout organizations. The assumption has been that people will effectively use information that is available and at their fingertips to make sound and informed decisions that support strategic objectives and add value to the organization. There is ample research that supports this assumption, and companies do enjoy increased productivity and efficiency when employees are provided tools and given access to data bases, the internet, or other repositories of information that make available data or information to assist the decision-making process.[13] Companies spend billions of dollars, not only on the technology but also on training so that employees make the best use of the investment in technology. However, making more informed decisions using information is only part of the equation. Taking information and combining it with inherent tacit knowledge into actionable knowledge is much more difficult. Research shows that only between 10% and 20% of the total body of knowledge in an organization is explicit in nature and can be captured and shared throughout the organization using various forms of technology.[14,15] If this is true, then most organizations are just scratching the surface of the intellectual and experiential potential that exists within their organization.

Learning organizations

In 1990, Peter Senge described what a learning organization looks like and predicted the benefits that might be gained from organizational learning.[2] Senge suggested that organizations are essentially a collective of many intellectual assets and biographies that when combined generate innovative ideas to solve problems or create new products or provide answers to questions that single individuals may not be capable of doing. We all know the old saying that two minds are better than one, and if that is true, then ten minds should be better than two. The trick is getting people to actually collaborate and share what they know. Facilitating a learning organization has become another buzz word among executives, but it is easier said than done. For too many organizations, facilitating a learning organization remains just that… a buzz word… without specific action or substance. It sounds good in a mission statement and speeches but without specific actions, remains hollow and does not truly generate value for the organization. Decades after Senge introduced the concept of a learning organization, executives worldwide still struggle with converting theory to action.

Knowledge creation

21st century organizations have become so large and complex that the relevant knowledge needed to make effective decisions is difficult to access. Innovative ideas are distributed throughout the organization and contained in the minds of individuals with different biographies, personalities, skill sets, and mental models. Individuals within the organization represent various educational backgrounds, diverse experiences, and abilities relevant to creating actionable knowledge that can be harnessed to accelerate decision-making or innovate or solve a problem in a way that adds value to the organization. Knowledge for knowledge's sake may not necessarily be valuable. Therefore, knowledge contained in the collective must be actionable and shared through the social interaction of numerous individuals with diverse biographies.[3,4,5,10] Leaders must establish conditions or a safe space that is described in Japanese as *ba*. *Ba* facilitates the sharing of tacit knowledge throughout the organization in order to gain access to that 80% to 90% of the body of knowledge that exists in all organizations. *Ba* is a safe space which may be physical or virtual, where participants may share what they know without fear of ridicule or retaliation.[4] Without *ba*, members of the organization will not trust each other enough to share their tacit knowledge. Leaders who are successful in bringing diverse biographies together will benefit from leveraging individual abilities and tacit knowledge to add value by focusing fresh insight and experiences to a problem-solving situation or to innovate.[10]

Over the past two decades, Ikujiro Nonaka and his associates drew from deeply rooted Eastern (oriental) culture to develop and promote the theory of knowledge conversion from tacit to explicit and back to tacit in a dynamic process originating at the individual level and spiraling throughout the organization both horizontally and vertically.[3,4,5,6,7,8,9,10] From a practical viewpoint, organizations that could tap into just a small percentage of the massive body of tacit knowledge would gain a significant competitive advantage over competitors through accelerated effective and decisive decision-making, accelerated development of process improvement, accelerated development of innovative products, and much more that depends on special tacit knowledge. Central to knowledge creation theory is the process of Socialization, Externalization, Combination, and Internalization (SECI) that outlines and describes a dynamic cyclical process of converting tacit knowledge to explicit knowledge and back again to new tacit knowledge that adds to the body of organizational knowledge. Completing a SECI cycle adds to the body of organizational knowledge, thereby enhancing the organization's ability to act.[14] The SECI cycle illustrated in Figure 4.2 describes the four-step dynamic process of a continuous cycle of knowledge conversion, creation, and regeneration.

1. Socialization – occurs when people interact on an individual level to share personal experiences or tacit knowledge with others. We have all sat in the break room and said, "If I were in charge, we would...." This is the beginning of the process of harnessing the vast reservoir of knowledge in an organization.
2. Externalization – occurs when tacit knowledge is converted to an explicit form and distributed and assimilated by a larger community, beyond the immediate social group. People with the basic knowledge are typically not the senior executives. We all know who knows the most about what is going on at operational levels, and it is not the CEO. But these people are typically not decision-makers able to take decisive action. Therefore, they must convert the tacit knowledge or idea into a form that can be shared with a wider audience of decision-makers in the form of a memo or proposal.

Figure 4.2 – The SECI Cycle

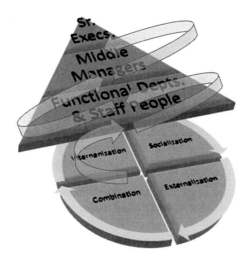

3. Combination – occurs when pieces of knowledge that have been shared with a wider audience or decision-makers are reconstituted to create something new and more complex. A wider group of individuals add their knowledge and practical experience to the original idea so that something new emerges in the form of innovation or process improvement or some action that adds value to the organization.

4. Internalization – occurs when the organizational decision-makers formalize and institutionalize the new idea in the form of revised procedures or new product or action. People then absorb the recombined knowledge (procedure or innovation) into their existing knowledge base to yield new knowledge that is unlike the original knowledge set. Then the process repeats as in a few months people again sitting in the break room say, "Remember that change we made a few months ago.... well, I have a better idea that improves the new (existing) one....".

"Test fast, fail fast, adjust fast" – **Tom Peters**

The Continuous Loop Model for Management

Western Style Linear Thinking Process

Assume that leaders of the organization are able to create an environment where people exist in *ba* and share their valuable tacit knowledge. How can this flow of knowledge be channeled in a way that benefits all stakeholders of the organization? The accumulation of knowledge must be focused to achieve some outcome that adds value to the organization. Otherwise, what is the purpose? The SECI model is routed in social structures and beliefs that are characteristic of Eastern societies (China, Korea, Japan, etc.) that emphasize and value group effort and collaboration. Western societies and resultant thinking in Europe and America are generally grounded in the protestant work ethic mode of thought which emphasizes individual achievement over that of the group. Western managers are generally conditioned by society to think in a linear fashion ... one step at a time... followed by another logical step or action... and so on. While there is nothing inherently wrong with this style of thinking, unanticipated events or occurrences that disrupt the logical flow of events create havoc. Many of us have witnessed or experienced projects that came to a screeching halt when confronted with an unanticipated event or change as managers scratch their heads wondering what to do next. To illustrate this linear thinking, I borrowed the value stream diagram from the six-sigma toolbox. The SIPOC (Supplier, Input, Process, Output, Customer) model shown in Figure 4.3 illustrates the typically Western linear thought process. The flow or logical thinking and resulting sequence from input to output can also be applied to tasks such as project management where each stage represents a milestone in the project timeline. The challenges before leaders and managers are to find a way to advance quickly from one step to another and react quickly and decisively when unanticipated events occur, or conditions change. Too often, unanticipated events or changing conditions result in costly delays as leaders and managers scratch their heads wondering how to respond when the answer lies embedded somewhere within the tacit body of knowledge in their organizations.

Figure 4.3 – 6-Sigma Value Stream – SIPOC

What if, rather than defining the "customer" as someone external to the organization who pays for some product or service, we define "customer" as anyone or group of people engaged within or without the organization who gains value from some activity. If we make that change to our thinking, then the output becomes any action or resulting product that adds value to the organization as a whole. This could be things like strategic plans, budgets, process improvements, completing a project on time and under budget, or ideas for new products and much more. If the target output changes, then the source of supply for the input must also change. Suppliers are not only vendors who provide goods or services for ultimate resale but anyone who has special knowledge needed to contribute to the development of the final item of value. Suppliers may be other management, individuals within the organization at any level, or people outside of the organization who have special knowledge. Special knowledge may come from anywhere inside or outside of the organization. People at any level of the organization may have special tacit knowledge that can contribute to adding value to whatever is the output. Is it possible to accelerate the creation of new knowledge by accessing the vast tacit knowledge base in organizations and focus the new knowledge on tasks that add value?

Combining the best of Eastern and Western Thought

If the goal of management is to create new knowledge to quickly solve problems, make decisions, develop new products or processes, etc., in order to gain a competitive advantage, then merging the best elements of Eastern and Western thought might offer a practical approach. Creating an environment where people at all levels of the organization feel safe to share their tacit knowledge (environment of *ba*) will enable the first step of the SECI cycle: socialization. People will openly and willingly share what they know. Their special knowledge will become available to management through the process of externalization to be combined and eventually internalized in the form of implementation of a new process or product. Once the *ba* environment exists and the SECI cycle results in ideas and innovation, management's challenge is to focus the resulting flood of ideas on value adding tasks. The Continuous Loop Management Model (CLM) shown in Figure 4.4 offers a visualization of the merged Eastern style SECI cycle with the Western style six-sigma SIPOC.[11,16]

Figure 4.4 – The Continuous Loop Management Model

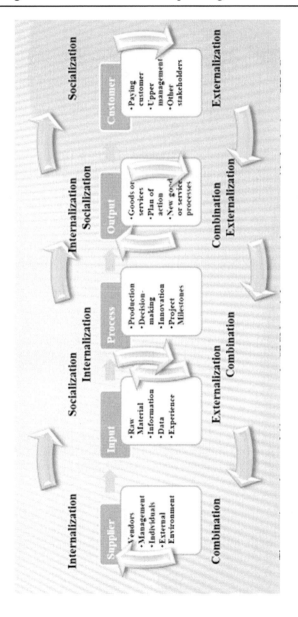

Overlapping SECI cycles represent the sharing of tacit knowledge from one step in the SIPOC process to the next step. Since each SECI cycle represents the creating of some new nugget of knowledge that supports the decision-making process, speeding up the completion of SECI cycles accelerates the knowledge creation and decision-making process and eventually the emergence of new solutions to problems, process improvements, or new products.... whatever the eventual outcome. Accelerating the rate of new knowledge creation and decision-making through time enables the organization to essentially get smarter, faster, than the competition. Applying the concepts of the Continuous Loop Management Model helps executives and managers to progress more quickly and effectively through the SIPOC stages not only to create output that adds value but also to respond to unanticipated changes more quickly. How many times have projects progressed from one milestone to the next to project completion following the schedule or work breakdown structure as it was planned on day one? The answer from almost everyone who has ever participated in a project is... almost never. If the SIPOC steps are defined as project milestones, then the Continuous Loop Management Model offers a practical way to quickly identify those unanticipated conditions that tend to bring a project or a strategic initiative to a screeching halt, then access the tacit knowledge base to respond to the problem and keep the project moving forward on schedule. The Continuous Loop Management Model offers a roadmap for executives and managers to follow Tom Peters' advice, "test fast, fail fast, adjust fast." Speed is the key to success in the VUCA world. Organizations must make strategic and operational decisions fast, develop new approaches fast, adjust to unanticipated events and change fast.

What have we learned... where do we go from here?

In my classes I ask students to discuss how the CLM model might be applied effectively in the organizations that they work for. Many, if not most, reply that they already use this type of process and cite the "open door policy" or "project teams" or "action committees." I ask, how many times have people gone into the CEO or owner's office and sat down to share an idea or a gripe? The answer is almost always "never." Similarly, when I ask, what really changed as a result of the team or committee, the answer is usually "not much, really." Deeper probing typically reveals that very little of the tacit knowledge in the organization is actually being converted to action. Most of the time, these policies, teams, or committees are little more than window dressing designed to make people feel as if they are making a contribution and allow managers to claim that they are "people, people" and leveraging their "most valuable asset." The reasons that these common techniques do not actually work are many, including fear, title intimidation, social norms, personalities, and an infinite number of unspoken and unseen beliefs, values, and shared assumptions within the group. So, what attributes must an organization cultivate in order to make the Continuous Loop Management Model work effectively? What does an organization look like that enables the SECI cycle to begin to tap into the tacit knowledge base of an organization? What is needed to create *ba*? What are the benefits of *ba* and how does this shape strategy?

Thinking Exercises

1. Select five publicly held companies in each of three industries for fifteen companies in total. Calculate the market capitalization to book value ratio for each. Discuss why the ratio between industries might be different.
2. Select one company in each industry used in #1, then explain why investors do or do not pay a premium that the ratio between market capitalization and book value represents. What is it that creates value or lack of value for each company? Explain your logic.
3. Consider Tom Peters well-known "test fast, fail fast, adjust fast" statement. How might this be relevant in the development and execution of strategies? Explain your reasoning.
4. Using the organization that you work for or one that you know well, identify and discuss unseen or unspoken beliefs and values, or shared assumptions that are held by people in the organization that inhibit the flow of knowledge throughout the organization. Explain your reasoning. Some examples are good.

Suggested Reading

Nonaka, I., & K. Ichijo. *Knowledge Creation and Management: New Challenges for Managers*. New York, NY: Oxford University Press, 2007.

Nonaka, I., & H. Takeuchi. *The Knowledge-creating Company: How Japanese Companies Create the Dynamics of Innovation*. New York, NY: Oxford University Press, 1995.

CHAPTER 5

ORGANIZATIONAL CULTURE...
THE KEY TO THE KINGDOM

So, what attributes must an organization cultivate in order to make the Continuous Loop Management Model work effectively? What does an organization look like that enables the SECI cycle to tap into the tacit knowledge base of an organization? What is needed to create *ba*?

I ask these questions in my classes, and students typically respond with comments like "we already do this with regular department meetings" or "my company has a suggestion box..." or "we have an idea committee that ..." or some similarly structured management action. When asked how effective these meetings are in generating new and innovative ideas, the answer is typically "not very good" because the manager typically takes charge (as managers must do to assert their power). Lower-level people attend the meeting and enjoy a company bought lunch but keep the really unique ideas to themselves for any number of unseen and unspoken reasons. After the meeting, the manager goes to his/her boss and accepts congratulations for whatever idea or suggestion that emerged, if any. In the end, little typically gets done, yet management feels good and goes along fat, dumb, and happy as they bask in the image of accomplishment. This routine is repeated thousands of times every day at companies throughout the world as managers are rewarded while employees who have the really valuable ideas feel left out and unfulfilled. We have found in our research that many unseen and generally unaccounted for interferences creep into the subconscious mindsets (the culture) of groups of people that prevent knowledge sharing and the emergence of innovation and ideas.[1,2,3]

Organizational Culture – what is it?

Recognition of the powerful influence that organizational culture has on organizational performance has been steadily growing for several decades. Numerous books and research papers have been published using a variety of models and methods attempting to assess various dimensions and the strengths of those dimensions within the organization. While there is no universally accepted definition of organizational culture, there appears to be wide agreement with Edgar Schein's definition of organizational culture as a set of beliefs, values, and shared assumptions "invented, discovered, or developed by a given group as it learns to cope with its problems of external adaptation and internal integration – that has worked well enough to be considered... the correct way to perceive, think, and feel in relation to those problems" (p. 9).[4] Geert Hofstede observed that organizational culture consists of core values that are often unconscious and rarely discussable.[5] These descriptions and many variants appear throughout the literature on organizational cultures. Many researchers and authors have demonstrated the power of culture on organizational performance using both qualitative and quantitative methods.

Schein went on to identify three distinct levels of organizational culture that can be observed by other people:

- Artifacts and behaviors – which include any tangible, overt or verbally identifiable elements in any organization. Architecture, furniture, dress code, and office jokes, all represent organizational artifacts. Artifacts are the visible elements in a culture, and they can be recognized by people not part of the culture. Similarly, outsiders observe behaviors that reflect the underlying values and beliefs of a group of people.
- Espoused values – are the organization's stated values and rules of behavior. Espoused values dictate how members of the organization represent the organization both to themselves and to others. This is often expressed in official philosophies and public statements of identity like mission or vision statements. These statements are often a projection for the future, of what the members hope to become or hope that the organization becomes. Examples of this would be employee professionalism, or a "family first" mantra or a statement about making the world a better place to live. Trouble may, and often does, arise if espoused values by leaders are not in line with the deeper tacit assumptions of the culture that exist in the minds of employees. Trouble develops if employees perceive those leaders are demonstrating "do as I say, not as I do" behaviors.
- Shared basic assumptions – are the deeply embedded, taken-for-granted behaviors which are usually unconscious, but constitute the essence of culture. These shared basic assumptions are typically so well integrated in the office dynamic that they are hard to recognize from within as people simply follow along with "this is how we do things around here."

We all observe people's behavior or how they are dressed and act, and then make judgments based on this observable evidence about their underlying beliefs and values. The same can be said for organizations. Walking into an office space, we observe the layout and decoration, how people are dressed, and how they address each other, and we can gain some insight into the underlying beliefs, values, and shared assumptions (the culture) of the group. When beginning work at a new organization, it is natural for new hires to want to fit in and be accepted. Existing members of the group want the new person to assimilate quickly so the indoctrination begins with "this is how we do things here" starting on day one. Many textbooks, particularly those on strategy, tend to discuss both the visible and invisible dimensions of organizational culture as one thing, blurring the distinction. When students begin looking at organizational culture, they tend to focus on the obvious, visible, parts of the culture without asking "why" do people act or dress in a certain way. What are the underlying beliefs and values that generate certain behaviors or shape decisions? For this reason, I prefer to discuss organizational culture as having two distinct parts: culture and climate.[6]

Figure 5.1 – Climate vs. Culture

As shown in Figure 5.1, the climate part of organizational culture is made up of the visible and observable behaviors, artifacts, and norms that people in an organization display and react to. The culture part of organizational culture is made up of the invisible, unconscious and rarely discussable, set of beliefs, values and shared assumptions of the group as a whole. The characteristics of the organizational culture can be observed and evaluated by assessing the climate. People at companies with strong and unique cultures like Southwest Airlines or Starbucks demonstrate a climate that gives insight into the culture. When researching Southwest Airlines, for example, students typically find stories of Herb Kelleher, co-founder and CEO, attending employee functions dressed as Elvis Presley or Hokey Day where employees volunteer their time to assist flight crews to turn around flights quickly or flight attendants pulling out a guitar and singing the required safety directions at the beginning of a flight. What do these behaviors suggest about the underlying beliefs and values (the culture) of the thousands of employees as a group at Southwest Airlines? The powerful, unseen force that is the culture, shapes employees' behaviors at Southwest Airlines in a way that typically, but not always, results in superior customer service which is an outcome or part of the climate. Southwest Airlines' hiring philosophy of "hire for attitude" begins the process of assimilation into the culture as people who are not a good fit are never hired in the first place. Starbucks has a similar approach that typically results in excellent service for customers.

As Southwest Airlines has developed a healthy culture, the culture at some organizations evolves into a toxic environment as people learn early in the organization's development "what works" and then pass that along to new hires. As new hires assimilate into organizations, they may be told "it is ok to cheat on expense statements.... everybody does it" or "don't trust Bob" or "never contradict the boss" or.... and the list goes on and on. Good people can be corrupted in an attempt to fit into the organization. For an extreme example of how good people can be corrupted by a culture that was established at the top of the organization and promoted throughout, I encourage students to research Enron and watch the documentary "The Smartest Guys in the Room." Cultures can be healthy and good, like Southwest Airlines, or toxic and eventually destructive like Enron. It is up to employees to recognize the difference and make value judgments and either buy into the existing culture or reject it and go elsewhere.

This is not an easy task because there are actually many cultures at work in an organization, which are dynamic and many times competing. Organizational culture is not monolithic and is actually a dynamic interplay of many sets of beliefs, values, and assumptions. Many cultural subsets exist from the organizational level to the individual level, creating a dynamic interplay throughout the organization. Some of these subsets are shown in Figure 5.2. While an organization may have an overarching set of beliefs and values and assumptions, Schein observed that departments or disciplines within an organization develop unique sets of cultural values and worldviews due to training and education that shape behaviors and the decision-making process. Think about the differences that you have observed in your personal lives among people in accounting/finance, engineering, information technology, or marketing/sales. People with different personality traits and interests gravitate into these fields, then they are indoctrinated with "this is how engineers think and act" throughout the educational process which is further reinforced when they join a company with other engineers. Added to this already complicated mix are individual cultural differences due to national heritage, ethnic background, religion, social status, education, and much more. The result for the organization when these cultures interact is a dynamic and complex hodgepodge of values and beliefs that manifest themselves through behaviors, artifacts, and norms that begin at the top and extend to the most entry-level employee. Every executive and manager who has attended business school sat through organizational behavior classes so they have been introduced to these ideas, yet many choose to ignore or forget the learning when they are promoted to "manager."

Figure 5.2 – Subsets of Organizational Culture

Company Culture

Dept. Culture

National Culture

Social Culture

Ethnic Culture

Educational Training

Turning a blind eye… the DaimlerChrysler case

Peter Drucker famously observed that "Culture eats strategy for breakfast." Yet despite the widely accepted recognition that culture is a powerful force in determining the success or failure of organizational initiatives, including strategic plans, executives and managers seemingly fail to take affirmative action in dealing with cultural issues that interfere with the effective execution of well-designed plans. Cultural sensitivity courses are not adequate. For example, we found that in the context of cross-national mergers and acquisitions, 90% of executives acknowledge that culture was a key factor in the success or failure of the venture. Despite this recognition, less than 10% took specific actions to address cultural disconnections either in the due diligence or implementation phases of the project.[7] Executives explored financial and operational issues and established wide-ranging goals for operations, financial performance, quality, and market penetration yet rarely focused on the culture with the result that nearly 80% of cross-national mergers and acquisitions fail. We continue to ask "why" do executives give lip service to the importance of culture yet apparently bury their heads in the sand when it comes to acting? I find it amazing that seemingly intelligent and highly educated business executives will close their eyes and be blind to the obvious... culture is important. Deeply entrenched cultural difference can sabotage the best plan developed using classical techniques. One of the best recent examples of how cultural disconnections can scuttle strategic initiatives is the failed merger between Chrysler and Daimler-Benz.

On paper, the 1998 "merger of equals" between US-based Chrysler and German giant Daimler-Benz had all the attributes needed for success, using traditional strategic thinking and methods. Synergies created by taking advantage of the best attributes of each company were expected to position the new company, DaimlerChrysler, as the third largest car company in the world. This would give DaimlerChrysler a competitive advantage over the existing US market leaders, Ford and General Motors. At the time, Chrysler controlled about 23% of the US car market while Daimler-Benz earned just a 1% market share.[8] Chrysler's strategy was to focus on highly efficient production processes, low-cost design, and product development which made Chrysler one of the world's most profitable car manufacturers appealing to the masses. Daimler-Benz, on the other hand, was renowned for quality engineering and meticulous manufacturing which made Daimler-Benz cars more expensive and they targeted the higher-end, more selective and affluent buyers. Merging Chrysler's efficient manufacturing and extensive distribution network in the USA with Daimler-Benz's engineering expertise and attention to quality was expected to give DaimlerChrysler a competitive advantage over both Ford and General Motors. To classically trained and educated engineers, CEOs Robert Eaton (Chrysler) and Jürgen Schrempf (Daimler-Benz) this was a match made in heaven. The goal was to unite the companies and combine the best of their unique know-how and different manufacturing processes, share distribution channels, and share technological expertise by working together. The SWOTs, GAP analysis, Porter's Forces, and financials analysis all indicated that this "merger of equals" had all the makings for a landmark deal.... a true game changer in the auto industry.

The post-merger-integration (PMI) plan followed the classical formula of three phases; a start-up phase, a project-implementation phase, and a business transformation phase complete with measurable goals and objectives for each phase. There was apparently some discussion of integrating the different national cultures, but those discussions were apparently overwhelmed and relegated to the back bench by goals for market share, production, and financial objectives. In a "merger of equals" the expectation was that the cultures would merge and blend to create a new, shared, corporate culture.[8] Psychologists generally, and classically, compartmentalize the cultural integration process into three phases; shock, stress (psychological), and the willingness to solve the problems.[9] At the beginning observers of the two organizations did not expect problems. After all, the organizations and people did not look all that different; they look like us, they talk like us, they have the same focus of attention, and their English is excellent.[10] However, significant differences became apparent, and while the merger was not foredoomed from the beginning, these fundamental differences when not addressed in the PMI doomed the venture to failure in the long run.

"Coming together is a beginning; keeping together is progress; working together is success." **– Henry Ford**

During the post-merger integration process, millions of dollars were spent on workshops focusing on cultural sensitivity covering topics like "Sexual Harassment in the American Workplace" and "German Dining Etiquette." Measurable goals dealing with "unconscious and rarely discussable" basic values and beliefs making up the different cultures were not established. A budget was established to fund the many workshops, but fundamental differences in business practices and philosophy were never addressed.[10] There were fundamental differences in values, beliefs, and morals that quickly became apparent in day-to-day work that affected decision-making and performance at all levels of the new company. For example, Chrysler's values include a focus on efficiency and productivity, empowerment of employees, and equal rights among the staff. Conversely, the Germanic Daimler-Benz culture is authoritarian and bureaucratic, with centralized decision-making, and a focus on quality at any cost. The decision-making process at Daimler-Benz is methodical, analytical, and measured with more weight given to individuals of rank or reputation. By contrast, the decision-making process at Chrysler was, to the Germans, haphazard and undisciplined as creativity was encouraged and solicited from anyone with a voice.[8] To the Germans, the Americans must have looked like a disorganized mob, so why would they value any opinions or suggestions the Americans had to contribute?

Basic approaches to work in the two companies were very different; a lot of red tape (German) versus no red tape (American); very long and detailed reports and lengthy debate (German) versus reports with the minimum necessary details followed by a quick decision (American). The approaches to product development were significantly different with Americans favoring the trial-and-error method to find a solution to a problem which gave the Germans an image of chaos and disorganization. The German approach was to develop detailed plans ahead of time and then execute a precise implementation of the plans which looked slow and ponderous to the Americans.

Significant differences in basic organizational designs and processes emerged that are a result of the different national backgrounds and historical experience. America is a country of immigrants with a frontier spirit that emphasizes individualism. Americans instinctively rely on themselves instead of relying on others in reaching a goal. Everyone is responsible for his or her own success or failure which is why employment contracts are negotiated individually. Americans tend to be highly pragmatic and focus on efficiency, resulting in a set of values and shared assumptions on performance that is goal and performance oriented. Results count for more than how the results were achieved. We all know the old saying "time is money" so if the trial-and-error approach is the fastest way to solve a problem, that is how the Americans will approach finding a solution. Using Hofstede's dimensions, American society is founded on equality, and power distance is small compared to German society. Because of the emphasis on individualism, Americans tend to rely less on groups or teams, are more short-term oriented, and willing to take risks and be more flexible than their German counterparts.[8]

German society, on the other hand, exhibits a greater power distance in business relationships. German organizations are very hierarchical, and decisions are made by people with the highest authority or rank. In my own personal interactions with German business organizations, it is easy to identify the highest-ranking German in the room because he does all, or most, of the talking. Others rarely interrupt or contradict the ranking person in the meeting even if they have a different opinion. Also, the highest-ranking person makes the final decision and... that is that. As a reflection of their cultural heritage, Germans tend to be less individualistic and are more team-oriented. As they tend to be more risk averse, the Germans see teams or groups as a sort of security or protection or buffer, and they become highly skeptical of novel ideas that might represent high risk.[8]

None of these cultural observations are new. They are well known by anyone who has ever worked closely with Americans and Germans in any industry. In retrospect, we can see that without addressing these very fundamental differences in values, beliefs, and shared assumptions the merger of Chrysler and Daimler-Benz was doomed from the outset.

"The effectiveness of organizations could be doubled if managers discovered how to tap into the unrealized potential in their workforce." – **Douglas McGregor**

Why does this happen?

I believe there are many reasons for this apparently illogical behavior. Tom Peters observed that, "What gets measured gets done" and business schools worldwide have developed curricula that emphasize data-driven decision-making. Take a good look at the AACSB (Association to Advance Collegiate Schools of Business)[11] accreditation criteria that emphasize quantitative research and standards that focus on quantitative research, research, research. As one of the most influential accrediting bodies for business schools worldwide, if not the single MOST influential, AACSB criteria drive curricula and shape behavior and thinking for millions of business school faculties and students across the globe. Accreditation criteria that award points for publications are a strong force helping to create the "publish or perish" environment that exists in many, if not most, major universities with minimal influence on the educational experience for students.

Having attended many conferences of academics from major universities worldwide where PhD students or associate professors hoping to advance to assistant professor proudly present the results of their research, one cannot help but be impressed by the worthless nature of much of the so-called "research." For example, while attending the Academy of Management Annual Meetings several years ago, a PhD student from a major Midwest university presented his research. He had compared the curricula of many AACSB accredited university business schools to the AACSB accreditation criteria. After extensive data collection and statistical analysis, he determined that there was a high correlation between the curricula content and the AACSB accreditation criteria. Think about that for a moment. If the university curricula did NOT comply with AACSB accreditation criteria, would they be accredited? The answer of course is no, so naturally there is a high correlation. If there was not a high degree of correlation between the criteria and the curriculum, the university would not be accredited. For this nugget of knowledge, the student received a PhD and has most likely gone on to pass on his highly developed critical thinking skills at some other AACSB accredited university.

"The trouble with the world is not that people know too little; it's that they know so many things that just aren't so." – **Mark Twain**

At universities worldwide, course curricula at both the undergraduate and graduate levels focus on data-driven decision-making which indoctrinates students with the unconscious and rarely discussable belief that executives must base decisions on hard data. Combine that conditioning with the overwhelming demand by stakeholders for quantitative proof of performance to earn bonuses, promotions, or recognition. Therefore, executives instinctively shy away from intangibles that are difficult to measure and even more difficult to understand or explain. Unconscious and rarely discussable values, beliefs, and shared assumptions held by a group of people cannot be seen or measured directly. They can only be inferred by observing behaviors, norms, and artifacts that are visible but difficult to measure directly. Universities typically include a class on organizational behavior and may touch on the subject of organizational culture in other classes, but the overwhelming focus is on data and measurable processes leaving graduates with the impression that intangibles, like culture, are relatively unimportant because they are difficult to quantify. Human nature is to avoid what you do not understand or feel comfortable with, so executives with MBAs from highly regarded universities avoid the issue in the absence of a tool to quantify the intangible. Besides, the executive's quarterly bonus is based on profits or other performance measures.... not changes in unconscious and rarely discussable values and beliefs held by employees.

The annual "employee survey" is a common event in many companies which I suggest implies that people need fixing rather than the management systems or leadership. The annual "employee survey" is done to try to control leaders and give executives cover for missing communications and unclear strategies that are always at the top of the list of problem areas identified by employees. Consultants earn a vast amount of money in fees administering the annual "employee survey." Then executives spend an afternoon evaluating the results and congratulating themselves on the progress over the past year, pronounce grand sounding initiatives for the next year, then return to their offices and wait another 365 days to repeat the exercise. Rather than an annual exercise of questionable value, diagnostics should be an infrequent feedback tool for organizational development. What is needed is a methodology and tools to help quantify many key intangibles of organizational culture along with other heretofore invisible dimensions that drive performance and the ability of organizations to adapt and change strategies in the VUCA 21st century. The methodology and tools must be practical in order to be applied, simple to understand, easy to administer, and yield insight into previously unknown and invisible values and beliefs that promote or interfere with the performance of the group.

Organizational Culture as part of a Dynamic System

Most of the popular instruments used to assess organizational culture use models that view organizational culture as a standalone dimension. Many proposed models such as the competing values framework (CVF) popularized by Kim Cameron and Robert Quinn, the Denison model, and Schein's layered framework are joined by a host of other models.[12,13,14] Popular instruments such as the organizational culture inventory (OCI), the organizational culture assessment instrument (OCAI), the culture gap survey (CGS), the organizational beliefs questionnaire (OBQ), the corporate culture survey (CCS), Denison's organizational culture survey, and the Great Place To Work Institute© methodology attempt to provide insight into many beliefs and values held by a group of people but ignore how the culture interacts with other key elements of the organization.[13,15]

Research based on the Great Place to Work Institute© (GPTW) culture model demonstrates that companies with higher levels of certain cultural attributes significantly outperform competitors with lower levels of these attributes. The GPTW model shown in Figure 5.3 has five dimensions: credibility, respect, fairness (collectively called the trust index), camaraderie, and pride. The logic goes something like this. If management members do what they say, then they will be perceived as credible. If people are treated with respect and fairly, then people will trust each other and management… forming the trust index. If people like each other and being together, then camaraderie will be high, and if people take pride in both the organization's goals and the work they do, then, taken together… trust, camaraderie, and pride…. the organization has a healthy culture. Research demonstrates that companies with higher levels of trust, camaraderie, and pride significantly outperform competitors. [15] The reason, I suggest, is that people are in an environment where they are willing to share their special tacit knowledge to create new knowledge. This environment where people share what they know enables knowledge to be shared from which emerge ideas and innovation that result in a competitive advantage for their company.[15] While the GPTW surveys can be beneficial if executives understand the meaning and take actions, I can attest from personal experience that this does not happen. Knowing that people do not trust management, or do not like being around each other, or do not take pride in the organization, or what they do is one thing but taking action to change the situation is another thing altogether. Issuing corporate directives attached to managerial bonus plans to increase the level of trust from one year to the next rings hollow with managers at operational levels. Without a clearer definition and addressing underlying issues that inhibit trust, for example, little will get done.

> Figure 5.3 – The Great Place to Work model

With this in mind, I suggest that viewing culture as a standalone organizational attribute is a major contributing factor to the low success rate of change initiatives that have been estimated at only between 20% to 30%.[16] Decades ago, Ludwig von Bertalanffy described organizations as dynamic systems where all parts are inextricably connected with each part dependent on and influenced by the others. Since Descartes, the evolution of the "scientific method" was built on the basic assumption that a system could be broken down into its individual components for analysis. After that, the system could be understood by adding up all the various subcomponents in a linear fashion.[17] The "scientific method" essentially assumes that systems are closed systems. This means that the components of the system and the system in total exist in isolation and are unaffected by outside forces. In 1951, Bertalanffy described organizations as dynamic systems where all parts are inextricably connected with each part dependent on and influenced by the others like a living organism. Rather than a system being the sum of the parts, the functions of a total system are determined by the complex interactions among all its components.[18] Bertalanffy's general systems theory (GST) assumes that components of the system and the system itself are open to environmental forces that shape and influence both the components and the system in its entirety. Alfred Kuhn observed that within social systems, like a company, communication or the flow of information and knowledge among the various components of the system and the system as a whole provides the energy for the system.[19] Decisions made by all members that influence or are influenced by the system generate outcomes which can be readily observed. According to Kuhn, "Culture is communicated, learned patterns…and the society [organization] in a collective of people having a common body and process of culture." (p. 154, 156). According to Kuhn, subcultures can only be interpreted when viewed relative to all the other subcomponents of the system, and culture must be viewed as a pattern of behaviors within the system. Therefore, the study of the social interactions that power the system consists of interpreting "communicated, learned patterns common to relatively large groups (of people)" (p. 157).

With regard to organizational systems, David Walonick suggested that healthy organizational systems must change through time in order to remain healthy and productive.[17] However, since organizational systems are open, they are sensitive to changes in the general environment as well as to internal environmental changes. The ability of all parts of the organizational system to anticipate, sense, and adapt to environmental change is a key factor for success. Decisions powered by the flow of information and knowledge throughout the system become observable outcomes with which to evaluate the health of the system (organization). Systems theory forces scholars and company managers to expand the scope of their thinking to consider how the flow of information and resulting decisions affect all the subcomponents of the system, the system as a whole, and the general environment.[17]

Organizations must be viewed holistically. Effective change initiatives require conscious actions and reactions with all parts of the dynamic system of organizational management. While the great body of knowledge lies within the tacit knowledge base of people in an organization, they must be organized, lead, and have access to relevant and timely information in order to make effective and speedy decisions on suggestions for improvement and change. In order to improve on the 70% to 80% failure rate of change initiatives, it is necessary to assess "unconscious and rarely discussable" dimensions of leadership, systems, and culture that permeate all elements of an organization. It is necessary for executives to gain insight into many heretofore unseen dimensions of these key components of every organization in order to form targeted actions to deal with these invisible issues which inhibit the free flow of knowledge and stifle change. The dynamic that is organizational culture is much more complex than the GPTW model suggests. Gaining actionable insight into organizational culture requires a much deeper dive into the underlying beliefs, values, and shared assumptions that exist throughout the organization that shape behaviors, norms, and artifacts accepted within the organization. The question surrounding organizational culture then becomes twofold: "what are the critical 'unconscious and rarely discussable' dimensions?" and "can they be measured?" If critical dimensions of organizational culture can be measured, then can they be harnessed to give companies a competitive strategic advantage by being more agile and adaptable when confronted with unanticipated and accelerated change? After nearly two decades of observation and research, my colleague, Lukas Michel and I, suggest that the answer is an emphatic **YES!**

What have we learned? ... Where do we go from here?

Designing an organization to be agile should be a major focus of senior executives. Whether the executives are exploiting core competencies through mergers, acquisitions, reorganizations, and cost reductions or exploring new innovative opportunities, the organization must be flexible and agile. In today's VUCA world, designing organizations to sense change, come up with effective responses, and execute them quickly is a necessary strategic capability. The first step toward designing an agile organization is gaining insight into the underlying "unconscious and rarely discussable" dimensions of leadership, systems, and culture that either enable or stifle knowledge sharing and the ability of the organization to be agile. Transitioning from a product/competitor to a Delta Model strategic approach requires senior executives to have an ambidextrous mentality. However, rigid bureaucratic organizations and toxic cultures that stifle knowledge sharing will make any strategic move into the 21st century very difficult, if not impossible. Senior executives must also consciously design organizations to be agile. For this, we need a model of what an agile organization looks like as well as tools to assist executives to gain insight into those pesky "unconscious and rarely discussable" dimensions of the organizational culture that inhibit or promote agile capabilities.

Thinking Exercises

1. Research the Quinn, Schein, and Great Place to Work models of organizational culture. Create a chart to compare and contrast the various elements. Discuss which one provides insight that would be useful and actionable for an executive who thinks that there are issues within the culture. Explain your reasoning.
2. Look up the Great Place to Work list of 100 Best Companies in the USA. Identify one company that has been on the list for each of the past three years. Then do some research to identify what makes the culture good. Discuss how the positive elements of the culture in your company help the company to be successful.
3. Consider Peter Drucker's well-known statement that "Culture eats strategy for breakfast." Do you think that Drucker is right? If not, why not? Explain your reasoning.
4. How might "unconscious, and rarely discussable" shared assumptions in an organization help or hinder the ability of an organization to adapt and change? Explain your reasoning.
5. Using the organization that you work for or one that you know well, choose one of the three models from question #1 and apply it to your organization. Explain how and why you think your groupings make sense. Explain your reasoning.

Suggested Reading

Finkelstein, S. *The DaimlerChrysler Merger*. Dartmouth University, Tuck School of Business, 2002.

McLean, B., & P. Elkind. *The Smartest Guys in the Room: The Amazing Rise and Scandalous Fall of Enron*. New York, NY: The Penguin Group, 2003. Also recommended viewing the documentary based on the book released in 2005.

Schein, E. *Organizational Culture and Leadership*. San Francisco: Jossey-Bass, 1985.

CHAPTER 6

THE PERFORMANCE TRIANGLE....
MODEL FOR AGILE STRATEGY

The Performance Triangle Model

Our work on the Performance Triangle Model (PTM) for agile organizational design in a turbulent world emerged from nearly twenty years of observation and research with over 200 organizations worldwide.[1,2] My friend and colleague, Lukas Michel, provided the foundational framework for the concepts of agile management in his groundbreaking book *The Performance Triangle; Diagnostic Mentoring to Manage Organizations and People for Superior Performance in Turbulent Times* in 2013. We have continued to build on the original foundations with additional data, research, and new knowledge to develop a workable and practical methodology with tools to help executives to design and mold organizations that can be successful in the VUCA 21st century. The data collected, collated, and analyzed show that 78% of problems with performance, innovation and growth in organizations can be avoided if senior executives consciously design their organization to be agile. We have long argued that agile thinking and strategies should originate in the boardroom and flow from there to the C-suite then throughout the entire organization. Agile principles, beliefs, values and attitudes, center around people and the massive body of tacit knowledge embedded within their minds and experience. Agile principles and capabilities include developing the ability to facilitate change, collaboration through the organizations vertically and horizontally, a focus on excellence, engaging in interactive dialogue and conversation at all levels, self-organization, and continuous improvement as a way of life. Agile concepts originated with IT around the need to develop better software, faster, and more efficiency. Social technologies such as scrum, Kanban, six-sigma, and lean helped to establish new and more effective ways of working together to improve the delivery of products or services. The general idea in these methodologies is to decrease response time by empowering teams to self-organize and act within the scope of their own domain, department, work group, or project team. Agile management originated as a bottom-up culture change from those who do the work. On the other hand, comprehensive culture change needs to be led from the very top and adopted by everyone from top to bottom of the organization chart. When one considers that organizational culture exists in the minds of people in their values, beliefs, and shared assumptions, changing the culture is easier said than done. We can all relate to the difficulty of changing the culture if we reflect on how difficult it is to change the fundamental beliefs and values of just one person, let alone magnify that by hundreds or thousands of people. Clearly, anytime that business leaders say they need to evaluate and change the culture of the organization, they are in for a long and hard journey that is more likely to fail than succeed.

For years, we have argued that agile management is led from the top and gives companies a competitive strategic and tactical advantage. In our 2017/18 agile management design study we gathered and compiled data from senior executives representing 220 companies worldwide. Results from the study revealed how implementing agile management capabilities helps organizations to achieve six multidimensional goals:

- to get work done more efficiently,
- to create value for all stakeholders,
- to be specific and target critical needs,
- to incorporate processes that are hard to copy,
- to avoid short-cuts, and
- to deeply embed agile philosophies throughout the people.[3]

Our first agile management design study was done in 2008 and repeated in 2013. With the results from the 2017/18 study, we can now paint a picture of what agile attributes top, middle, and bottom tier companies have developed and where they are in what we call "agile maturity." Agile maturity is a measure of how effectively the organizations have adapted and institutionalized agile concepts and practices. In other words, Nonaka would use the SECI process to say that the organization "internalized" the power of new agile management knowledge and techniques. Sun Tzu would include internalizing agile management principles and structure as a key factor (methods and discipline) needed for success on the battlefield that is the 21st century business environment.

"There ought to be ways of reforming a business, other than merely putting more money into it." – **Winston Churchill**

The Performance Triangle Model (PTM) illustrated in Figure 6.1 is a visual representation of a dynamic system of culture, leadership, and systems that is powered by people who work in an environment that nurtures healthy relationships, collaboration, and a strong sense of purpose, and share their unique and valuable tacit knowledge. Culture is a major component of the dynamic system and cannot be effectively changed without recognizing and addressing key elements of the ENTIRE system. Since the culture resides in the minds and experiences of people, people become the focus of attention because power for the entire PTM system comes from the ability of people to maximize their inherent capabilities to fuel change. However, culture with all its intangibles and people with all of their idiosyncrasies and uncertainties make actively creating a people-centric management design very difficult. Senior executives intrinsically know that "people are our most valuable asset" and the corporate mission or vision statement says this. But where does the CEO begin to gain insight into what is going on in the minds of people so he/she can roll out another initiative? CEOs spend vast sums of money with consulting firms like Deloitte Consulting, Accenture, or McKinsey who use their canned methodology to generate advice for the CEO on issues he was probably already aware of. As a former CFO, I issued many checks to consulting firms that promoted the "flavor of the month" strategy to address people issues and rarely felt that I got my money's worth. As a result, companies try one method then another typically without getting to the root cause of the problems that are being observed and certainly not adding value by helping the CEO to maximize the potential of people to create an agile organization. In order to avoid this aimless wandering and fruitless expenditure of cash, CEOs need a workable model and advisors who take a diagnostic approach. Think of it as a doctor.

Figure 6.1 – The Performance Triangle

Source: Adapted from Michel, L. (2013). *The Performance Triangle: Diagnostic Mentoring to Manage Organizations and People for Superior Performance in Turbulent Times*, London, UK: LID

How would you feel if you went to a doctor who prescribed pills or procedures without first taking your blood pressure or listening to your heart? I suspect, you would not have much confidence in the doctor's diagnosis, yet this is exactly what business executives do when confronted with culture and people. While teaching university courses we constantly emphasize the need for management action. All the vast amount of data, information, and resulting knowledge without resulting action is worthless to an organization. If you know what is going on and why and what to do about it, and then do nothing, the effort was worthless. The first step in the process is having a practical model that asks questions that delve deep into the underlying values, beliefs, and shared assumptions that make up the critical elements of the culture. Take the pulse, blood pressure, and heartbeat that power the organization.... the people. So, we have developed a workable and practical model for organizational agility and success along with a validated diagnostic instrument to assess the strength of multiple dimensions that drive the PTM system.[4] This allows executives to assess the strengths and weaknesses within the culture and take targeted action quickly and efficiently to create an agile organization that will be given a strategic advantage.

"You can analyze the past, but you have to design the future" – **Edward de Bono**

Over the decades, we have observed countless organizations in which unseen beliefs and shared assumptions infect large segments of an organization, interfering with knowledge sharing and the decision-making process like a virus in the human body. Bertalanffy was right in using the analogy of a living organism to describe organizational dynamics. We can all relate that we, as humans, will not perform at our peak if we have a migraine headache or stomachache, or definitely with a broken bone. The same thing applies to an organization. If one department or individual does not perform well, the whole organization suffers with under performance. Maybe, more importantly, if information and critical knowledge are not shared among departments or individuals, the whole organization suffers. These interferences or organizational viruses are almost always unknown to senior executives and derail or sabotage the most well-conceived strategic plan or action. In which major company will low-level staff employees walk into the CEO's office and tell him or her that they do not trust their boss or that their manager's actions are not consistent with the stated mission or value statements of the company? In most cases, executives would be wise to identify and address the interferences and eliminate the viruses BEFORE spending valuable energy and resources on change initiatives with a low probability of success. We contend that armed with insight into many "unconscious and rarely discussable" beliefs, values, and shared assumptions embedded within the employee population, executives will be able to take targeted and effective actions to design agile organizations that will be successful in a VUCA 21st century environment and dramatically increase the probability of a successful change initiative.

How do we measure success?

In the 20th century, success was traditionally measured using tangible assets, and for-profit companies still measure success by stock price, earnings per share (EPS), return on assets (ROA), etc. This can be broken down to functional departments where marketing might use market share as a measure while finance might use investment income. While such tangible, financial measures are important, relevant, and necessary particularly to investors and business owners, we prefer to define success by attributes of successful organizations that we have observed. What are the underlying or fundamental capabilities and organizational beliefs that drive performance yielding results in increased market share or profits? What are the underlying behaviors that are driven by beliefs and values which result in innovations, process improvements, or ideas that bring value to the organization? All these measures are outcomes… the result of hundreds or maybe thousands of people inside and outside of the organization whose combined talents and special knowledge yield innovative products or profits or improved client service if the organization is a service or governmental agency. By defining success by attributes rather than financial performance or tangible assets, we can include not-for-profit organizations, governmental agencies, private companies, and functional departments or business units in addition to for-profit companies. It is necessary to first identify and understand the underlying organizational environment and conditions that enable people, including managers and leaders, to made decisions and take actions that generate desirable results. There is an old philosophical saying that "If you ask 'why' five times, you can get to the root cause of any problem or question." Taiichi Ohno applied and refined this "5 whys" thinking process to business during the 1950s at Toyota and helped to propel Toyota to the global automotive powerhouse it is today.[5] We have applied a similar 5-why process in interviews with executives to gather increasingly insightful data, allowing us to dig deeper into the underlying conditions needed for success in a VUCA world. After nearly two decades of study and asking "why?" we have observed that top tier companies have strong foundations in responsiveness, alignment, capabilities, motivation, and cleverness. These underlying core attributes, we believe, help companies to accelerate the rate of new knowledge creation and be agile so they can adapt and change quickly in a VUCA world. The logic goes as follows.

- If you are **responsive** to your customers' needs, requests, and expectations, and changes in the environment…. You might be successful!
- If your people and managers are **aligned** in their goals and aspirations with all working toward the same common objective… You might be successful!
- If the people in your organization have the right set of **capabilities**, skills, expertise and tools needed to quickly and efficiently deliver the company's products or services…. You might be successful!
- If your employees throughout the organization are **motivated** and inspired to perform above management's expectation and over deliver on customers' expectations…. You might be successful!
- If your employees are empowered and have the freedom to use their innate **creativity** and tacit knowledge to meet or exceed management and customers' expectations within reasonable boundaries… You might be successful!

In our view, motivated employees armed with the essential needed capabilities who have personal goals and objectives aligned with organizational goals and are empowered and encouraged to use their cleverness and creativity to be responsive to customers and clients will make any organization successful. Results from our 2017/18 study displayed in Figure 6.2 show that top tier organizations with a score of 82 out of 100 have adopted and implemented the elements of the Performance Triangle Model in ways that help them to have a score that is 49% higher than bottom tier organizations. These organizations have developed environments where people at all levels are able to utilize their innate skills and unique knowledge to perform at their peak. Top tier companies have created a dynamic operating environment where

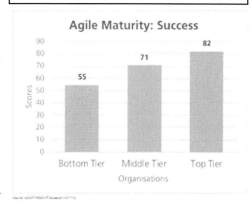

Figure 6.2 – Agility Study Results

leadership, systems and a culture enable people to get work done quickly and effectively. These companies have also made it possible for people to find purpose and take pride in what they do and the organizational mission and vision, to collaborate openly across organizational boundaries and to connect with others who have special knowledge inside and outside the organization to enhance knowledge and cooperation. Essentially, these top tier companies are finding ways to institutionalize management practices and structures that combine parts of the Great Place to Work Institute culture model with Nonaka's SECI cycle for knowledge creation in a dynamic system that the Performance Triangle Model helps to visualize.

The success scores are nearly independent of context, organization size, management model, life cycle, structure, type of company, or industry. Our population of over 200 companies includes mature massive multinationals along with startups, public and private companies along with governmental agencies and not-for-profit organizations, banks, manufacturing companies, and service companies. The broad population allows us to generalize and suggest that the underlying success capabilities that we have identified apply equally across a broad spectrum of organizations. This means that regardless of the specifics of an organization, those that have chosen an agile design are clearly more successful than those organizations that have not invested in implementing agile management principles. Agile designs identify, and then seek to eliminate interferences that inhibit knowledge sharing to unlock the latent potential and capabilities inside of people and ultimately... the organization.

What is next?

Agile management is not simply some new theory or digital tool like some software program or a new way to organize work like lean or six-sigma. The Performance Triangle Model and associated tools explore the root capabilities and underlying beliefs, values, and shared assumption that enable an organization to be agile. In the past century, a management style and structure that worked might be effective for decades. The emergence of General Motors Corporation in the 20th century as the world's largest industrial enterprise is a good example. GM's growth and success are largely credited to Alfred P. Sloan. Alfred Sloan became the president of General Motors in 1923 and retired as its chairman in 1956. Sloan is credited by many for introducing the concept and practice of planned obsolescence by establishing annual styling changes with a modest improvement in engineering so that customers felt a need to buy the latest and greatest car because it looked different or had some new feature. Sloan also continued a practice begun by the founders of GM of acquiring smaller car companies. He established a pricing structure by brand in which (from lowest to highest priced) Chevrolet, Pontiac, Oldsmobile, Buick and Cadillac, were referred to as the ladder of success. The intent was for models not to compete against each other and customers could be kept in the GM "family" as their buying power and preferences changed as they aged.[6] These strategies, along with Ford's resistance to the change (another excellent example of failed 20th century management philosophies) in the 1920s, propelled GM to become the largest car manufacturer in the world by the early 1930s. GM retained this dominant position for over 70 years until being overtaken by Toyota. Under Sloan's direction, GM became the largest industrial enterprise the world had ever known. Sloan designed and built huge hierarchal management structures, and then became famous for managing diverse operations with financial statistics such as return on investment. Promotions, salaries, and bonuses were based almost entirely on a manager's ability to hit financial targets that had been set by the corporate office and assigned to all segments of the organization, with little or no input. Research in recent decades has shown that such rigid and formalized management structures are essentially anti-change and effective as long as change is happening very slowly… like a glacier… As Figure 6.3 shows, by 2017 General Motors and Ford ranked 4th and 5th in worldwide vehicle production after Toyota, the Volkswagen Group, and Hyundai.[7]

Figure 6.3 – World Motor Vehicle Production

WORLD RANKING OF MANUFACTURERS

Rang	GROUP	Year 2016 SUM	Year 2017 SUM
	Total	94 020 883	96 922 080
1	TOYOTA	10 213 486	10 466 051
2	VOLKSWAGEN	10 126 281	10 382 334
3	HYUNDAI	7 889 538	7 218 391
4	G.M.	6 971 710	6 856 880
5	FORD	6 457 773	6 386 818
6	NISSAN	5 556 241	5 769 277
7	HONDA	4 999 266	5 236 842
8	FIAT	4 681 457	4 600 847
9	RENAULT	3 373 278	4 153 589
10	PSA	3 152 787	3 649 742

Source: OICA correspondents survey, 2020

"So much of what we call management consists of making it difficult for people to work" – **Peter Drucker**

Terry Howerton, founder and CEO of TechNexus, the venture collaborative, suggested that most of today's large companies will cease to exist or be replaced during the next ten years. Many large companies have failed to develop the core competencies needed to sense threatening emerging technologies, make operations more efficient, or form hard-to-break bonds with customers. Most CEOs seem to recognize that the rapid pace of change in technology and society is a serious threat to their company's future... and their own. Howerton cited a few statistics to make the point that senior executives must develop the ability to "see around corners," meaning they must be able to sense threats early enough to take effective action.

- Nearly 75% of the companies in the Fortune 1,000 have been replaced in the past 10 years.
- In the upcoming decade, over half of the Fortune 500 companies will cease to exist.
- Only 20% of the chief strategy officers in large companies feel that they are highly prepared to react to the coming disruptions.[8]

However, the future need not be so bleak because many Fortune 500 and middle-market CEOs say that they recognize the need for agility in order to be competitive in the future. Visionary CEOs are trying out a variety of strategies like corporate venture capital, accelerators and innovation labs. Executives throughout the world are realizing that change is never easy, and it takes collaboration among people both internal and external to the company to maintain a competitive edge. While this is a good first step, we suggest that executives must dig deeper and ask the right questions using the 5-why technique. Who in your organization is the first to sense changes in customer expectations? Where do ideas for innovation come from? Who knows how to make some process more efficient? Most likely, it is not the CEO who is far removed from the everyday interactions with customers, suppliers, and the many stakeholders who are a driving force for the organization. More likely, the people who interact with customers, suppliers, and stakeholders are the ones who sense when change is in the wind. The challenge for senior executives is "how to become aware of the observations that are being sensed by the people in closest contact."

The results of our 2018 agile management study confirm that there is a huge untapped potential to make organizations nimbler and faster. The trick for the executive is to ask the right questions. If you do not ask the right question, you will not get the right answer. We have developed a diagnostic assessment tool with questions to assess the perceived intensity of the dimensions for success within the employee population that are the foundation of the Performance Triangle Model. This is just the first step. Feedback from people within an organization on these questions should prompt further "why?" questions. Answers to these questions will help executives to gain insight into whether the organization has the agile capabilities to be successful and to be one of the 50% of the Fortune 500 companies that will still be around in 10 years.

- **Responsiveness** – Is the organization flexible and able to react to changes in the environment?
- **Alignment** – Is the direction of the organization clear? Does the structure fit the strategy? Is it shared broadly and are employees aligned to support the strategies?
- **Capabilities** – Does the organization have the competencies and skills needed to deliver on promises?
- **Motivation** – Are employees throughout the organization inspired to perform above and beyond expectations?
- **Cleverness** – Are employees empowered to be creative and use their creativity to meet expectations or demands from clients or customers within boundaries that do not stifle creativity?

We feel that if the answer to these questions is yes, then the organization will likely be successful and have advanced on the agility maturity scale enough to still exist a decade from now. Essentially, if people are equipped with proper capabilities, are aligned and motivated to excel, and empowered to use their innate creativity to react to changes; the organization will be successful. Unfortunately, if (for example) well-intentioned rules and regulations stifle creativity or if actions in one department interfere with the ability of another department to align with corporate strategy, senior executives will rarely be aware of the condition. Few employees will walk into the CEO's office and say "you are killing me with unnecessary rules" in any organization. The first step toward designing an agile organization for success is to ask the right questions, then dig deeper into the dimensions of the Performance Triangle Model to gain more granular insight and develop actionable plans to address those pesky "unconscious and rarely discussed" values, beliefs, and shared assumptions that interfere with knowledge sharing and the ability of CEOs to "see around corners."

Thinking Exercises

1. Reflect on the five elements of success in the Performance Triangle Model. Discuss how and why each might, or might not, promote success for both for-profit and not-for-profit organizations. Are there others that should be added to the list? Explain your reasoning.

2. How might the measures for success be different for for-profit, not-for-profit, and governmental organizations? Explain how and why.

3. Look up the Great Place to Work list of 100 Best Companies in the USA. Select one for-profit and one not-for-profit organization. Research each organization and try to estimate the levels or strength of each dimension of success. Explain your reasoning.

4. Using the organization that you work for or one that you know well, evaluate the strength of each dimension of success. Explain how and why you think that the measures of success are strong or weak. Explain your reasoning.

Suggested Reading

Michel, L. *The Performance Triangle: Diagnostic Mentoring to Manage Organizations and People for Superior Performance in Turbulent Times*. London, UK: LID Publishing Ltd., 2013.

Sloan, A. P. *My Years with General Motors*. Garden City, NY: Doubleday, 1964.

CHAPTER 7

THE PERFORMANCE TRIANGLE MODEL ....
POWERED BY LIMITLESS ENERGY
FROM PEOPLE

Quick Review... getting up to speed

Introduced in Chapter Six, the Performance Triangle Model (PTM) for agile organizational design in a turbulent world emerged after nearly twenty years of observation and research with over 200 organizations worldwide.[1,2] The PTM illustrated in Figure 7.1 describes a dynamic system of leadership, systems, and culture that is powered by people. Notice that people are at the center of the PTM triangle. There is a reason for this. All dynamic systems require power from some source to operate. Electric power generating systems are powered by nuclear fission, coal, gas, hydro power, or the sun. Cars and trucks are powered by gasoline, diesel fuels, and increasingly by electricity. Living organisms are powered by foods eaten and then converted through chemical processes into energy or in the case of plants water and nutrients are converted to life-giving energy through the process of photosynthesis that is powered by the sun. In each instance, fuel is converted to energy that is transmitted throughout the system to make the car move or the living organism grow. All

Figure 7.1 – The Performance Triangle

Source: Adapted from Michel, L. (2013). *The Performance Triangle: Diagnostic Mentoring to Manage Organizations and People for Superior Performance in Turbulent Times*, London, UK: LID

dynamic systems require an energy source and a mechanism to transmit that energy throughout the system. Management systems are no different. Management systems are powered by people who generate new knowledge with their tacit experiences, creative thinking, and socialization skills. However, it has not always been this way. The recognition and appreciation that people are a critical force that can give an organization a competitive advantage emerged during the last half of the 20th century but remains an elusive management concept. Practical methods or approaches to harnessing the power of people remain an emergent topic in both academic and business practice worlds. As with cars and trucks, the engineering and management focus throughout much of the last century was primarily on developing the most efficient ways to harness energy to yield the greatest output and control the behaviors of people. I suggest that success in the 21st century is finding the "right" balance between efficiency and control in an environment that enables people to use their tacit knowledge and experience for the betterment of the organization and society as a whole.

A little history... how we got here

Early 20th Century – "scientific management" and bureaucracy

At the beginning of the industrial age, over a century ago, Fredrick Winslow Taylor developed and introduced "scientific management" in his groundbreaking 1901 book *Principles of Scientific Management*.[3] The fundamental idea behind "scientific management" was to improve efficiency by employing highly specific "command and control" practices to shape the behaviors of workers to achieve higher levels of productivity. Greater efficiency in the Taylor philosophy, called Taylorism, was achieved by assigning workers specific targets or quotas and then offering incentives to follow specific procedures and meet predetermined standards which were assigned by managers. Taylor's view was that workers were motivated by basic instincts which were primarily driven by money. Therefore, workers would only respond to financial incentives tied to specific performance standards. The influence of Taylorism can still be seen and felt today as companies set performance goals, financial incentives, and productivity improvement programs like six-sigma. By the middle of the last century Taylorism began accumulating critics who questioned his approach by pointing out issues like resistance to control and disputes,[4] dehumanizing on ethical grounds,[5,6] and the introduction of democratic processes that encouraged worker participation, dialogue, and methods to improve performance without trampling on workers' human rights.[7] The Taylor "scientific management" model with the emphasis on highly bureaucratic "command and control" style organizations that were promoted by the German sociologist Max Weber dominated management thinking and practices throughout the 20th century.

"Bureaucratic administration means fundamentally domination through knowledge." – Max Weber

Max Weber wrote that the modern bureaucracy in both the public and private sectors relies on the following principles. "First, it is based on the general principle of precisely defined and organized across-the-board competencies of the various offices. These competencies are underpinned by rules, laws, or administrative regulations"(p. 77).[8,9] For Weber, this meant the following:

1. A rigid division of labor to identify the regular tasks and duties of everyone in the particular bureaucratic system,
2. Regulations that describe firmly and clearly established hierarchal chains of command and the duties of each position as well as the power that the position has to coerce others to comply with rules, regulations, and edicts, and
3. People should be hired with the specific, certified, qualifications needed to effectively perform regular and continuous duties assigned to a specific position.

Weber emphasized that these three principles "...constitute the essence of bureaucratic administration ... in the public sector. In the private sector, these three aspects constitute the essence of a bureaucratic management of a private company" (p. 77). In Weber's view the primary principles or characteristics of an effective bureaucratic organization consisted of the following,

1. Specialized roles for people up and down the hierarchy and throughout the organization.
2. Recruitment of new workers and promotions based on merit tested through open competition.
3. Uniform principles (job descriptions and duties) for hiring new employees, promotions, and transfers throughout the administrative system.
4. Careerism (the policy or practice of advancing one's career often at the expense of one's integrity, personal life, ethics, etc.) with a systematic salary structure.

5. A rigid hierarchy with clearly defined and specific responsibilities and accountability.
6. Forced regulation of official conduct to strict rules of discipline and control.
7. Supremacy of abstract rules and regulations that govern all aspects of behavior and job performance.
8. Impersonal authority (e.g., it's not personal, it's just business).
9. Political neutrality (e.g., don't take sides in disputes).

The combined writings by both Taylor and Weber profoundly influenced management thinking and techniques throughout the 20th century and are still practiced today. I suspect that many of you can recognize many adaptations of Taylorism and Weber's command and control bureaucratic organizations where you work or in organizations that you know well today. Around the middle of the 20th century, the human relations movement began to emerge that advocated the concept of treating people as human beings to improve performance.

"The way you see them is the way you treat them and the way you treat them is the way they often become." – **Zig Ziglar**

Mid-20th Century – Human Relations and Motivation

In the 1940s, the famous Hawthorne experiments conducted by Elton Mayo caused Mayo and others to begin questioning the prevailing assumptions that shaped economic and behavioral theory; (1) That natural society consists of a horde of unorganized individuals; (2) That every individual acts in a manner calculated to secure his self-interests; and (3) That every individual thinks logically, to the best of his ability, in the service of this aim.[10] Mayo concluded that business leaders believed that the only way to effectively motivate people was through financial incentives. However, Mayo's studies showed that workers' performance was also linked to social interactions in the workplace and money was **NOT** the only motivation for workers. As a result, Mayo suggested that providing a supporting and accommodating work environment should be a manager's primary task in order to maximize human potential.

During the 1950s and 1960s, the writings of Abraham Maslow and Fredrick Herzberg reinforced Mayo's findings and firmly demonstrated that people were motivated by things other than money. Maslow's hierarchy of needs summarized in Figure 7.2 proposed that people are motivated to achieve certain basic needs and that some needs take precedence over others.

Figure 7.2 – Maslow's Hierarchy of Needs

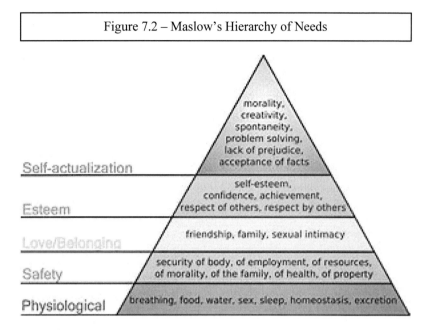

Our most basic need is for physical survival, and this will be the first thing that motivates our behavior. Once that level is fulfilled, the next level up is what motivates us, and so on. Maslow theorized that human needs are arranged in a hierarchy in which needs from one level must be met before people can advance psychologically to the next higher level.[11,12] Herzberg developed the two-factor theory (also known as Herzberg's motivation-hygiene theory or dual-factor theory) based on the results from interviews with 203 engineers and accountants in the Pittsburg, Pennsylvania, area. The two-factor theory states that there are certain factors in the workplace that cause job satisfaction while a separate set of factors causes dissatisfaction, all of which act independently of each other. The two-factor theory distinguishes between motivators and hygiene factors:

- **Motivators** – Examples of motivators include challenging work, recognition for one's performance and accomplishments, responsibility, the opportunity to take on tasks or projects that are meaningful and satisfying, involvement in decision-making, and a sense of importance to an organization. Motivators give workers positive satisfaction, arising from the intrinsic conditions of the job itself, such as recognition, achievement, or personal growth.

- **Hygiene factors** – Examples of hygiene factors include status or job title, job security, salary, fringe benefits, workplace conditions, paid insurance, and paid vacations. Hygiene factors do not result in positive satisfaction or lead to higher motivation. However, the absence of these factors leads to high levels of dissatisfaction. The term "hygiene" is used in the sense that these are the minimum expectations or maintenance factors that workers expect to receive. These factors are extrinsic to the work itself and include aspects such as company policies, supervisory practices, or wages/salary. The threat of punishment to make someone do something is also a hygiene factor.

According to Herzberg, hygiene factors, or more accurately the lack of satisfactory hygiene factors, are the primary causes of employee dissatisfaction in the workplace. Workplace dissatisfaction can only be removed if the employee's hygiene factors are satisfied. There are several ways that this can be done, but some of the most important ways to decrease dissatisfaction would be to pay reasonable wages, ensure job security to employees, and create a positive culture in the workplace. Herzberg considered the following hygiene factors from highest to lowest importance: (1) company policy, (2) supervision, (3) an employee's relationship with their boss, (4) work conditions, (5) salary, and (6) relationships with peers.[13,14] Notice that salary (wages or compensation) is relatively low on the list.

"The ingenuity of the average worker is sufficient to outwit any system of controls devised by management." – **Douglas McGregor**

Later 20th Century – Theory X and Y

In 1960, Douglas McGregor's highly influential book, *The Human Side of Enterprise*, summed up much of the prior work on employee motivation by grouping managerial styles based on how managers view typical workers into two general categories that he called Theory X and Theory Y (see Figure 7.3). These fundamental assumptions about human nature and what motivates workers shape the manager's style when organizing work and dealing with employees.

Theory X style managers assume that the typical worker has little ambition, avoids responsibility, and is more interested in achieving individual goals than those of the company. In general, Theory X style managers believe their employees are less intelligent, lazier, and work solely

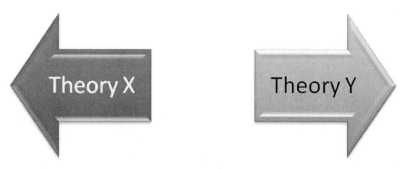

Figure 7.3 – Theory X vs. Theory Y

Attitude

We dislike work, find it boring, and will avoid it if we can.	We need to work and want to take an interest in it. Under the right conditions, we can enjoy it

Direction

We must be forced or coerced to make the right effort.	We will direct ourselves towards a target that we accept.

Responsibility

We would rather be directed than accept responsibility, which we avoid.	We will seek and accept responsibility, under the right conditions

Motivation

We are motivated mainly by money and fears about their job security.	Under the right conditions, we are motivated by the desire to realize our own potential.

Creativity

Most of us have little creativity – except when it comes to getting around rules.	We are highly creative creatures – but are rarely recognized as such or given the opportunity to be.

for the money.[15] Management fundamentally believes that employees' work ethic and motivation are based on their own self-interest. Managers who believe that employees operate in this manner are more likely to use rewards or punishments as motivation.[16] With these underlying assumptions of what motivates workers, Theory X managers believe that the typical workforce operates more efficiently with a hands-on approach by management.[15] Theory X managers believe that all actions should be traceable to the individual responsible which allows the individual to receive either a direct reward or a reprimand, depending on the outcome of the task or assignment.[16]

I suspect that many of you have observed this style of management... the dictatorial micro-manager. Theory Y managers assume employees are internally motivated, enjoy their job, and work to better themselves and the organization without a direct reward in return. These managers view their employees as one of the most valuable assets to the company and design the structure and shape the culture around this fundamental assumption. Under Theory Y, employees additionally tend to take full responsibility for their work and do not need close supervision to generate a quality product or service. It is important to note, however, that employees must obtain the manager's approval before performing certain tasks.[15] Obtaining prior approval for special tasks or performing by following predetermined instructions provides assurance that work is done efficiently, productively, and in line with company standards.

As shown in Figure 7.3 the differences in how managers view human nature result in very different, almost diametrically opposed, management styles. Theory Y managers tend to relate to employees on a more personal level, as opposed to a more directive or incentive-based relationship exhibited by Theory X managers.[15] As a result, people who work for Theory Y managers may have a better relationship with their boss which creates a healthier workplace atmosphere. In comparison to Theory X, Theory Y encourages a more democratic work environment where employees are empowered to design and perform and coordinate their work to manage their own workloads or projects.[17]

"Above all, it is necessary to recognize that knowledge cannot be pumped into human beings the way grease is forced into a machine. The individual may learn; he is not taught." **– Douglas McGregor, The Human Side of Enterprise**

Although Theory Y enables more creativity and discussion, the Theory Y style does have its weaknesses. While there is a more personal and individualistic atmosphere, this opens the possibility for more error in terms of consistency and uniformity for both products and services.[17] The workplace may lack uniform rules and practices, which could be potentially harmful to the quality standards of the product or strict guidelines of the company.

According to McGregor, there are two opposing approaches to implementing Theory X: the hard approach and the soft approach. Managers using the hard approach depend on close supervision, intimidation, and immediate punishment.[15] The hard approach can potentially result in a hostile, minimally cooperative workforce that may cause resentment towards management. Managers using a hard approach are always looking for mistakes from employees because they do not trust the employees' work. The hard approach results in an "us versus them" atmosphere in the workplace where the shared perception is management versus employees.[16]

The soft approach is characterized by leniency with less strict rules to create a more positive morale and cooperation with employees. However, implementing a system that is too soft could result in an entitled, low-output workforce. McGregor believed that both ends of the Theory X spectrum were too extreme for efficient real-world application. McGregor felt that an approach located in the middle would be the most effective implementation of Theory X.[16] As managers and supervisors are in almost complete control of the routine work, the Theory X approach produces a more systematic and uniform product or workflow.[15] Theory X can be beneficial in a workplace with an assembly line or manual labor. Using Theory X in repetitive or manual labor workplaces enables employees to specialize in specific work areas or tasks, allowing the company to mass-produce a higher quantity and quality of work in volume.[15]

The 1980s and 1990s – Goals and Objectives

Management practices in the last few decades of the 20th century were dominated by the idea of goal orientation where an employee's behavior and resulting productive output could be shaped by incentives designed to promote actions that supported corporate goals and objectives. The application of goal-oriented practices considered the emergent human relations concepts and took into account the growing individualism among highly educated "knowledge workers" who are motivated by intrinsic rewards and quality of work rather than extrinsic rewards for meaningless tasks. The need for self-direction and the need to develop specific competencies gained more importance in management practices. Finding a balance between the desire to control behaviors and performance and motivate employees while at the same time providing sufficient freedom for employees to utilize their unique talents and abilities emerged in a variety of forms. Six-sigma and lean strategies were applied primarily to improve productivity in manufacturing operations while management by objectives (MBO) became a popular strategy throughout all functions within many organizations.

PDSA and Six-sigma

The plan, do, study, and act (PDSA) process illustrated in Figure 7.4, initially popularized by W. Edwards Deming, became a fundamental component of six-sigma and lean practices. Six-sigma in particular, focuses on the science of measuring variability in the production process, setting standards that if maintained provided reasonable assurance that the desired quality levels would be achieved. The process is actually fairly simple.

Figure 7.4 – The PDSA Process

- Plan the manufacturing process with standards or specifications designed to meet a desired level of quality. Then measure performance against the desired specifications and make plans to correct any deviation.
- Implement the corrective actions to make a small change toward meeting the standard or goal.
- Study the results from the change.
- Make further changes and improvements in the process needed to zero in on the desired tolerances in the product.

However, six-sigma methodologies that were popularized by General Electric in the 1980s paid little attention to the human or behavioral aspect of performance. Six-sigma was, and still is, an updated and modernized version of Taylor's "scientific management." While it is popular and useful in many companies to help improve productivity, the methodology's lack of attention to the human aspect is perceived as a weakness by many scholars and managers.

Management by Objectives (MBO)

Management by objectives (MBO), also known as management by results (MBR), was first conceptualized by Peter Drucker in his 1954 book *The Practice of Management*.[18] However, the concepts were not widely applied until the later part of the 20th century with the capabilities enabled by computer technology that did not exist in the mid-1950s. Management by objectives is the process of defining specific objectives and quantifiable goals within an organization that management can communicate and cascade to employees at all levels, and then deciding how to achieve each objective in sequence. The idea is that managers and employees at all levels will identify and set goals that, if achieved, will support and advance the company's strategic objectives. This process allows managers to break down the work that needs to be done one step at a time to allow for a calm, yet productive work environment. MBO, in theory, also helps employees to see their accomplishments as they achieve each objective, which reinforces a positive work environment and sense of achievement.[19] An important part of MBO is the measurement and comparison of an employee's actual performance with the goals set. In theory, employees are more likely to be highly motivated and fulfill their responsibilities when they have been personally involved with the goal-setting process and choosing the course of action to be followed. The MBO system can be described as a process whereby the superior and subordinate jointly identify common goals, define everyone's major areas of responsibility in terms of the quantifiable results expected of him or her, and use these measures as guides for operating the unit and assessing the contribution of each employee.

"Management by objectives works if you first think through your objectives. 90% of the time you haven't." – **Peter Drucker**

The Balanced Scorecard

The balanced scorecard methodology was introduced in the 1990s as a way to align the actions and behaviors of all employees within an organization with the corporate strategic plan. The fundamental idea behind the balanced scorecard methodology is that success depends on more than just financial achievements. This approach defines financial and nonfinancial attributes that are believed to be necessary for the superior performance needed to execute the corporate strategic plans. The characteristic feature of the balanced scorecard and its many variations is the inclusion of a mixture of financial and nonfinancial measures, each of which is compared to a target value that is contained in a report. The report illustrated by the example in Figure 7.5, is not intended to be a replacement for traditional financial or operational reports but a compilation of key performance indicators (KPIs) that highlights the most relevant actions needed for superior performance and to advance the overall strategic plan. The intention is to translate the overall strategic mission and vision into measurable goals throughout the organization which, if achieved, will support the overall strategic vision and move the organization forward.

Figure 7.5 – Example of the Balanced Scorecard

Simple Balanced Scorecard Indicators Dashboard

Financial

Objectives	Target	Current
Maintain Probability	+.05%	-.02%
Reduce Operating Costs	+50k	-35
Minimize Debt	300k red	200k red
Efficient Billings	3 days	4 days

How we maintain our current financial strategies.

Learning and Growth

How we maintain our learning and growth strategies.

Current	Target	Objectives
3 new	4 new	Open New Regions
-20k	-18k	Reduce Operating Costs
11 new	10 new	Recruit Partners
1 new YTD	3 new	Innovative Products

Vision, Goals Strategy

Customer

Objectives	Target	Current
High Cast	4.55/5	4.52/2
Retain Customers	340	337
Fulfill Customer Needs	3/10	2.6/10
Loyalty Program	27% repeat	28% repeat

How we increase our success and maintain our customer strategies.

Internal Process

Internal initiatives and strategies designed to increase internal performance.

Current	Target	Objectives
77%	75%	Puperless office efforts
82%	65%	Centralize IT
12 empty	0 empty	Fill Empty FTEs
27% attr.	3% attr.	Employee Retention

Popularized by Harvard's Robert Kaplan and David Norton, the balanced scorecard approach suggested that the corporate strategy should drive all actions and behaviors and proposed methods that focused on choosing measures and targets associated with the main activities required to implement the vision and strategy.[20] Kaplan and Norton's proposed methodology emerged in a form that included financial measures as well as three categories of nonfinancial measures: customers, internal business processes, and learning and growth. Regular measures of targets compared to actual or current results were intended to focus employees on the "right" actions or behaviors and motivate employees to meet the targets. The design of a balanced scorecard is about the identification of a small number of financial and nonfinancial measures and attaching targets to them. When the difference between target and actual are reviewed, it is possible to determine whether current performance meets expectations and reinforces the strategic plan. By alerting managers to areas where performance deviates from expectations, employees can be encouraged to focus their attention on the key areas and hopefully trigger a behavioral change leading to improved performance.

The original thinking behind a balanced scorecard was to focus attention on information relating to the execution of a strategy, but through time there has been a blurring of the boundaries between conventional strategic planning activities and "command and control" activities with those needed to design an effective balanced scorecard. This is illustrated by the four steps that Kaplan and Norton identified as necessary to design a balanced scorecard in the late 1990s:

- Translating the vision and strategy into measurable operational goals,
- Communicating the strategy and vision, and then linking it to individual performance,
- Business planning and setting targets throughout the organization, and
- Feedback and learning followed by adjusting the strategy accordingly.

These steps go far beyond the relatively simple task of identifying a small number of financial and nonfinancial measures (KPIs) but illustrate how the resulting balanced scorecard should integrate with the wider business management process. Having personally implemented several balanced scorecards, some weaknesses and issues have emerged. The process of translating the strategic vision and goals into individual behaviors requires a strong understanding of and appreciation for human nature and motivation, which are absent in many managers. The result is that many KPIs lead to unintended consequences by reinforcing behaviors that are counterproductive. Another weakness in the balanced scorecard approach is that gathering and collating large quantities of detailed data for reporting require dedicated computing and human resources. In many organizations, it was found that the cost to manage the balanced scorecard process exceeded the benefit. One company that I was associated with was introduced to the balanced scorecard by a senior engineer who was a newly minted executive MBA. He convinced the owners that this approach was the latest and greatest method to motivate people and gain a competitive advantage. The process was rolled out and then discarded after 18 months when it was realized that behaviors were changing that were not intended and it was not cost effective.

The 21st Century .... Talent in search of a playing field

The underlying assumptions that drove management thinking and styles for dealing with people and motivation in the 20th century were dominated by the basic belief that the interests of the organization and the individual were different. Therefore, management philosophy was shaped by the belief that individuals were more likely to behave in ways that were in their personal interest rather than the interests of the organization. While the proliferation of human relations and Theory Y gained acceptance in the last quarter of the century, organizations and management theory remained focused on the need to control individuals either through formal mechanisms or by absorbing them into the culture or values of the organization. Employees' need for self-direction and to develop the competencies required for self-directive approaches gained in acceptance but remains an ideal rather than a reality in many, if not most, organizations.

Figure 7.6 – People, Potential, and Interferences

Potential	Understand	Create	Achieve	Contribute	Do "right"
Employees...	need feedback on where and how work is being done	need freedom to make decisions	are motivated by a sense of higher purpose	must have clear priorities	understand accepted norms and are empowered to take action
In a work environment with ...	unlimited access to key pieces of information	unlimited opportunities and encouraged to take risks		limited managerial oversight and limited resources	growing temptations
As compared to ...	critical information is limited to top managers	leaders making all decisions	increased pressures leaders who actively try to motivate to force performance	employees who just execute a job	managers who control what gets done
And face interferences from management due to...	lack of information	lack of opportunities and fear of taking a risk	lack of a sense of higher purpose	conflicting goals and lack of resources	lack of boundaries

Source: Adapted from Michel, L. (2013). *The Performance Triangle: Diagnostic Mentoring to Manage Organizations and People for Superior Performance in Turbulent Times*, London, UK: LID Publishing Ltd.

More recent thinking on motivation now suggests that knowledgeable people and knowledge workers are responsible and want to contribute to the success of the organization. Managers who accept this view of employee motivation can harness self-determination, self-control, self-initiative, and self-responsibility to advance the organization rather than using traditional "command and control" structures and practices. Forward-thinking leaders view talented and knowledgeable people as searching for a playing field where they can apply their gifts and talents for the benefit of the organization and themselves. The goals of the organization and the individual are not a zero-sum game. Summarized in Figure 7.5, both can be winners if people understand, create, achieve, contribute, and do what is "right" without managerial interferences that limit the productive use of their energy and abilities.

People must understand what is expected and how they are doing relative to the expectations. This requires an effective and constant feedback loop between the manager and the employee. Employees must be given the right information at the right time in an environment where they can separate the irrelevant from the relevant information to help them choose from alternative actions to effectively address specific situations. In too many organizations, key pieces of information are held by top managers; employees get distorted or conflicting feedback or no feedback at all on their performance. The result is that people make the best decision using flawed or missing information that does not support organizational or personal goals.

People instinctively want to create and innovate to find new ways of doing things. Innate human curiosity and a desire for new things power continuous improvement, but experimentation is inherently risky. As children, humans are curious about the world around them and ways to change it. However, as adults, our curiosity is constrained by rules and norms, limited resources, and a lack of opportunities in the organization. In many organizations, taking a risk is a formula for career destruction prompting people to just exist and slide by advance. We observed this in one organization where a new CEO was spending large sums of money on consultants and various leadership and process improvement programs while getting nowhere. After working with the company's top 18 executives, it was discovered that there was the perception among the executive team that they would be penalized if a risky project failed to deliver on expectations. Since each program involved risk, no corporate initiatives were going to work since the lower-level executives would not try to make them work. This "unconscious and rarely discussable" interference in the culture doomed every initiative to failure. We suggested that the CEO should take a year to try to change this shared assumption before spending more money on consultants with expensive change programs.

"If you want to kill innovation, reward it." – Alfie Kohn

People instinctively want to achieve and be recognized for their accomplishments. Achievements can yield tangible rewards, but the personal satisfaction of being able to say "I did it" can also be a powerful motivator. With a clear sense of purpose, both organizational and personal, people have an immense ability to accomplish feats not even imagined. Unfortunately, the main obstacle to unleashing the vast creative ability of people and achievements are the managers themselves who actively work to motivate people, and then try to direct their actions. This prevents people from finding a higher purpose for their efforts as commands are given without explanation so that the work does not make sense. Developing a sense of purpose that fuels the natural human desire for achievement requires managers to clearly explain what is to be done and why it is to be done, and then arm employees with the right information to make effective decisions.

The Center of the Performance Triangle Model .... People

Recall that people are at the center of the Performance Triangle Model. All systems need power to go, and if the PTM represents a dynamic system, then people represent the fuel that powers the system. Effective utilization of the innate human attributes needed to power the systems depends on creating an environment that permits... no ... encourages ... people to unleash limitless quantities of creativity and problem-solving abilities. While there are many factors that enable or inhibit the unleashing of natural ability, we have identified four factors that we believe are particularly powerful: focus, awareness, trust, and choice.

Focus of Attention

In an attempt to "manage" people in a way that demands compliance and helps to produce consistency and reliability in products and services, management develops and applies layer upon layer of rules, processes, and structure. While it is logical and helpful in many ways, this holdover from 20th century management philosophy in many cases creates an atmosphere where rules, paperwork, and processes become a hindrance rather than a method for performance improvement. Management structure, in many cases, causes people to focus their attention on "filling out the form, and be sure all of the blocks are checked" or "finish the report on time with no obvious mistakes." Too often these forms or reports were reasonable in a prior time and place but are no longer relevant. Yet, people are forced to focus their attention on these activities whether they contribute value or not. In my career, I was interrupted many times by the "boss" and directed to stop what I was doing and focus on some immediate task that had to be done by the end of the day, many times without explanation or reasoning why. The effect was to redirect my focus from the routine task which put me behind schedule to get the routine task done and introduced possibilities of errors in an attempt to refocus and make up for lost time. I suspect that many of you have experienced this dynamic.

Managers should periodically and critically reevaluate the need for many routine activities and then eliminate or modify those that do not add value to the end product or service. Such a process eliminates many interferences and would allow people to focus their attention on what is important. It is impossible to unleash creativity and innovation with interferences that prevent people from focusing their attention. We encourage managers to ask the following questions regularly and be honest with themselves.

Are people allowed to focus attention and energy on tasks? Are interferences preventing people from focusing their abilities to complete tasks?

Awareness

Every day, people at all levels of any organization are engaged with customers, suppliers, and other stakeholders. From the CEO to the guy on the shipping dock, people are in constant contact with elements of both the internal and external environment and must make on-the-spot decisions and take actions that collectively determine the success or failure of the organization as a whole. Traditional performance measurement methodologies and motivational strategies assume that senior management can shape behaviors and decisions in a way to force actions that advance and support the corporate objectives. However, experience has shown that it is impossible for senior managers to anticipate every possible variable or situation faced daily by people throughout the organization. As a result, people are forced to make decisions and take actions without being aware of how the decision might affect some other part of the organization or add value. Many well-intended decisions or actions lead to unintended consequences for the person making the decision or the customer/client, or some other stakeholder because the decision-maker was not aware of some important piece of information.

In order for people to make informed decisions and take decisive actions, they must be aware of relationships or conditions that are tangential to their immediate job. Managers must create an environment where critical information and knowledge are widely shared across the organizations so that people are aware of possible conflicts or issues…. before making a decision and taking action! Many companies develop a long-range strategic plan that is approved by the board of directors, then lock it up and do not share the plan with key decision-makers. The Neolithic thought was that some competitor might find some information from the strategic plan so it had to be locked up. In today's world, all stakeholders should know the plan and your competitors probably already know your plan. I personally worked for six years as vice-president of finance and operations for the largest business unit of a publicly traded company and almost daily made decisions that affected the company's performance and success. Yet, despite having quarterly review meetings at the corporate headquarters, I never saw the company's strategic plan. We developed our own strategic plan at the business unit level and shared it with all our people, yet we never knew if it supported and advanced the corporate strategic plan. If it did not, we probably would have been informed, after the fact. This was no way to run a ship. We encourage managers and senior executives to ask the following question regularly and be honest with themselves:

Are people aware of forces that influence actions and decisions? If the answer is "no," you might consider improving communications so that people can align their actions with those of the company's strategy and goals.

"There are managers so preoccupied with their e-mail messages that they never look up from their screens to see what's happening in the non-digital world." – **Mihaly Csikszentmihalyi**

Trust

Research in the fields of organizational behavior and organizational dynamics over the past 25 years consistently identifies trust as the single most powerful force to enable or stop the flow of knowledge throughout an organization. The research confirms what is intrinsically logical, that I won't share what I know with you if I don't trust you and you won't share what you know with me if you don't trust me. While painfully obvious to most of us, it remains a mystery to me how so many managers and people at all levels do things (actions or inactions) that destroy the trust among employees, supervisors, and upper management. The widely read 100 Best Places to Work is published in *Fortune Magazine* every year is compiled by the Great Place to Work (GPTW) Institute headquartered in San Francisco. The GPTW Institute is hired by thousands of companies to conduct extensive surveys that explore elements of the organizational culture. A key element of the GPTW model is the Trust Index© which is collectively:

credibility, respect, and fairness. The logic is simple and seemingly obvious; if management says what it means and does what it says, management will be credible. If you are treated with respect and dignity and if you are treated fairly, you might trust someone or the organization. My own research published in 2012 and 2013 provided empirical evidence supporting this intrinsically logical perception.[21,22] If there is a low level of trust within an organization whereby employees do not share what they know with other employees or managers, the flow of critical knowledge stops… completely. In our experience, when this happens, upper management is unlikely to be aware of the problem or the damage it causes or how their actions or inactions inadvertently contributed to creating an atmosphere lacking in trust. Employees will never enter the boss' office, close the door, and tell him or her that they do not trust them or anyone else for that matter. The vast majority of people tend to shun and avoid confrontation so what needs to be said, never is said, and the manager goes on his or her merry way oblivious to the underlying beliefs that are so damaging. We encourage managers and senior executives to routinely and regularly try to gain insight into the unseen "unconscious and rarely discussed" level of trust in their organizations either by employing confidential surveys or by (here is a novel thought for some managers) getting out of their office and walking around to talk to people and get to know them. Only after a relationship is established will people open up with their true thoughts and perceptions. We encourage managers and executives to ask the following questions in any way that will facilitate honest and truthful responses.

Do people trust co-workers and management to be treated fairly and with respect? Is management credible? If the response to either of these questions is "no," then management might do well to look at themselves with a critical and objective eye because in virtually every situation that we have found, the results of these perceptions are behaviors, actions or inactions which may be inadvertent. We all know from our personal relationships that trust is hard to earn but very easy to lose and once lost, even more difficult to regain. Managers may have to take years to undo damage and increase the level of trust throughout an organization, but without trust, all initiatives especially change initiatives will yield few if any results.

Choice

One of the keys to releasing the massive reservoir of energy in people is giving them freedom of choice. People must have freedom to choose from multiple possible solutions to problems or the choice to find a solution of their own that best fits the situation. Basic to enabling people to have choice is the freedom to say "no." For people to truly have choice, they must be allowed to say "no" when the available or conventional options do not fit the situation. Choice is about moving the situation and ultimately the entire organization in the right direction to add value. Without choice, there is no free will.

Making effective and timely choices requires that the decision-makers have options and awareness of the advantages or disadvantages and potential consequences of the choice. People who are in immediate contact with customers or suppliers make choices daily and must feel in control of their lives through accountability. Both employees and supervisors or managers must trust each other such that each is accountable for the effectiveness of the on-the-spot decision that may be made. Employees must have a degree of freedom to make a contribution, and rules, or boundaries must be flexible enough to allow sufficient room to move.

Freedom of choice requires people to be able to focus their attention on the problem or question at hand, have awareness of the options, pros and cons, and potential consequences, and trust in themselves and their superiors for support, even if the outcome turns out to be less than optimal. Giving people the room to move does not mean that there should be no boundaries. Every space is defined by boundaries, but the boundaries must be large enough to allow for a wide playing field and flexible enough to adapt to unexpected changes. A lack of space needed for freedom of choice limits the opportunities and the ability of people to use their talents. A lack of opportunity to perform leads to a lack of commitment from people. Essentially, giving people choice requires a synthesis of all the elements of effective people-centric management practices. When people become truly free to make effective choices, the organization has speed to react quickly to the daily onslaught of problems and issues as well as to identify and implement longer range solutions to nagging problems.

Managers indoctrinated with bureaucratic theory and the need to enforce conformity and consistency tend to build highly structured organizations bounded by mountains of rules, restrictions, and processes. While these structures might have been effective at one time, chances are that changes in the environment and the employee population have degraded the effectiveness of the management structure. However, managers will rarely be aware that their actions and rules are degrading operational efficiencies and inadvertently fighting the organization's ability to change.

We encourage managers and leaders to frequently ask the following questions, and then to be objective and introspective with the answers because they may not like the responses.

The key question regarding trust is, "Are people allowed freedom to use their own creative ability to solve problems, respond to customers, or to be innovative?" It may not be easy to solicit honest feedback if there is a lack of trust within the organization so managers and senior leaders must carve time from their busy schedules to engage with employees to establish personal relationships. This needs to be done **BEFORE** a crisis emerges because forming solid, trusting relationships takes time. If managers wait until after a crisis emerges, it is too late.

So, what have we learned? …. What is next?

If people provide power for an agile management system, then what are they powering? Mechanical and biological systems are made up of multiple components or organs that must work in harmony to achieve maximum performance outcomes. If any one part is out of balance or not functioning properly, the system will degrade and fail to deliver superior results. In Chapter Eight, we will explore the major organizational components that provide balance and superior results in a VUCA world and offer insightful questions that managers and leaders should ask. Assessment of all dimensions of the Performance Triangle Model should be continuous and ongoing so that managers and leaders can make small adjustments needed to adapt to subtle changes both internally and externally to the organization.

Thinking Exercises

1. Compare and contrast Taylor's "scientific management" and Weber's bureaucratic management with McGregor's Theory X and Y. How are they similar and different? What are the strengths and weaknesses of each? Explain your reasoning.
2. The balanced scorecard and management by objectives (MBO) approaches represent a management approach assuming that people will respond positively to goals and objectives. In your experience and opinion, is this assumption valid? Explain your reasoning.
3. The people part of the Performance Triangle encourages managers to create environments that enable people to focus their attention and energy, be aware of what is going on around them, and trust each other

and themselves in an environment where they have freedom to make choices. How is this different from Taylor and Weber? What are the advantages and disadvantages of each approach? Explain your reasoning.

4. How might the dimensions of people in the PTM help or hinder the development and execution of strategy in response to rapid and unexpected changes? Explain your reasoning.

5. What role does "self-responsibility", i.e., people taking responsibility for the outcomes for their actions, have in effectively utilizing the power of people? Explain your reasoning.

6. Using the organization that you work for or one that you know well, evaluate the strength of each dimension of the people part of the Performance Triangle. Explain how and why you think that the dimensions for people are strong or weak, and then discuss how each benefit or hurts the organization's ability to adapt and change. Explain your reasoning.

Suggested Reading

Michel, L. *The Performance Triangle: Diagnostic Mentoring to Manage Organizations and People for Superior Performance in Turbulent Times*. London, UK: LID Publishing Ltd., 2013.

Michel, L. *People-centric Management: How Managers Use Four Levers to Bring Out Greatness of Others*. London, UK: LID Publishing Ltd., 2020.

CHAPTER 8

BALANCING THE FORCES: SYSTEMS, LEADERSHIP, AND CULTURE

Quick Review… getting up to speed

In this chapter, we continue to build out the Performance Triangle Model (PTM) for agile organizational design in a turbulent world.[1,2] The PTM describes a dynamic system of leadership, systems, and culture that is powered by people. In Chapter Six we defined successful organizations as those with the following characteristics:

- **Responsiveness** – The ability to respond quickly and effectively to stakeholders' demands and expectations,
- **Alignment** – When employees and other internal stakeholders share common goals and aspirations,
- **Capabilities** – The organization has developed the skills, expertise, and tools needed to quickly and efficiently deliver the organization's products or services,
- **Motivation** – Employees throughout the organization are inspired to exceed the expectations of management and customers.
- **Cleverness** – Employees are empowered to be creative and use their creativity to meet expectations or demands from clients or customers within boundaries that do not stifle creativity.

In our view, organizations of virtually any type that have these characteristics are likely to be successful.

In Chapter Seven, I discussed how people provide the power to the dynamic PTM system. Widely accepted and still dominant management practices developed in the last century fail to promote self-responsibility that is needed to harness the full potential of knowledge workers in the 21st century. Management practices that enable people to reach their full potential in the current century create an environment that enables the following people-centric attributes:

- **Focus of Attention** – People must be free of distractions or interferences, typically created by management, to focus their abilities and expertise on their work,
- **Awareness** – People must be aware of what is happening around them in order to respond to the specific needs of stakeholders, quickly and efficiently,
- **Trust** – People must trust their managers, co-workers, others both internal and external to the organization, and (maybe most importantly) their own abilities and judgment,
- **Choice** – People must have freedom of choice to choose the best action in response to some demand and the freedom to say "no" if prescribed actions are inappropriate or ineffective.

Fundamental to creating an environment where a collective of people develop these attributes is the recognition that people are self-responsible and want to do the "right" thing for stakeholders and willing to stand by their decisions. Self-responsibility also means that managers must be self-responsible and accept decisions made by others and celebrate rather than punish the occasional decision that might yield less than desirable results.

A Balancing Act

We all know what happens when the tires of the car are out of balance or alignment. That annoying vibration, noise, and pull to one side of the road or the other make the vehicle more difficult to drive, accelerates the wear and tear on the tires, and reduce the gas mileage among other things. All of these reduce the efficiency of the vehicle and comfort for the passengers. Like tire balance or tire alignment in a car, organizations need balance between three essential components of the organizational system to maximize performance: systems, leadership, and culture. Too often, I, and I suspect most of you, have seen or experienced organizations where one or more of these components either dominate the others or are too weak to be an influence. How often have you been told "the system won't let me do it" or "it will take weeks or months to get a decision" … the system is dominating. How about "I have been waiting for my boss to make a decision for weeks" …. weak leadership. One of my personal favorites that I have observed personally "it is ok to fudge on expense statements because everyone does it and it is just the way we do things here" … flawed culture. So, what happens when these components become out of balance? Figure 8.1 illustrates the key parts of the Performance Triangle Model that need to be in balance.

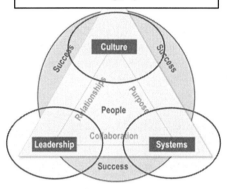

Figure 8.1 – Balance – Culture, Leadership, Systems

Source: Adapted from Michel, L. (2013). *The Performance Triangle: Diagnostic Mentoring to Manage Organizations and People for Superior Performance in Turbulent Times*, London, UK: LID Publishing Ltd.

Operating Modes

"theory in use" vs. "espoused theory"

Chris Argyris and Donald Schön explained how many, if not most, people and the resulting organizations that they manage have a disconnect between what they say they do or want to do and what they actually do.[3] According to Argyris and Schön, "espoused theory" represents what people say they do or want to do and, in most cases, people believe they are doing what they say. "Theory in use" describes what people actually do. In many, if not most cases, what people say is not necessarily what they do. This disconnect is natural and, in most cases, people are unaware of the difference. However, others are painfully aware of the disconnect which leads to an erosion of trust in management and weakens leadership. In our research we have found that organizational structures operate in different modes that range from high levels of traditional command and control to agile, people-centric organizations. Robert Simons proposed a simple-to-understand model with four levers of control that is helpful to illustrate the difference between what executives think they do and what actually happens.[4] Figure 8.2 illustrates the merging of Simons' model with our findings and observations to describe the disconnect between traditional 20th century command and control management styles and 21st century agile, people-centric management styles.

Span of control defines the tangible and intangible resources including financial assets and people that you have direct access to in order to meet organizational goals. *Span of accountability* defines the range of performance metrics that focuses attention on actions needed to meet specific metrics. Many detailed metrics limit the trade-offs available for actions while few metrics allow a much wider range of accountability and flexibility to take effective actions in unusual cases. *Span of influence* defines the range of interactions inside or outside of the organization. I have worked in companies where one could almost be fired for talking to someone in accounting, for example. Limiting an individual's span of influence limits his or her ability to gain the access needed, and potentially critical information contained in another part of the organization or outside of the organization. *Span of support* defines the amount of allowable collaboration with other parts of the organization. Like limiting an individual's span of influence, a limited span of support creates functional siloes that prevent effective knowledge sharing and create inefficiencies.

Figure 8.2 – Accountability Levers of Control

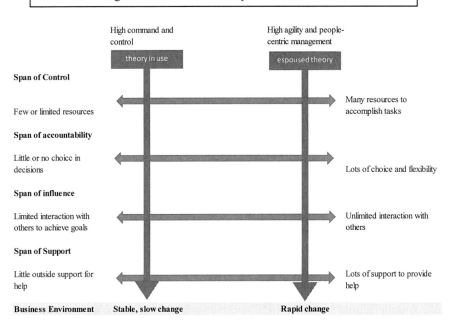

What we have found in our research is that many executives and managers espouse to be in a people-centric operating mode. Yet they either inherit command and control style organizations that are embedded in the systems, leadership style, and culture of the organization or they unwittingly create such highly structured organizations in control mode because that is what they were taught in the MBA program or because of their own insecure need to "be in charge." The difference between the espoused and in use theory weakens trust in leaders and creates interferences in the organization that prevent people from reaching their full potential. The result is the organization as a whole does not reach its full potential.

Having said all of this, it is important to recognize that not all organizations necessarily need to be at the agile people-centric side of the operating mode scale. Organizations in a stable environment where change is slow may be successful with a strong command and control structure, but how many organizations in today's rapidly changing global society exist in environments that are not changing rapidly?

Unless you are the founder or early leader of a young organization, you will be inheriting existing management systems with routines, rules, and procedures which shape leadership styles, your behavior, and the underlying beliefs, values, and shared assumptions (the culture) of everyone in the organization. Therefore, systems are a powerful force for good or evil.

"You cannot understand a system unless you change it." – **Kurt Lewin**

Systems

When they hear the word "systems," most people typically think of computer-based systems with databases crammed with data that are made available to a wide range of people for the purpose of improving efficiency and performance. Our definition of "systems" is much broader with systems helping to provide the organization with a unified self-determined purpose and function to support leadership and the organization at all levels and functions. Systems are intended to get the right information to the right people at the right time. In order to do this, systems include rules, routines, and tools for discipline. Proper rigor, delegation, and internal control enable an environment where people can maximize their potential and do good work. Systems provide needed structure to encourage personal responsibility and accountability, help allocate vital resources, and provide a means for people to find purpose, and a shared way of doing things more efficiently. This is at least the theory on how systems are supposed to work. Unfortunately, in too many organizations it does not work this way.

Organizations are "social systems in which all members contribute to shaping the organization in both interaction and meaning-giving processes".[5] What this means is that control systems must go beyond traditional models of human behavior and bureaucracy that communicate distrust and negatively impact morale and engagement. Effective systems enable sound decision-making, enhance trust, help create meaning and purpose, and enable collaboration throughout the organization.

Leadership is the work of developing the potential of people, not systems. Weak leaders demand, depend on, and hide behind systems like incentive plans to motivate people. In many, if not most organizations, the systems that evolve over time generally weaken accountability and discourage employee engagement which is the reverse of their intended purpose. Ineffective leaders replace interactive leadership with procedures, processes, and tools, but the fundamental purpose for developing systems is to enable accountability for routines, replicability, predictability, and consistency. These are particularly important as organizations become larger and more complex. It is also important that systems are context driven. One size does not fit all and "best practices" in one context rarely transfer successfully into a different context or organization. In the 21st century VUCA world it becomes critically important to continually evaluate existing systems to see if they are generating the intended outcomes. If the answer is "no", it is necessary to dig into the primary elements of effective systems to understand why, so that corrective action can be taken.... Quickly and effectively. The PTM model identifies three basic elements of systems that should be diagnosed if they are not yielding the desired results: rules, routines, and tools (see Figure 8.3). These basic elements directly shape the ability of people to attain flow (see Chapter Seven) and influence trust between the leaders and people who power the organization.

Figure 8.3 – Elements of Systems

Rules

Nobody would disagree that we need rules. However, finding the balance between having too many rules that restrict the ability of people to make effective or timely decisions and not enough rules so that chaos results is a challenge for all leaders. In ambiguous times when the future is unclear, rules must allow choice in the decision-making process rather than strictly following standard operating procedures. Rules that might have been reasonable and appropriate several years ago might be out of step in the current ambiguous environment which leads to an infection in the system and a lack of discipline. As a result, people instinctively look for ways to get around rules to meet the current needs. Leaders must frequently and objectively investigate to find out if the rules set the right balance between self-determination and motivation with control.

Experienced people in all functions, and knowledge workers in particular, accumulate a library of mental models and patterns over the years that helps to interpret what is happening and make sense of the situation. These mental models and patterns are not facts and cannot be captured in rules or procedures.[6] Mental models are critical in knowledge-based work because systems can only capture a limited amount of data or information pertaining to a specific situation. Tacit knowledge (see Chapter Three) is essential for designing and using tools and routines because rules must enable knowledge workers to apply their mental models and tacit knowledge to a specific situation. This means that the rules must enable choice rather than promote blind compliance to standard operating procedures.

Rules are enforced and compliance evaluated with a variety of measurement instruments and techniques. Virtually all organizations have some sort of traditional financial performance measurements. Yet, we know that much of the performance and value in 21st century organizations are intangible and cannot be captured using traditional financial measures (see Chapter Four). Many organizations have adopted methods attempting to measure nonfinancial performance. Leaders may choose from a host of possible approaches such as the balanced scorecard,[7] the performance prism,[8] and the delta project,[9] among many. A well-designed and effective performance measurement system is flexible, simple, and allows users to choose what works for them. Too often, we have observed that the corporate executives choose a measurement model and then forces standardized metrics across all functions or parts of the organization. This standardization ultimately defeats the intended fundamental purpose of the system which is to detect weak signals of possible trouble and then facilitate a powerful response in volatile and uncertain times. So, I have a few nuggets of advice:

- **Be cautious about using balanced scorecards and MBO**. The idea is to incentivize behaviors with metrics that reinforce corporate strategy. Unfortunately, in many cases managers develop metrics that reinforce behaviors that are counterproductive. This is because managers are not psychologists or knowledgeable on human behavior, plus these topics get little or no coverage in university curricula. The result is that balanced scorecards and related **M**anagement **B**y **O**bjectives' methodologies become rigid and inflexible as leaders become preoccupied with meeting targets rather than having productive and insightful conversations on strategy.

- **Be wary of using benchmarks.** Benchmarking is a common practice in many organizations and can be useful particularly if you are lagging behind top tier competitors in your business segment. However, in a rapidly changing environment benchmarking can be detrimental because we know that "best practices" are contextual and typically successful because of unique circumstances in the originating organization that cannot be duplicated. Additionally, as performance improves, continued benchmarking can lead to mediocrity. Jeffrey Pfeffer said it nicely, "We have been benchmarking the wrong things. Instead of benchmarking what others do, we ought to copy how they think" (pp. 6-7).[10]

- **Be careful to choose the "right" metrics and avoid over-regulating.** In many organizations, IT or finance dominates the choice of measurement tools. Business intelligence is a common fad but be sure to select metrics that have meaning at the point where work is being done. Be cautious about using measurements that can be added to corporate totals because these are rarely relevant to front-line workers and generally just make executives feel good. Front-line units should have a method of reporting insights on market changes and performance to communicate weak signals to upper management.

- **THINK!... don't just measure.** First, differentiate accuracy from precision. Precision means that the numbers add up, but accuracy is about getting relevant information on the right question to the right people at the right time to make an informed decision. Precision does not equal accuracy. Second, ask yourself what actions add value and measure them. But remember that value today comes from intangibles. Third, manage your business not the scorecard. Do the right thing and let the numbers fall where they may. Fourth, use your tacit knowledge, intuition, and judgment. Lots of data does not automatically lead you to the best decision. Fifth, only generate data that you are going to use. More is not necessarily better. In many situations, less is more.

- **Engage everyone when designing the performance measurement system.** Performance measurement and scorecards can be immensely helpful if they help people to focus their efforts on what matters, adds value, and works. Choose key performance indicators (KPI) in collaboration with the departments, teams, and individuals doing the work so the system is meaningful and secures support.
- **Reevaluate the measurement system regularly.** What is important today may not be relevant one or two years down the road. The environment changes, markets change, people change, issues change, technology changes, and more, so objectively review your measurement system and avoid getting into a rut. Do not be afraid to ask questions and make change to remain relevant.

"Management by objectives works if you first think through your objectives. 90% of the time you haven't" – **Peter Drucker**

Routines

As the complexity of organizations grows, routines should help to create awareness more than enforce control. Traditionally, leaders address increasing complexity by breaking down the complex organization into component parts, then setting goals for each component and delegating decision-making. Increasing complexity typically leads to layers of bureaucratic routines and managerial processes that may make sense when implemented but quickly become ineffective as the organization grows and the environment and needs change. If one of the primary goals of having routines is to help create awareness that aids the decision-making process, then routines must be considered more of a learning process than a telling process. The difference is like that of a teacher who lectures for 45 minutes and then dismisses the class, compared to a teacher who engages students in constructive dialogue on the various topics. The task for leaders in an agile management environment is to find the right balance between enabling learning and the need for control.

Before the Civil War, General Thomas "Stonewall" Jackson was a professor of artillery tactics at the Virginia Military Institute. While his effectiveness on the battlefield is legendary, his effectiveness as a teacher is questionable. Professor Jackson would devote countless hours to writing his lectures and then memorizing them before the class. If a student asked a question, Jackson would mentally rewind his lecture to the section in the lecture that contained the answer, then continue reciting the lecture from that point onward. This routine certainly discouraged follow ups or dialogue as well as general inquiry, but Jackson had complete control of his students and the class.[11]

In simple situations with little change or variation, processes and checklists for people to follow can be helpful. However, in more complex situations with more variability and change, this approach breaks down as people apply their tacit knowledge to take shortcuts or to go around the process. The result is a loss of credibility for those leaders or managers who create or blindly enforce the routines that lead to a disastrous culture where "let's work around the system" becomes a widely shared assumption and "the way we do things around here." Effective leaders and managers use good judgment and objective inquiry to challenge existing routines and then modify and replace procedures that do not make sense. Interestingly, while totally inflexible as a teacher, Jackson, the commander, challenged many widely accepted military axioms of the day and then adopted routines that made his command arguably one of the most effective fighting units on either side during the Civil War and, as some experts argue, one of the best in history. Routines both in the military context and business must help to create a learning environment and awareness of the many competing forces so that people use their tacit knowledge to adapt to a specific situation. Agile routines help people have meaning through effective feedback, help create a bottom-up strategy by raising awareness for what is important, and value adding, and help to create and implement effective performance planning and business reviews that help people align their behavior and focus their abilities on activities that really matter. I have a few pieces of advice on routines for agile organizations.

- **Remove the management control bureaucracy and barriers to knowledge sharing and collaboration.** Bureaucracy drains the energy from the organization that could be used to capture business opportunities and add value. Keep details at the level where work is being done and do not attempt to aggregate data up the chain of command because this does not add value and prevents ownership where the work is being done. The research is clear: "People rewarded for individual performance shared the least information; those rewarded for team performance shared more; and those rewarded for company performance shared the most."[12]
- **Raise awareness through performance feedback.** People must get relevant and timely information on their own performance and how they contribute to the performance of others to create awareness. Direct and immediate feedback that does not reach the

people who are doing the work is worthless. Feedback must be self-explanatory and honest, geared to performance or behavior, not the individual.

- **Adopt a flexible strategy development routine.** Avoid sticking to a predetermined calendar. Keep strategy development flexible to react to the unexpected because customers, clients, governments, technology, and more do not stick to a company cycle so you must be able to evaluate and change strategies quickly. Avoid making planning the goal. I worked for a company that took 4 months to develop annual targets, then another 4 months in mid-year evaluating and revising the targets. We spent 8 months developing goals, then only 4 months managing operations to meet the goals. This drained energy from the organization and distracted attention from getting things done.
- **Engage people throughout the organization in strategy development.** In most companies, strategy development is limited to the top level of management, yet people doing the day-to-day work with clients or customers really know what is going on.
- **Use the strategy planning process to allocate resources to the best opportunities.** In many companies, units or departments use the planning process to bargain for resources. Those who make the most noise get the most resources. Separate the strategic planning process from the resource allocation process to allocate resources to the opportunities to provide the best value and return for your bucks.
- **Avoid setting outrageous targets.** Rather than establishing BHAGs (Big Harry Audacious Goals) or, one of my pet peeves, stretch goals with little credibility, allow employees to participate and set achievable goals with personal ownership. In my experience, BHAGs and stretch goals are, more often than not, more detrimental to morale and performance than beneficial.
- **Avoid linking performance evaluations and rewards to fixed targets.** This routine encourages the gaming of the system rather than working on things that add value. People will naturally negotiate for lower performance measures to increase the chance of being rewarded which ensures mediocrity rather than superior performance. Also, avoid using detailed, standardized forms for individual performance evaluation. A handwritten note with personal commitments for the employee will be much more effective.

Tools

To respond to increasing volatility and rate of change, people need tools which should help focus their attention on the issues at hand. In stable, slowly changing conditions, static hard goals, rigid outside command and control, and structured collaboration organized by leaders work just fine. However, faced with rapidly changing market dynamics, tools should be flexible to help people focus on what is important, enable self-initiative and encourage goal-achievement. Too often we see people using tools that might have been appropriately designed in an environment that is long gone. The result is that people make good decisions with irrelevant, inefficient, or ineffective tools that are woefully out of date. Therefore, the decision fails to yield the intended result. So, while management may feel like it has control, employee morale and engagement are falling as are customer satisfaction and corporate performance. Executives may go along fat, dumb, and happy while the floor is deteriorating under them. Agile leaders frequently question existing tools to see if they are helping employees to focus their attention rather than just enforcing control.

Key performance indicators (KPIs) are popular in western business operations and can be very helpful in today's fast-moving environment. Properly designed and executed KPIs are actually essential keys to effective people-centric leadership that is the basis of agile management. Effective agile leadership depends on having relevant observation points as a tool that focus people's attention on doing good work. However, a problem arises in many companies when performance indicators are accompanied by hard performance targets. These are very different, and targets come along with many undesirable side effects that have already been discussed. Potentially beneficial tools like the balanced scorecard have proven to be unmanageable or unproductive because of the ambition of leaders to use the tool as a lever to enforce control… producing the opposite of the desired effect. Too much control acts like having the emergency brake on a car engaged while trying to accelerate.

An easily overlooked element to agile people-centric leadership is corporate strategy. When enabling self-responsible and self-initiated work, people doing the work must be able to identify with the grand purpose of the organization to rally behind the strategy. High identification with the company's strategy signals that employees have found their purpose and are ready to perform at their peak. Clear strategy also helps people to focus proper attention on tasks that add value for clients and the company. Traditionally, strategy implementation means the creation of performance plans with a vast array of financial reports that organizational units use to prove to management that they are making their numbers. Many times, however, the targets or budgets are not clearly linked to what is important to get done. When this happens, making the numbers becomes the objective rather than doing the things that are really meaningful. Mission and vision statements form the foundation for strategy and provide a framework for people to gauge their decisions and behaviors. These define the boundaries for risk that the organization is willing to accept and set the boundaries for opportunities that are beyond the scope of the organizations and establish clarity for accountability. Self-responsible knowledge workers need to know the boundaries and be trusted to work within those boundaries. Here are a few topics to consider when evaluating tools within an organization.

- **Avoid using KPIs as targets.** People will focus their attention on meeting targets rather than the actions that drive performance. Focus of attention is what matters, not arbitrary goals intended to drive performance. Also, be cautious about using financial results to measure performance because there are too many variables between individual performance and financial outcomes like time lags, complex relationships, customer expectations, economic forces, etc.

- **Limit measures to seven, plus or minus two.** Research shows that people can remember seven things.[13] Five is enough variety to stimulate creativity, but nine decreases focus from the important things. Also, don't let performance measurement reports sit on the boss' desk. Make them available to the people doing the work so they can focus on improvement.

- **Avoid changing strategy too often.** Strategy provides long-term direction for the organization. Changing course too often communicates to stakeholders that management is indecisive, and stakeholders will not know what the company stands for, which inhibits focus. When strategies are agreed upon, be sure they are clearly communicated to all stakeholders in simple terms that people can understand. In many companies, strategic documents are developed by some strategy "priesthood" that is divorced from the other 99.9% of the organization. Then, the resulting strategy document is locked up out of fear that competitors might get it and find some secret. In reality, all stakeholders must know your strategy.... and your competitors probably knew it anyway.

- **Establish action plans rather than targets.** Action plans communicate what needs to be done rather than the hoped-for outcome. People-centric leaders develop collaborative action plans, then let people focus on the action and use their tacit knowledge and creativity to find the best way to do the task. The numbers will fall out naturally. Also, use the KISS (Keep It Simple Stupid) method so that self-directed people understand it.

- **Be cautious with individual performance incentive systems.** Quoting Jeffrey Pfeffer again, "Individual incentive pay in reality undermines the performance of both the individual and the organization. Many studies strongly suggest that this form of reward undermines teamwork, encourages a short-term focus, and leads people to believe that pay is not related to performance at all but to having the 'right' relationships and an ingratiating personality."[14] Base pay should be based on long-term relative performance of peer groups or promote profit-sharing where employees share in the success of larger groups rather than on themselves, individually.

- **Keep structures clear and simple.** Keep job descriptions simple, flexible, and limited to the essentials. Ask employees to articulate their duties and have a dialogue with them to reinforce their role. A simple one-page job description allows for a high degree of flexibility and speed when circumstances call for a quick response. Encourage self-responsible people to focus their abilities and creativity on the issue to come up with a response that works. Don't pen them in.

- **Talk the talk and walk the walk.** Senior leaders must embody the vision and values of the organization. People inside and outside of the organization constantly observe and evaluate the behavior of senior leaders, and if their actions do not match their talk, then distrust and confusion emerge, which interferes with knowledge sharing and focus of attention.

"The challenge of leadership is to be strong, but not rude; be kind, but not weak; be bold, but not bully; be thoughtful, but not lazy; be humble, but not timid; be proud, but not arrogant; have humour, but without folly." – **Jim Rohn**

Leadership

Leaders are constantly challenged by uncertainties and ambiguities that question their strategic decisions. They are torn between their convictions on direction and control and the temptation and need to adapt and change. The conflict between direction and control, and adaptation and change, is a constant headache for senior leaders. However, in today's fast-moving environment it becomes essential that organizations develop the ability to rapidly make sense of changing market and environmental situations. This requires leaders to trust in their own abilities and the capabilities of the organization to find the right balance between stability in direction and quick reaction.

Mobilizing all the resources, and most importantly people, to focus on one direction requires people to have a shared context and purpose that promote healthy relationships. Healthy relationships facilitate effective collaboration that is absolutely essential in changing situations to find and execute effective responses to change. With clarity on context and shared purpose, leaders can trust people to use their knowledge to think, decide, act, and behave in ways that support the strategy and add value.

Leadership is a strange thing. Good leadership is difficult to define and appreciate but painfully obvious when it is not there. Everyone knows what a good leader looks like but typically only thinks about it when leadership is poor. People have a finely tuned sense for authenticity, and they can tell when leaders are play-acting, tweaking the truth, or not being what they really are. When people sense any of these, among other behaviors, they begin second-guessing statements and decisions, lose respect for the leader, and become cynical.

Effective leadership is based on trust. Leaders must trust their people in order to build relationships, and people must trust their leaders and the people they work with in order to collaborate effectively. Leaders who successfully create an environment and culture with high levels of trust where people take pride in what they do and like socializing with others achieve superior performance.[15,16] With systems designed with agile and people-centric principles driving rules, routines, tools, and interactions, leaders facilitate a culture based on trust that allows people to use their tacit knowledge and creativity to unleash potential with minimal interference from management.[17] In the people-centric environment illustrated in Figure 8.4, leadership is inextricably connected with systems through interactions and relationships among people. Agile leaders recognize these relationships and then engage with people to establish trust and design systems that allow choice, create awareness, and focus attention on what matters.

Fundamental assumptions about people and human nature profoundly influence individual leadership styles. Traditional managers and most college curricula assume that managers must motivate and decide what needs to be done, tell people what to do and how to do it, review and judge the outcomes and performance, sit on top of the hierarchy, provide instructions, assume responsibility, set rules, and have the power to change things. This approach is often successful, but if managers assume that people want to create, understand what is going on, achieve, do right, and contribute, then managers must adopt a very different approach. To enable these positive attributes of people, managers must raise their level of interaction to inspire as leaders. Leaders (as opposed to managers) interact positively with people, to facilitate collaboration rather than command collaboration, and establish a supportive work environment based on trust.

Figure 8.4 – The Leadership, People, and Systems Linkage

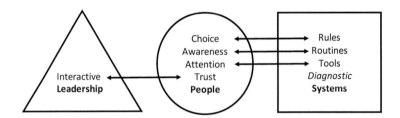

In the modern business environment where knowledge creation and knowledge sharing are essential, dynamic knowledge sharing can only take place through developing healthy interpersonal relationships and communications that facilitate, rather than direct collaboration. In an environment where processes translate knowledge into productive action, and decision-making is delegated, healthy and frequent interactions with teams and people are crucial. To enable the exchange of knowledge, leaders (as opposed to managers) engage in productive dialogue and foster a culture of openness, trust, and collaboration.[18] Leaders must be diligent to create a safe space free of ridicule, sarcasm, and cynicism, which the Japanese call *Ba,* where people can share what they know without fear of repercussions.[19] Leaders must facilitate channels of communication with productive dialogue (a productive exchange of ideas between two people on a specific topic) as opposed to discussion or conversation (talking among two or more people without a specific point like a story or joke). The PTM identifies five communications practices shown in Figure 8.5 where facilitating open and honest dialogue is needed to explore deep questions which are essential for agile people-centric organizations. Effective 21st century leaders engage with people in productive dialogue to gain insight into the following topics and questions:

- Sense-making – What is going on and what does it mean?
- Strategy Conversation – Why are we going there? Why is our strategy "the" strategy?
- Performance Conversion – Are we on track?
- Contribution Dialogue – What do we need to do next and what is my part?
- Risk Dialogue – How can we contribute and what are the boundaries?

*"The Pessimist complains about the wind. The Optimist expects it to change. The Leader adjusts the sails." – **John Maxwell***

Sense-making

Sense-making is more than just being able to connect the dots to gain some level of understanding of a situation. Sense-making is an elevated awareness of what is important and what is happening… before it becomes a problem. Leaders with developed abilities to sense what is happening focus on the now, measurement, and perceptions to gain an understanding of what is happening. Effective leaders have an aptitude for learning, a sense of objective reality, and a focus that is facilitated with relevant and timely information from systems along with effective and timely feedback processes. For feedback information to be effective it must be immediate (timely), consistent, self-directed, honest, controlled, and focused on behaviors or performance, not the person. Here are a few things to consider about sense-making:

Figure 8.5 – Dimensions of Leadership

- **Avoid collecting data that is not used** – Data that is not used or does not translate into information and action is useless and a waste of resources. Too much data can lead to information overload or paralysis by analysis which wastes time and introduces interferences that take away focus, leading to distorted feedback and faulty decisions.
- **Develop sense-making techniques to help establish trust** – Sense-making does not happen in isolation and is based on effective communication. Knowledge sharing and sharing insights to look at a situation from multiple angles result in information that can be relied upon.
- **Provide feedback on outcomes** – Feedback is essential for learning and relies heavily on sense-making. Let people know the results or consequences of their actions but keep it simple and easy to understand.

Strategy Conversation

Strategy conversations should be part of the daily leadership routine to help to create a shared intent throughout the organization. An attractive strategy that is well communicated helps employees to direct their efforts and decisions toward what matters. The conversations should be open for productive dialogue (as opposed to discussion or lecture), and for new ideas that focus on the future, opportunities, and options. Clearly, effective strategy conversations demand a high level of trust throughout the organization. Here are some thoughts on strategy conversations:

- **Do not restrict strategy conversations to the leadership team** – People on the front line dealing with customers or clients are most knowledgeable about customer dynamics and have the greatest ability to execute a strategy. Everybody needs to understand the strategy to help convert it to action. Avoid the annual off-site strategy event. It is typically a waste of time and money.
- **Avoid strategy decisions by committees that are far removed from clients** – Strategy and budgeting decisions are too often restricted to "home office" executives where the political fights for resources and power dominate in traditional organizations. Also, decisions made by a committee create an atmosphere where innovative approaches are difficult to gain favor because of inherent risks. In addition, committee decisions relieve individual members of responsibility and risk. Decisions on strategy and

resource allocation should be made by people on the front line who are responsible for the results.

- **Be aware of bias** – Through time the mindset of "this is how we do things around here" can dominate and cloud the decision-making process. Such bias repeated over time can create undesired thought patterns that become part of a dysfunctional culture. A classic example of this is Kodak. Kodak engineers were the first to develop digital photography in the mid-1970s. Kodak executives, the majority of whom had spent most, if not all, of their careers at Kodak, rejected the new technology because "real photography is done with chemicals to get the best results." The Kodak engineers took their ideas elsewhere… and the rest is history.

- **Set the stage for constructive debate and encourage creative thinking** – Organize strategy meetings to include a diverse set of people with different backgrounds who can offer alternative perspectives. Attendance of meetings should be limited to a core group of people who will be responsible for the implementation of the strategy, but the core group should actively engage with a supporting cast of specialists with insight, clients with a voice, and employees with a voice. All participants should be encouraged to offer new ideas in the *Ba* created by senior leaders.

Performance conversation

Frequent and honest performance conversations serve to clarify expectations for individuals and teams. Performance conversations engage people and organizational units in productive dialogue that helps to establish a shared agenda. Effective, people-centric leaders use performance conversations to translate organizational strategy into concrete and achievable objectives, review performance against pre-agreed objectives, and agree on actions in response to changing dynamics. In the PTM vision, performance conversations tap into the tacit expertise of people and close discussions with agreement on actions to be taken and measured. Here are a few points to consider:

- **Avoid focusing on mistakes and appraisals** – It seems to be a normal human reaction to focus on mistakes or errors, but this too often erodes trust which is essential to tapping into human potential. There is no room for assigning blame when the primary purpose is to help translate strategy into action and superior performance. Use performance metrics as a framework to guide the conversation to identify productive actions rather than as a hammer to gain control.

- **Stop the controlling manager from driving the conversation** – This is supposed to be a two-way dialogue between people or business units with a shared agenda to help find innovative actions in response to a changing environment or unexpected events. In this situation the relationship must be more like that of two trusting partners rather than supervisor/subordinate. Subordinates know their place on the organization chart; they do not need to be constantly reminded.

- **Create the right atmosphere** – More than two people may need to be involved so the organizer must create an atmosphere of trust...*Ba*... where there is a free exchange of ideas and opinions without fear of repercussions. When the session is over, be sure that everyone commits to specific actions.

"The supreme quality for leadership is unquestionably integrity. Without it, no real success is possible, no matter whether it is on a section gang, a football field, in an army, or in an office." – **General Dwight D. Eisenhower**

Contribution Dialogue

It is widely recognized that 75% of managers do more to demotivate their people than help them make sense of what is going on and find purpose that leads to engagement. The performance dialogue is an ongoing conversation between a manager (acting more like a leader) and an individual and a direct report on how that individual can contribute to help meet organizational goals. It is based on trust and seeks to secure mutual agreement on what both the manager and the report should be focusing their attention on. This exchange of ideas helps individual alignment and secures personal responsibility for both. Think about these points:

- **Use this dialogue to establish trust and reliable relationships** – Too often, performance discussions focus on detailed objectives or stretch goals that result in long justifications for not reaching set targets. The justifications get even longer and more convoluted when goals are linked to incentive programs. Engage in a two-way exchange of ideas that focuses attention on the "right" things that both the employee and manager can take responsibility for.

- **Rely on responsibility rather than motivation** – There is no need to attempt to motivate people with extensive and detailed performance objectives if the contribution dialogue focuses the employee's attention only on personal commitment. Extensive performance reviews contribute little to the contribution dialogue because they are after the fact and are, therefore, of little value. Reviews should be conducted selectively at key decision points and seek to focus attention for both the employee and manager on what matters.
- **Use contribution and performance dialogue to learn** – Agile people-centric organizations rely on self-responsibility rather than control mechanisms. Self-responsible people must learn where they fit in, what is going on around them, and what resources they have available to perform effectively.

Risk dialogue

The risk dialogue has two major components; daily coaching with employees on the potential risks of actions and the boundaries that the organization is willing to accept and a corporate conversation about the limits of risk that the organization will accept. Essentially, risk dialogue among employees at all levels helps people understand the organization's tolerance for risk-taking. This is especially important in a time of change since any attempt at change, large or small, involves a risk that it will not work. Conversations on risks should be separate from strategy conversations because strategy emphasizes creativity which requires freedom of thought without restraints while risk conversations revolve around things that can go wrong. These are very different mental attitudes and should be kept separate if at all possible.

Distorted perceptions about risk can creep into an organization and kill any change initiative or innovation. We had an international client with operations in six countries that was experiencing loss of market share, a rash of accidents related to safety issues, and declining operational efficiencies. The new CEO had engaged a series of consultants who implemented leadership, marketing, and efficiency improvement programs without any results. After gathering information on risk dialogue, among other elements of the PTM, we discovered that there was a significant disconnect between the CEO and his top executives. The perception of the executives was that if they attempted to change something and it failed, they would be penalized if not fired. The result was that nobody tried anything, and despite spending large sums of money with consultants, nothing ever changed. In our work with hundreds of companies, we have found that risk dialogue is one of the most important conversations to have when trying to navigate rapid change. Consider the following regarding risk dialogue:

- **Avoid making risks the only conversation** – We have observed many organizations with a strong "command and control" management style make potential risks the dominant discussion point. This results in a risk averse culture where people are afraid of making decisions or taking actions. Obsession on potential risks kills any chance for growth or change. Risk dialogue in its proper perspective helps leaders consider the possible consequences of actions that will help prevent costly detours, but it should not stifle action or innovation… or experimentation.
- **Use risk dialogue to establish trust** – Clear boundaries help people make effective and timely decisions, adapt behaviors, and take action. When people have clear boundaries, they operate in an environment of greater trust… in their decisions and support from superiors.
- **Interesting observation** – We have observed significant differences in risk dialogue and tolerance for risk among industries. Size does not seem to matter, but businesses with high initial investment requirements like industrial companies clearly show a greater intolerance for risk (they do not take risks) while banks and insurance companies rank toward the bottom of the risk-taking scale (willing to risk your money).

"In linear times, an organization's culture is its greatest asset. However, in exponential and disruptive times, some parts of that same culture can become large liabilities, creating persistent resistance to pressing change and renewal." — **Gyan Nagpal, The Future Ready Organization: How Dynamic Capability Management is Reshaping the Modern Workplace**

Culture

In Chapter Five, I explained how organizational culture is the invisible force that hinders or enables knowledge sharing. By now, you should have gotten the message that the ability of an organization's leaders to tap into the vast tacit knowledge base within their organizations is essential for success in the 21st century knowledge economy.[15,16] You should have also realized the importance of trust throughout the organization in agile people-centric organizations. You cannot see or quantify trust, but we all know when there is a lack of it or when trust prevails. I concluded Chapter Five by stating that "organizational culture is much more complex than the GPTW model suggests [or any other existing model] and requires a much deeper dive into the underlying beliefs, values, and shared assumptions ... that drive behaviors, norms, and artifacts of every aspect of the organization." I went further, to say, "The first step toward designing an agile organization is gaining insight into the underlying 'unconscious and rarely discussable' dimensions of leadership, systems, and culture that either enable or stifle knowledge sharing and the ability of the organization to be agile." The cultural dimension of the Performance Triangle Model shown in Figure 8.6 identifies five "unconscious and rarely discussable" attributes that we find are critical for an agile people-centric organization.[1,2]

- Understanding – What is our shared understanding of reality; past and current? Do people understand what it takes to be successful in the current environment?
- Intent – What is our shared idea, view, and direction on what is needed to be successful?
- Agenda – Do we share the same vision on what actions are needed to get things done? Are we all on the same page?
- Aspirations – Do we share the same sense of purpose to achieve success?
- Norms – Do we share the same values on what gets us ahead and what are our shared boundaries? Do we do what we say we do?

Cues for the organizational culture come from the top of the hierarchy, and then diffuse throughout the organization through socialization.[14] Senior leaders set the tone and the example. The culture shapes the collective mindset, decisions, behaviors, and actions of everyone in the organization. Displayed prominently in corporate mission and vision statements, then shared throughout the organization through stories and language, these commonly held values, beliefs, and assumptions become points of identification and orientation for everyone in the organization.[20] Consequently, culture has a stabilizing effect on an organization by giving meaning to work and helping to make the environment more predictable. However, we all know that changing the fundamental beliefs and values of one person is a difficult task and changing the beliefs and values of a large group of people is REALLY difficult.

John Kotter and James Heskett wrote in *Corporate Culture and Performance*: "Cultures that encourage inappropriate behavior and inhibit change to more appropriate strategies tend to emerge slowly and quietly over a period of years, usually when firms are performing well."[21] When things are going well, we tend to look the other way or excuse certain behaviors with, "if it ain't broke, don't fix it." But when the eventual downturn occurs in the normal business cycle, these "interferences" that have crept into the mindset of the people become glaring problems. Kotter and Heskett went on to observe that "Once these cultures exist, they can be enormously difficult to change because they are often invisible to the people involved, because they help support the existing power structure in the firm."

Figure 8.6 – Dimensions of Culture

A vibrant and healthy culture establishes a shared context throughout the organization with a shared agenda, shared common language, shared mental models, trusting relationships, and a common purpose which serves as a common ground for all operations. A shared context provides the framework for everyone to get on board and move in the same direction. A shared context depends on the exchange of knowledge, shared beliefs, and a common organizational history. It depends on shared assumptions that help people throughout the organization to set expectations on what others will do and clarifies roles and behavioral ground rules in advance. However, a shared context is always imperfect and constantly eroding as original plans, goals, and roles keep changing to degrade the shared context.

In a VUCA environment, identifying and changing cultural interferences and degrading context may be critical for the CEO, but where to start? Figure 8.6 illustrates the dimensions of culture to consider based on the Performance Triangle Model.

"Understanding depends on the quality of the relationship." – **Max Frisch**

Understanding

When people have a shared understanding of what their role is and what needs to be done, the decision-making process speeds up. In a VUCA world, speed in getting things done is critical when responding to challenging situations. Leaders can rely on teams and individuals to make quick and effective decisions that result in positive outcomes when everyone shares a clear understanding of what is needed. In the leadership section, I talked about the need for sense-making which is the tool that allows people to detect weak signals, then amplify the signals and separate the noise from what is important. However, highly developed sensing does little good if people do not understand what the signals mean or what to do with the information. A shared understanding is a precondition for senior leaders and everyone throughout the organization to absorb critical information and quickly take action that supports organizational objectives. Consider the following on shared understanding.

- **Not everyone understands the same thing** – People filter information through their own perceptions and will come to different conclusions on what is to be done. In agile organizations, everyone must be on the same page and dialogue must be continuous so that leaders can intercept misconceptions early and redirect people who are wandering outside of the lines. People need relevant and timely information (see systems) so managers should not hold information on their desks; rather, it should be widely disseminated. Managers must engage with people to help interpret information which helps to solidify a shared understanding of what it means and what needs to be done and done quickly. Speed is essential and understanding depends on developing high quality relationships.
- **Avoid groupthink** – Many times management teams are overly influenced by dominant leaders who monopolize the discussion. The result is that groups tend to reinforce each other's perceptions or misconceptions which leads to missed opportunities or flawed decisions. Current reality, success, and rigid routines and practices can create blind spots that prevent people from looking at situations from alternative perspectives.
- **As organizations grow, a shared understanding gets lost** – People come and go as the organization grows and becomes more

complex. Individuals and teams with different mental models come and go which through time dulls the sense-making ability of the organization. The process of translating data into information, insights, and actionable knowledge must be continuously refreshed and updated so that people maintain a shared understanding which may change through time, but it is critically important that everyone shares the same understanding, wherever it leads.

Intent

A shared intent among all the people in an organization strengthens the alignment toward a common purpose. Strategy conversations (see leadership) are the tool to get people to think about the future and help design an organization that fits with the requirements needed to execute the strategy. When people have a shared intent, they are more able to focus their attention on (see people) and direct their energy at what is important. Self-responsibility, not motivation, is the fuel that drives dedicated and purposeful behavior that is guided by a widely shared intent. The credibility of management teams declines if they fail to visibly demonstrate a shared intent. Think about the following observations on shared intent.

- **Be clear and unambiguous when articulating intent** – The objective of a shared intent is to provide clarity and uniformity on the direction for the organization. It is very difficult to create a shared intent throughout the organization if the management team cannot agree on the strategy, mission, or vision. Disagreement on the shared intent by the leadership team can be toxic for the organization which will be even more damaging when agreements are just talking points rather than actions.
- **Use strategy conversations to create a shared intent** – Frequent and intense communications on strategy should be shared throughout the organization to help everyone to interpret the strategy in order to shape and align personal actions and behaviors. Employees will be more motivated and engaged when they become aligned with the organization's purpose and goals. Strategy conversations should not be limited to off-site meetings. Informal gatherings, coffee chats, and structured workshops with all employees on strategy help to create a shared intent.

Agenda

A shared agenda helps organizations to harness the vast reservoir of talent and capabilities to generate a competitive advantage. Leadership bundles the energy of people through performance conversations (see leadership) which are the primary tool to help coordinate their activities with a shared agenda. A shared agenda gives the organization the ability to effectively use the company's resources to achieve organizational goals. Here are some tips to help create a shared agenda.

- **Avoid getting bogged down with competing priorities** – Different functional departments or business units have different priorities. The idea is to get everyone walking in one direction to negotiate agreements on the agenda, so the agenda serves as a guide to deal with competing priorities. Also, avoid getting bogged down with daily details. Keep the big picture in front of you.
- **Be accountable** – Accountability means being accountable for both the things being done and the things that are not being done. Too many times, people agree to an agenda item with a "yes" in the meeting while secretly thinking "no" in anticipation of its defection or failure. When this happens, the result is "an organized lack of accountability" which is a true virus in many modern organizations that can infect the whole organization.

Aspirations

The desire to achieve is a fundamental element for motivation. This desire is the source of will power needed to push ourselves to maximize our capabilities. Too frequently we see organizational structures and managers who create an environment where people are more focused on how efficiently things get done rather than on why they are being done. Focusing on HOW rather than WHY distracts people from purposeful action which reinforces the higher objectives and personal aspirations that are proven to be powerful motivators. In high-performing, goal-oriented organizations, these desires and shared aspirations need to be aligned with everyone moving in the same direction.

Commonly shared aspirations help to direct people's attention toward the vision and values of the organization. They help to give people a common sense of purpose which releases vast productive and creative energies. A lack of shared aspirations or conflicting aspirations lead to interferences that disrupt knowledge sharing and create demotivation instead of releasing the synergy of the collective of people. A shared aspiration among the leadership team strengthens credibility while conflicting aspirations among leaders will be quickly recognized by employees thereby undermining the credibility of the entire leadership team. Think about these things to avoid, and the practices to promote.

- **Ensure that all employees share the company's aspirations** – Employees who see things differently develop aspirations that are many times detrimental to the success of the organization. Multiple aspirations often result in endless debates or silent protests which slow the decision-making process and sabotage strategies. People need a shared sense of purpose which aligns with the vision and mission of the organization and helps them align their long-term goals. It is important to have frequent conversations with employees to review their ambitions. As new members join the team, and with changes in strategy and the organization, shared ambitions fade and lose their energy.

- **Give people the support, resources, and opportunity** – Ambitious personal goals can be a great motivator for individuals and the organization as a whole, but people need to have access to support and resources in order to take advantage of opportunities. If management does not provide support and resources, then the effort to align aspirations is for naught because it is just words. Bold ambitions might sound great, but if people are not given the resources they need to achieve these ambitions, they will say "why bother?"

- **Use contribution dialogue to create shared aspirations** – Frequent formal and ongoing informal dialogues with employees and teams solidify how personal aspirations align with contributions to the organization's success. Contribution dialogue (see leadership) reinforces how personal ambitions can be attained when people focus their attention on the "right" things. This requires constant reinforcement so that people can shape their daily decisions around the values and goals of the organization and know "what is in it for me?" and "how this will help me get ahead."

Norms

Shared norms help people to find the right balance between the duty to comply with standards, rules, and routines and the capability of getting the right things done without limiting their creative freedom. While expected norms of behavior are commonly articulated in corporate standards, rules, and ethical statements in employee handbooks, generally accepted, unwritten, norms of behavior permeate many organizations. In too many organizations, "this is how we do things here" or "it is ok because everyone does it" or "the boss does it, so why can't I?" ways of thinking lend tacit approval to inappropriate behavior. Senior executives will rarely be aware of these subversive shared norms while they continue to believe that people have followed the written rules and standards. I had an acquaintance in sales who frequently bragged about making several thousand tax-free dollars every month by padding his expense statements with extra mileage, inflated meals expenses, and more. I reminded him that the company will have trained people and processes to identify such cheating, and he justified his actions with "well, everyone does it, so it is ok." He was abruptly fired after about a year with the company and never explained why, but I have a strong suspicion that I know what happened. The unseen disconnect between written and unwritten norms can interfere with the best strategy and plans. Leaders and managers in agile people-centric organizations must be aware of these unwritten shared norms that infect the culture, and then be proactive to combat this insidious virus. Here are a few ideas to consider.

- **Set written norms of behavior that are credible and reasonable** – There are few things worse in an organization than written norms with explicit boundaries that are interpreted differently by different people. Written norms that are overly restricting or allow for too much interpretation encourage an environment where the norms are simply ignored which creates a toxic culture. Such an environment undermines the credibility of leaders who enforce the written rules. There is a balance between too much and too little which must be constantly evaluated and adjusted and communicated to people by example and constructive dialogue.
- **Be careful with using detailed operating procedures to set norms** – It is impossible to anticipate and set down in writing the proper response to every conceivable situation that employees will encounter. Lots of written rules will stifle the creative entrepreneurial capabilities of people. In many cases a set of general principles will be more effective because enforcing detailed rules becomes very difficult and often destroys the credibility of management.
- **Use risk dialogue to create and reinforce shared norms** – People must know the boundaries and behavioral expectations

regardless of whether the organization has detailed operating procedures or general principles. Managers must use risk dialogue (see leadership) with employees to help them interpret the norms as they pertain to their specific routines. This means that managers must establish healthy relationships and have continuous honest dialogue (as opposed to meaningless discussion or directives) with people throughout their organizations so that the norms become universally shared and part of the "unconscious and rarely discussable" culture. People just do right without thinking about it.

"Never confuse movement with action." – **Ernest Hemingway**

Closing thoughts on systems, leadership, and culture

I began this chapter with a brief discussion of operating modes which describe the general styles of management that are the levers for action. Agile, people-centric management styles operate in an enabling mode which means that leaders and managers create an environment where people are self-responsible with systems and cultural attributes that release the productive energy of employees. Traditional management models developed in the last century that still dominate management texts and university curricula promote structures that emphasize the command and control of people and processes. The fundamental traditional view of human nature is that people are not self-responsible; therefore, they must be told what to do and how to do it and be forced to comply with management either through punitive performance reviews or by being given tangible incentives. We talked briefly about how many leaders and managers say one thing but do something else. I suspect that you have all observed how differences in a manager's "espoused theory" and his or her "theory in use" create disruption and uncertainty in the organization that interfere with the organization's ability to be as successful as it could be.

The entire Performance Triangle Model is based on a fundamental belief that people are self-responsible and leaders must practice what they preach... meaning that the "espoused theory" is identical to the "theory in use." It is critically important to visualize all aspects of an organization as a dynamic system where each part influences the other. Notice in Figure 8.4 on the *People, Leadership, and Systems Linkage* illustration how the connecting arrows point both ways. This symbolizes the irrefutable fact that systems influence the behavior of people and leaders while at the same time people and leaders influence systems and how they are used. We believe it is impossible to make significant and lasting changes to one element without considering the equal and opposite effects on other parts of the dynamic organizational system. Similar to an amoeba, you cannot push one part of the system without creating a bulge somewhere else.

Think about riding a bike. You can expend a lot of energy peddling hard, but if you lose your balance, it is all for nothing. In the PTM, people provide the energy for the bike, but if the systems, leadership, and culture are out of balance, the organization will not maximize its potential. Like riding a bike, the organization may reach most of its goals but will have expended valuable people energy on the way and taken much longer to get there. By maintaining balance, the organization is able to harness the vast creative energy of people inside and outside of the organization, not only to reach the current goals but to identify and exploit opportunities that were not imagined.

Systems give the organization structure and the wherewithal for leaders and individuals at all levels to perform effectively. However, in many, if not most, unseen "unconscious and rarely discussable" interferences creep into an organization that inhibit knowledge sharing and the ability of self-responsible individuals to contribute to the success of the organization as much as they could. Fortunately, all is not lost because people-centric leaders can influence both the systems and the interferences that infect the culture of an organization. Agile, people-centric leaders have multiple tools and techniques to engage people in constructive conversations and dialogue to shape the fundamental dimensions of the culture that are necessary to release the vast productive energy of people. Notice how the connecting arrows in the Figure 8.7 illustration, *Leadership-Culture Interactions,* go both ways. This is by design to make the point that leaders must engage in open, two-way conversations and dialogue with people rather than one-way directives or discussion controlled by the supervisor. It takes time and effort for managers and leaders to create a trusting environment where people can freely and without fear share their understanding of what is going on, their intent, agenda, aspirations and ambitions, as well as those insidious unwritten norms that are the seeds of a toxic culture.

Using the bicycle analogy, your legs provide the energy to make the bike go, just as people provide the energy in an organization to make it go, and you must maintain balance in order not to fall. However, how is the energy transferred to the bicycle? The answer is…. by the chain attached to the pedals. In the next chapter we will discuss how energy is transferred from people throughout the PTM system to make agile organizations realize their potential as the world changes.

Figure 8.7 – Leadership-Culture Interactions

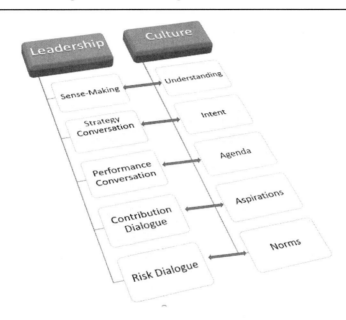

Thinking Exercises

1. Refer to Figure 8.2 and consider how differences between "espoused theory" and "theory in use" influence the various levers of control. How do these differences affect operational performance or success?
2. Consider the elements of the Performance Triangle Model for systems. How do these various elements influence the way that people think and act and make decisions? Explain your reasoning.
3. Refer to Figure 8.5, then think about some of the many conversations surrounding leadership that we recommend. How might these conversations promote constructive dialogue and help the organization to be more agile? Explain your reasoning.
4. Consider the culture dimensions of the Performance Triangle Model. Culture is contained in the "unspoken, rarely discussed' beliefs, values, and shared assumptions of a group of people. How might exploring the

various elements of culture through constructive dialogue help managers and leaders change the culture? Explain your reasoning.

5. Using the organization that you work for or one that you know well, evaluate the interaction of the three main points of the Performance Triangle Model. Are they complementary or do they interfere with performance? Explain your reasoning.

Suggested Reading

Axlrod, A. *Patton on Leadership: Strategic Lessons for Corporate Warfare.* Paramus, JJ, Prentice Hall Press, 1999.

Hayward, S. *Churchill on Leadership: Executive Success in the Face of Adversity.* Rocklin, CA: Prima Publishing, 1997.

Michel, L. *The Performance Triangle: Diagnostic Mentoring to Manage Organizations and People for Superior Performance in Turbulent Times.* London, UK: LID Publishing Ltd., 2013.

Michel, L. *People-centric Management: How Managers Use Four Levers to Bring Out Greatness of Others.* London, UK: LID Publishing Ltd., 2020.

Michel, L. *Agile by Choice: A Workbook for Leaders.* London, UK: LID Publishing Ltd., 2021.

Nold, H., & L. Michel. "Organizational Culture: A Systems Approach". In *21st Century Approaches to Management and Accounting Research.* London, UK: Intech, 2021. ISBN 978-1-83968-571-2.

CHAPTER 9

CONVERTING ENERGY TO ACTION: PURPOSE, RELATIONSHIPS, AND COLLABORATION

Quick Review… getting up to speed

In this chapter, we continue exploring the Performance Triangle Model (PTM) for agile management using people-centric techniques to harness and focus the vast reservoir of talent in organizations to add value and create success.[1,2] I have described how the PTM is a dynamic but balanced system of leadership, systems, and culture that is powered by people. Using the analogy of a bicycle, YOU provide the power to make the bike go with your legs similar to people in an organization. YOU must balance the bike to keep from falling over similar to how leadership, systems, and culture must be balanced in an organization. The question YOU should be asking now, which I will address in Chapter Nine, is the following: How is the energy transferred from the legs to the bike to propel it forward? In the PTM, the energy from people is transferred and distributed to the rest of the dynamic system when people share a common purpose and have healthy relationships, which promotes effective and efficient collaboration.

In Chapter Seven, I discussed how people provide the power to the dynamic PTM system. In successful 21st century organizations, value is created with intangibles resulting from innovation and the capability to react quickly and effectively to rapid change. Effective leaders and managers must actively engage with knowledge workers to create an environment where people are able to focus their tacit knowledge and talents on things that are important and add value. Essential to unleashing the vast potential of knowledge is the fundamental belief that people are self-responsible and want to do the "right" thing for stakeholders, and willing to stand by their decisions. They do not have to be TOLD what to do or how to do it. They just DO it. Self-responsibility applies equally to managers as well as subordinates in the sense that managers must accept the decisions made by others and celebrate creativity and experimentation even if the results do not necessarily turn out as hoped. Management must be aware of the critical attributes needed to allow people to realize their full potential using people-centric practices which enable the following four attributes:

- **Focus of Attention** – People must be free of distractions or interferences, typically created by management, to focus their abilities and expertise on their work,
- **Awareness** – People must be aware of what is happening around them in order to respond to the specific needs of stakeholders, quickly and efficiently,
- **Trust** – People must trust their managers and co-workers, others both internal and external to the organization, and (maybe most importantly) their own abilities and judgment,
- **Choice** – People must have freedom of choice to choose the best action in response to some demand and the freedom to say "no" if prescribed actions are inappropriate or ineffective.

In Chapter Eight, I discussed how there is a distinct difference in many, if not most, organizations between the leader's "espoused theory" (what s/he says s/he does) and the leader's "theory in use" (what s/he actually does).[3] Many executives claim that "people are our most valuable asset" and include flowery statements to illustrate this in vision and mission statements. Leaders worldwide make a big deal about employee engagement and how they are "all about the people." While this sounds great, in too many organizations, management has created highly structured command and control structures and processes designed to pigeonhole people into highly limiting jobs. Managers then try to ensure consistency and drive efficiency with highly restrictive job descriptions, performance goals, and performance reviews that are made worse with ill-conceived incentive programs. If leaders truly wish to maximize the potential of their "most valuable asset," they must actively seek to balance systems (rules, routines, tools), leadership (sense-making, strategy conversations, performance conversations, contribution dialogue, risk dialogue), and culture (understanding, intent, agenda, aspirations, norms). Serious people-centric leaders must recognize the dynamic relationships between people, systems, and leadership, and the organizational culture. They need to rethink many widely accepted management practices and behaviors, then actively engage with people throughout the organization in very different ways to unleash the vast potential of their "most valued asset" which is the key to agile organizations and success in the 21st century.

Energy Transfer

As the pedal, chain wheel, and chain in a bicycle enable leg energy to be converted to forward motion, purpose, relationships, and collaboration transfer energy from people throughout the rest of the PTM system, systems, leadership, and culture. In previous chapters I emphasized the need for trust throughout the organization to facilitate knowledge sharing. When everyone shares the same beliefs, values, and assumptions which are aligned with the organization's mission and vision, good things happen. Illustrated in Figure 9.1, the PTM identifies three critical "connectors" that serve to link all of the parts of the model and enable agile people-centric management styles to unleash, and then harness the power of people to maximize their potential and the potential of the organization.

"Accept the fact that we have to treat almost anybody as a volunteer..." – **Peter Drucker**

Figure 9.1 – Focus on Energy Transfer

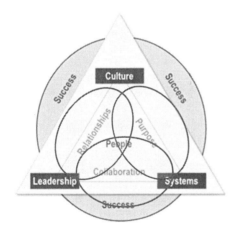

Source: Adapted from Michel, L. (2013). *The Performance Triangle: Diagnostic Mentoring to Manage Organizations and People for Superior Performance in Turbulent Times*, London, UK: LID

Purpose

If you look at the diagram of the Performance Triangle Model in Figure 9.1, you will notice purpose on the right side connecting culture with systems and intersecting with people in the middle of the triangle. Jürgen Habermas observed that "there is no administrative production of purpose."[4] In our workings with many executives we often hear comments along the lines of "When we lost sight of the purpose of our work, we started a discussion on motivation." People are internally motivated when there is a common purpose that is widely shared. People WANT to do good and be successful both personally and for the organization. However, through time, things change, and many organizations lose sight of the original purpose that inspired people to excel. When this happens, the natural reaction of traditionally trained managers is to try to motivate people. This comes in the form of both negative motivational techniques (if you don't reach your goals, you don't get a raise…or worse) and positive motivational techniques (there is a bonus for you if you exceed your goals). We have observed that both forms of motivation have many unintended consequences that defeat the purpose.

Every leader and manager in every organization wants employees to be committed to doing the best work possible and making a contribution. Unfortunately, lofty strategic plans and short-term goals do little to secure commitment from most employees. People make personal commitments because of their personal experience and relationships with supervisors, managers, and clients. All employees, whatever they are doing and whatever their level in the organization, always follow their own personal values, norms, and goals. Corporate guidelines can reinforce shared values, rituals, and myths, but purpose is created subjectively by individuals who decide what is important according to their own personal set of values. The fact is that every piece of work has a client, either internally or externally. Employees and supervisors must recognize this fact because without this realization there is no motivation for goal-oriented behavior or action. When people recognize that their efforts are meaningful, they work with greater energy, and are physically, mentally, and emotionally fully present.[5] Sadly, many organizational leaders and managers fail to recognize this basic human trait. They fail to realize that it is a shared path to produce a valuable customer experience that motivates people, not numerical targets generated by someone in an office, regardless of the potential monetary gain.[6] Purpose cannot be dictated or delivered. It must be found by each person individually according to his or her mental models and values. Here are a few suggestions on how to instill or maintain a strong sense of purpose that is widely shared throughout the organization.

- **Avoid job descriptions with a scope that is too narrow or limiting** – Work needs to make sense to self-responsible knowledge workers and give them room to grow personally and professionally. The vast majority of workers want to be creative and contribute, but narrow or overly restricting jobs deny employees the chance to be creative. Traditionally trained managers seek consistency and efficiency which narrow job descriptions can help to achieve. Unfortunately, restrictive jobs squash creativity and hide the contribution that an individual is making that might provide satisfaction. People-centric leaders recognize that job design has a huge impact on motivation and performance... then do something about it. Fredrick Herzberg said, "If you want someone to do a good job, then give them a good job to do" (p. 30).[7]

- **Avoid meaningless communications** – Distributing information by posting information on tough or "stretch" goals, important change projects, and dramatic scenarios typically have the opposite of the intended effect on most people. I worked for a company for many years with a CEO who, several times a year, would send out an email to everyone in the company for a "call to action" to address some problem or issue. The emails always contained an emotionally charged description of the possible danger with projections of doom and gloom if the answer to the problem were not found. The reaction from all other than the few people at the corporate office who were hoping to gain political favor from the CEO was "oh, no... here we go again." People can easily distinguish between corporate messaging and business reality. So, create an environment where leadership teams have an open dialogue and give people the opportunity to ask questions and get honest answers.

- **Give people the opportunity for emotional commitment** – Grand strategy plans, and vision and mission statements are formal statements that offer information on purpose, but real purpose comes from the daily routines and interactions with supervisors and others in the work group. Purpose results from doing something good. This demands that managers who demand performance must first provide purpose. Good leaders, at any level, help people on a daily basis to make sense of what is going on and why they are doing it. This is what instills in people a strong sense of purpose that gives them the motivation to go the extra mile and work very hard. Leaders inspire people with a higher purpose that goes beyond profits for the company.

"The price of greatness is responsibility." – **Winston Churchill**

Collaboration

As organizations increase in size and scope, they become more complex, making the need for close collaboration increasingly important for success. Traditionally trained managers with a highly developed need for command and control naturally add departments with specialized functions, geographic entities, services, customer groupings, and other structures that add complexity. Clearly, some divisions of labor and structure are needed for efficiency and accountability, but leaders must recognize that every new department or entity creates a new silo of knowledge and political intrigue as managers compete for recognition and resources. Organizational structures become hardened over time due to geographic separation, different disciplines and training, goals, and a tendency for people at all levels to hoard information and knowledge. Edgar Schein observed that different functional disciplines develop very different world views and mental models from indoctrination in schools to experience that result in many subcultures within an organization.[8] These differing mental models shape the decision-making process by people in different disciplines and interfere with collaboration. Few would argue that sales/marketing people have a very different perspective from those in accounting/finance which is different from the design engineer which is different from the manufacturing or production manager which is different from legal or human resources. These inherent differences contribute interference with effective collaboration in simple and complex organizations. Despite all these barriers to collaboration we need to find ways to get people to work together to solve problems quickly and effectively.

Complex organizations require collaboration on a shared problem. Virtually all problems or issues will affect many different segments of the organization but getting key people to recognize the potential impact on their organization (and the impact on their personal performance) can be difficult. Many times, ego or the natural differences in mental models interfere with the recognition that a problem can have consequences. Therefore, it becomes imperative that we, as diverse people, recognize that your problem is my problem, and my problem is your problem so that mutual dependency becomes personal. Breaking through these barriers and egos is a function of leadership and takes time and effort.

The challenge for people-centric leaders is threefold. First, leaders must be sure that the delegated actions needed to address the problem align with the overall goals of the company, not just personal ego, or reward. In traditional command and control type organizations goals are developed at the topmost levels then cascaded downward to various departments and ultimately to individuals. Senior leaders must keep an eye on lower-level collaborative teams to be sure that the problems being addressed do, in fact, support organizational goals. Second, individual actions needed to resolve the problem should complement, not interfere with, the actions of others in supporting roles. Leaders must establish clear boundaries around individual initiatives, and then be proactive to prevent others from infringing on the freedom of action of others. Third, the leader must act as a champion to reconcile the need for resources to solve the problem with competing demands from multiple segments in the organization or other problems. The leader needs to be able to relieve roadblocks so that the actions of collaborative teams can get the job done. The members of the team must know that their efforts will not be in vain…. otherwise, why bother.

Traditionally trained managers are taught any number of methods of control to solve the problem of lack of cooperation among individuals and segments. Promoting cooperation is generally considered as a core managerial task.[9] The challenge for managers comes from employees who have different goals that often conflict with the goals of the organization. There are essentially two ways to solve this conflict: (1) extrinsic motivation in which participants see solving the problem as a means to an end in the form of recognition to advance their career or monetary reward to pad their bank accounts; and (2) intrinsic motivation in which employees participate for their own sake because solving the problem is seen as personally rewarding or challenging.[10] We must remember that cooperation and collaboration are essential and the most effective ways to get things done in complex organizations, and I suggest that intrinsic motivation is a more powerful motivator for effective collaboration. Here are a few suggestions for people-centric managers to help facilitate effective collaboration.

- **Don't try to reduce complexity** – This is impossible, but it should not be ignored. Complexity can be navigated through effective delegation of decision-making. BUT effective delegation that promotes agility is a broad set of goals or boundaries rather than a limiting command and control list of dos and don'ts. Self-responsible people just need the boundaries; then you trust them to make effective decisions.
- **Be cautious about more knowledge sharing IT projects** – Just because information or knowledge is there does not mean that people will use it effectively, or at all. Knowledge sharing and collaboration between business units, functions, geographies, or departments do not happen because management mandates it. Knowledge sharing happens when self-interested people see the need and opportunity to collaborate and share resources.
- **Ask more questions than giving answers** – Asking questions rather than providing answers helps to create healthy relationships and allows employees to explore new ideas together. This is not necessarily a natural activity for many traditionally trained managers

who feel a need to establish superiority and it takes time and effort. However, taking the time to develop quality interactions is one of the most important capabilities needed to manage complexity and change.

- **Create cross-functional teams** – Creating effective cross-functional teams is more difficult than it sounds because of the cultural differences that I discussed earlier. Team leaders and team champions must work hard to navigate the difference in worldview and competing interests to bridge hierarchies and knock down barriers to getting things done.

- **Give teams room to move** – Effective collaboration needs space for creativity and performance. Give teams plenty of choices for possible actions and degrees of freedom and remove rules that limit the possibilities. Be careful when setting timelines and increase time for creative work. Innovative ideas do not just spring into people's heads. The light bulb goes on because of tacit knowledge sharing in a *Ba* environment that cannot be hurried.

- **Create ways to recognize effective collaboration and teams** – In most organizations the system of recognition focuses on individual contribution rather than that of a team. Routinely review managerial routines, tools, and principles looking for unintended barriers to collaboration. Sometimes it may be best to celebrate failure provided the team collaborated effectively, if the project does not turn out as hoped. People and teams learn from mistakes so the next time might be different if you don't kill the messenger.

"A leader is best when people barely know he exists." – **Lao Tzu, 4th Century BC, ancient Chinese philosopher**

Relationships

Obviously, relationships are the foundation of every interaction whether personal or business. Successful collaboration depends on people with healthy relationships who share a common purpose to get things done and innovate. This applies equally when interacting with people inside or outside of the organization…. any stakeholder. Moreover, leveraging healthy internal and external relationships becomes particularly critical in environments where the pace of change is high and there is a high degree of interdependent complexity. Not surprisingly, trust emerges as the single most powerful enabler or destroyer of healthy relationships. Yet, human relationships are absolutely essential when dealing with situations that require rapid change and the ability to withstand unexpected or unanticipated shocks. We can all relate to the fact that if I do not trust you and you do not trust me, neither of us will share what we know. When this happens, knowledge sharing and, therefore, effective collaboration comes to a screeching halt. Throw in diverse egos, conflicting agendas or aspirations, and goals and the organization come to a complete stop. Problem-solving, decision-making, and innovation, slow to glacial speed or to a complete standstill which can be a death knell in the 21st century business world. In the Performance Triangle Model, relationships connect leadership with people and culture. In a task-oriented world it is imperative for leaders to remember that reliable relationships are absolutely necessary to get just about anything done quickly and effectively. People-centric leaders who want to develop agile organizations must keep a few things in mind regarding relationships.

- **Relationships are a human need** – People have an instinctive desire for self-determination and to feel connected to others.[11] This shared connection is demonstrated by sharing thoughts and feelings.[12] Mutual understanding and respect strengthen intrinsic motivations to cooperate and get things done.[13] When human beings feel mutual respect, they have a heightened sense of autonomy (freedom to determine things for themselves) and increased ability to get a job done (job satisfaction), thereby reinforcing two basic human needs.[14]
- **Relationships are a two-way street** – At the most fundamental core of any culture are basic assumptions about the proper way for individuals to relate to each other when interacting for safety, for comfort, and to show respect. In organizational cultures, leaders set the example for others on how to relate to each other. Employees are very observant so leaders must be aware of how their interactions appear to others. If leaders desire an environment of mutual respect, they must treat everyone fairly and do what they say they do. This is not always easy and requires continuous effort, especially in times of crisis.
- **Be cautious with internal competitions** – As an athlete, I am fond of competition, but many times internal competition creates unintended consequences. The desire to win can unintentionally encourage silos and encourage people or departments to work in isolation thereby preventing the formation of healthy relationships, knowledge sharing, and effective collaboration. A little friendly competition can be healthy, but leaders must be very aware and

alert to detect when friendly competition becomes a blood sport, and then step in as referee or stop the competition entirely.

- **Promote interdependencies rather strict structures** – In complex organizations people, functional departments, and business units are inextricably dependent on each other for success. Agile leaders promote these interdependencies, using a variety of facilitation techniques to increase awareness of them and help units to establish productive working relationships to collaborate for the common good.

"If opportunity doesn't knock…. build a door." – **Milton Berle, comedian**

Connecting the dots…

In Chapter Four, I emphasized the need for speed to create new knowledge. I made the case that accelerating the rate of new knowledge creation gave organizations a competitive advantage. The logic goes something like this. If organizations can get smarter, faster, than the competition, they will accelerate the decision-making and innovation process which helps the organization to react more quickly to threats and opportunities. They also find solutions to problems more quickly, identify and implement process improvements more quickly to increase productivity, and innovate more quickly. Research has shown that only between 10 and 20% of the total body of knowledge in an organization is captured in an explicit form which can be easily shared via data bases, standard operating procedures, work instructions, memos, etc. Organizations worldwide spend untold billions of dollars to capture and share 10 to 20% of the knowledge that is in their organizations. The remaining 80 to 90% of knowledge is tacit in nature which exists in the minds and experiences of the people. The tacit nature of knowledge makes it difficult to share or replicate. We all know that if we do a task one time that takes 10 minutes the first try, it will take much less time after 100 repetitions. We just "learn" to do it better and faster. This is tacit knowledge. Most of us would be hard-pressed to convert what we do to get the job gone more quickly into explicit knowledge, work instructions or standard operating procedures. I asked, "what if companies have a process to access the massive tacit knowledge base?" I described a process of accessing the body of tacit knowledge in an organization, converting it to explicit knowledge, then implementing the new nugget of knowledge so the process can be repeated. The SECI (**S**ocialization, **E**xternalization, **C**ombination, **I**nternalization) cycle visualized by I. Nonaka provided a roadmap for the process.[15] The SECI model offers a visualization of a dynamic process that helps organizations to gain access to their tacit knowledge base.

Think back to Chapter Five where I made the point that organizational culture is critical to knowledge sharing and success. Throughout all of the subsequent chapters, I have repeatedly mentioned the need for knowledge sharing which is particularly critical for successful collaboration. For the SECI process to be workable, the organization must promote socialization; encouraging people to talk to each other and share what they know. However, most organizations, particularly those dominated by traditionally trained managers who develop and enforce restricting command and control systems, place people into limiting jobs with narrow boundaries and actively inhibit socialization. "Get to your workstation, focus on your job, ignore everyone else, and meet your goals" is the common attitude by such managers who see social interaction as an interference to productivity…. and their bonus or promotion. This is both a structural and cultural condition. Culture exists in the beliefs, values, and shared assumptions of a group of people. In Chapter Five I began exploring various models of organizational culture looking for one that would provide some direction on how to make the SECI process a reality. My research over many years led me to adopt the Great Place to Work© Institute model.

The Great Place to Work© Institute (GPTW) conducts culture surveys with tens of thousands of companies large and small, worldwide and shares the results of individual companies with company executives and publishes the 100 Best Places to Work list annually in *Fortune Magazine*. The GPTW culture model consists of five dimensions: credibility, fairness, and respect (collectively the Trust Index©), pride, and camaraderie.[16] Essentially, the thinking goes something like this; if managers say what they do and do what they say they are credible; if you are treated fairly and with respect, you are likely to trust someone. Additionally, people must take pride in their organizations and enjoy being with the people they work with and for. Organizations that can create a culture of trust, pride, and camaraderie enjoy an environment where people socialize, share what they know, and collaborate to solve problems and generate innovative ideas. Research demonstrates that organizations with higher values in these cultural attributes significantly outperform competitors.[17] I believe the reason for such success is because the culture creates an environment where people socialize and share their tacit knowledge; then leaders facilitate putting the emergent decisions and ideas into value adding action. Leaders have most likely never heard of the SECI cycle but without realizing it have created the environment that enables the SECI cycle to flourish. Apple,

Amazon, and other companies with a high ratio of market value to book value demonstrate the power of the SECI cycle and the culture that enables it (see Figure 4.1 in Chapter Four).

While organizational culture and accelerated knowledge creation are now becoming recognized as keys to superior performance and value generation in the 21st century, further research and reflection revealed a much larger dynamic system that contains innumerable interferences or

Figure 9.2 – Merging GPTW with PTM

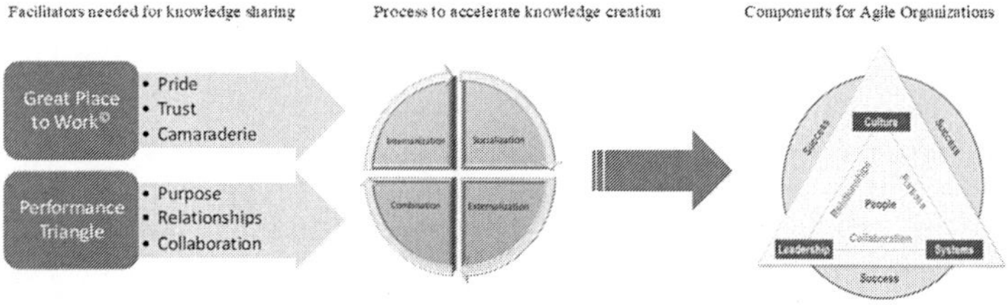

viruses that prevent knowledge sharing and inhibit performance. If you compare the dimensions of the GPTW culture model with the sides of the Performance Triangle Model as illustrated in Figure 9.2 you should see similarities which enable the SECI cycle to function that leads us to a much larger dynamic system in which organizations operate… the Performance Triangle.

When you compare the GPTW dimensions (pride, trust, camaraderie) with the sides of the Performance Triangle (purpose, relationships, collaboration) the similarities should be obvious. If you have pride in the values and mission of your organization that is widely shared throughout the organization, employees are likely to have a shared sense of purpose. As I have stated many times, trust is essential for healthy relationships. Certainly, people will collaborate more effectively if they share a sense of camaraderie and like being with one another.

Collectively, these shared, unseen, and rarely discussed attributes establish an environment that enables access to the tacit knowledge base in an organization which leads to the increased speed of decision-making, process improvements, innovation, and more. But organizational dynamics are more complex than any one dimension. An organization is like an amoeba in the sense that if you push in one place there will be a bulge somewhere else. The Performance Triangle Model builds on the root concept of knowledge sharing and organizational culture to include multiple dimensions that exist in all organizations in one form or another. All executives want their organizations to outperform the competition, but to do so, the executives must take a wholistic approach that views all the dynamic aspects of the organization, and then take actions to root out interfering viruses that prevent people and ultimately the organization from superior performance. Through time, interferences creep into organizations as managers seek to improve control and performance. Layers of procedures, processes, rules, customs, and more produce the unintended effect of strangling the flow of knowledge and stifling the self-responsibility that is essential for harnessing the capabilities of people. Managers must be aware of how those pesky interferences are preventing superior performance so they can take focused action to eliminate the interferences.

"So much of what we call management consists of making it difficult for people to work" – **Peter Drucker**

Models and theories are great, but the questions you should be asking now are, "How can executives become aware of those pesky interferences?" .... and .... "Is there a tool that executives can use to gain insight into those debilitating viruses?" Without a validated diagnostic instrument that identifies interferences in the organizational system, executives must just guess what is happening. Many times, executives can sense something is wrong which leads them to take a shotgun approach leading to multiple change initiatives, commonly called the "flavor of the month" approach. It is common knowledge that the vast majority of change initiatives fail to achieve goals, and those attempting to deal with intangibles like culture rarely succeed. Fortunately, there is just such a tool available for executives to diagnose their organizations and help them take target action rather than a hit and miss approach and hope for some improvement where the big winners are the consultants.

In Chapter Ten, I will introduce and explore the diagnostic instrument that has been developed and validated to give executives reliable insight into many of these pesky unseen viruses. Armed with the Agility Insights Diagnostic instrument, executives are able to visualize how unseen interferences affect performance using the Performance Triangle Model as the foundation to help interpret the results.

Thinking Exercises

1. Energy for the PTM system comes from people and is transferred throughout by the sides of the triangle: purpose, collaboration, and

relationships. In your own words, discuss how this energy transfer takes place and why it is important for an organization.

2. Winston Churchill said, "The price of greatness is responsibility …" What does this mean in the context of a people-centric manager and how might it influence the manager's interactions with employees?

3. Refer to Figure 9.2. In your own words, describe the similarities and differences between the GPTW and PTM connectors. How do these similarities and differences help or hinder companies in being agile? Explain your reasoning.

4. Consider Peter Drucker's quote, "So much of what we call management consists of making it difficult for people to work". What does this mean and how does this tendency affect organizational performance? What can managers do to make it easier for people to work?

5. Using the organization that you work for or one that you know well, evaluate the interaction of the three connectors of the Performance Triangle. Are they complementary or do they interfere with performance? Explain your reasoning. What would you do differently if you had the authority to change anything?

Suggested Reading

Kotter, J. *Leading Change*. Boston, MA: Harvard University Press, 1996.

Michel, L. *People-centric Management: How Managers Use Four Levers to Bring Out Greatness of Others*. London, UK: LID Publishing Ltd., 2020.

Michel, L. *Agile by Choice: A Workbook for Leaders*. London, UK: LID Publishing Ltd., 2021.

Nold, H., & L. Michel. "Organizational Culture: A Systems Approach". In *21st Century Approaches to Management and Accounting Research*. London, UK: Intech, 2021. ISBN 978-1-83968-571-2.

Schein, E. *Organizational Culture and Leadership,* 4th ed. San Francisco, CA: Jossey-Bass, 2010.

CHAPTER 10

CONVERTING THEORY TO ACTION: DIAGNOSTIC MENTORING

Quick Review… getting up to speed

In the prior nine chapters, I have walked you through a wide range of concepts and theories. Beginning with basic concepts on strategy development, I introduced you to emergent ideas related to knowledge creation and organizational culture and how these affects both the development and implementation of strategy. Actually, these ideas are not that new. Edgar Schein's seminal *Organizational Culture and Leadership* was first published in 1991.[1] Nonaka and Takeuchi's groundbreaking book *The Knowledge-creating Company: How Japanese Companies Create the Dynamics of Innovation* that introduced the SECI knowledge creation cycle came out in 1995.[2] Yet, after all these years these topics and how they influence strategic planning and implementation get little or no coverage in strategy textbooks. I have more than a dozen textbooks on strategy from multiple publishers in my office. Peter Drucker's widely acknowledged quote, "Culture eats strategy for breakfast" has been repeated in many forms by many authors worldwide, but precious little has been done to interpret what this means for college students or corporate executives. Less yet has been done to help provide executives with the tools to identify and understand the unseen, unconscious, and rarely discussed attributes within their organizations that can make or break the best strategic plan. Business school graduates continue to be indoctrinated with methods and processes developed in the last century that, while still useful and important, overlook the main drivers of value in the 21st century: knowledge creation, innovation, and speed in decision-making. In a volatile, uncertain, complex, and ambiguous (VUCA) world that defines the current business environment the traditional processes (SWOT, Porter's forces, the resource-based view, etc.) are inadequate for the rate of change that exists in virtually every industry. In a VUCA world, successful organizations create organizational structures and use philosophies that are people-centric so that the organization taps into the tacit knowledge base to become agile. New strategies like the Delta Model and ambidextrous thinking are needed along with institutional agility which allows the organization to adapt to rapid change without massive upheaval through ineffective change programs. Like Darwin's evolution of the species, organizations must evolve in almost unnoticeable increments to adapt to new environments, naturally and systematically. Unfortunately, corporate executives do not have eons to bring about change in their organizations. In today's world, executives must sense the need for change, develop and implement a plan, then internalize it within the organization in a year or two…. tops.

Charles Darwin

Source: WordPress.com

The Great Place to Work© model for organizational culture provides a useful framework to help gain an understanding for some of the most important dimensions of organizational culture that either enable or inhibit knowledge sharing. Research has demonstrated that the dimensions of the GPTW model; the Trust Index© (credibility, respect, fairness), pride, and camaraderie are significant forces for or against knowledge sharing.[3] Further research has demonstrated that companies with higher values in trust, pride, and camaraderie on the GPTW survey compared to competitors significantly outperform the competition in many key business measures.[4,5]

So, while knowledge sharing and organizational culture are important considerations for developing and executing strategic plans and institutional change, organizational dynamics are much more complicated. Over multiple chapters I introduced and discussed the Performance Triangle Model (PTM) for agile management using people-centric techniques to harness and focus the vast reservoir of talent and creativity in organizations to add value and create success.[6,7] I have described how the PTM is a dynamic but balanced system of leadership, systems, and culture that is powered by people. Productive and creative energy from people is transferred throughout the PTM system through a shared sense of purpose, healthy relationships, and effective collaboration. For each dimension of the Performance Triangle Model, I offered suggestions on dos and don'ts that managers should consider when attempting to create a more people-centric, agile organization. We left off the last chapter, Chapter Nine, by asking practical questions. If the various theories and models make sense, then what can an executive do about all this? Where do executives start? How can they know if they are making progress?

Fortunately, nearly 20 years of research with over 200 organizations worldwide has resulted in the development of a statistically validated diagnostic instrument. This diagnostic instrument gives executives insight into the underlying unseen and unconscious beliefs and values that infect organizations and prevent organizations and individuals from maximizing their potential. Once armed with insight into what is going on, executives can take targeted and effective action to eliminate the unseen viruses that are inhibiting change and performance. Instead of the one-size-fits-all, shotgun, approach promoted by consulting firms worldwide, we propose a more targeted approach. You would not return to a doctor who began prescribing drugs or treatments without first taking your blood pressure, other vitals, and thoroughly checking out your symptoms BEFORE prescribing treatments. Yet, this is exactly what corporate executives do when confronted with issues. Executives hire high profile, very expensive, consultants who do a superficial analysis of the organization and maybe the structure, and then prescribe actions taken from their predetermined, proprietary methodology. Corrective recommendations tend to be very similar despite the fact that organizations have very different issues and problems…hence… the one-size-fits-all methodology.

Would you go to either of these "doctors" … a second time?

Source: Shutterstock.com   *Source: Shutterstock.com*

To illustrate my point, I offer the following personal experience. For several years, I was a member of Financial Executives International (FEI) which is an organization for senior level financial executives to share insights, information, and support. In the city where I live, our FEI chapter would meet about once a quarter to listen to a guest speaker, have dinner (socialize), and share our experiences, challenges, and ideas with like-minded executives from various industries. At one point, strictly by chance my company and two others who were also FEI members from different industries engaged the same consultant to help find ways to address issues that all three companies were experiencing. All three companies were in different industries and experiencing very different problems and issues ranging from low morale and high turnover to supply chain disruptions. Several quarterly FEI meetings later, we shared notes while socializing over dinner and realized that the consultant had made almost identical recommendations to each company even though our issues and industries were very different. All three of us realized that the consultant had charged a lot of money for their one-size-fits-all proprietary methodology and then fit our problems into their specific model. The predictable result was that the consultant's recommendations yielded little in the way of concrete improvement. We all vowed never to use this consultant again, and I began looking more closely at other high-profile consultants only to realize that the one-size-fits-all methodology was standard operating procedure in the consulting business.

Because of this experience, the diagnostic approach evolved so that, like a doctor, it is possible to take the vitals or draw the blood of an organization, and then analyze the results. Based on the results of the diagnosis, senior executives can identify those unseen viruses which are "unspoken, and rarely discussed" elements of the culture. Executives can then take targeted action to eliminate the infections that are preventing the organization from changing or yielding superior performance. The first step is to diagnose the organization. This leads to an awareness of unseen and rarely discussed issues from which emerge targeted and effective actions to fix the root cause of the issues that can be seen. The idea is to fix the problem rather than apply a band aid.

Recognition of the underlying issues that cause interferences is just the first step in healing. Just like people who do not appreciate being told that their diet is poor or that the habits they have had for years are causing health problems and need to be changed, senior executives do not appreciate being told by outsiders that their organizations have problems, even if they know it. Therefore, our diagnostic mentoring approach centers around interpreting the results of the diagnostic, then asking probing questions so that executives come to their OWN realization of what is going on. I have seen too many situations where highly paid consultants TOLD executives that their organizations had problems and what to do about them. The executives all nodded their heads in agreement and then returned to their offices, closed the doors, and took no action. Human nature is such that people are more likely to get behind promoting and supporting an idea of their own. Likewise, the fragile egos of senior executives are injured when they are told that their organizations have significant problems. Executives may know it but being told about it becomes a hard pill to swallow. Therefore, it becomes essential for executives to understand what the data from the diagnostic say about their organizations, interpret the results in the context of their organizations, and then develop their own action plans where the executive can truthfully say "This was my idea." Coach the executives to gain understanding and insight and allow them to come to their own conclusions and have ownership of the resulting corrective action plans.

"While the journey seems long and hard at the beginning with perseverance and dedication the rewards at the end last a lifetime." — **William R. Francis via Baylor College of Medicine**

Figure 10.1 – The Performance Triangle

Source: Adapted from Michel, L. (2013). *The Performance Triangle: Diagnostic Mentoring to Manage Organizations and People for Superior Performance in Turbulent Times,* London, UK: LID

The doctor is IN!

Every trip to the doctor's office begins with questions... "What are your symptoms?", "Where does it hurt?", "Does this hurt?", "Do you feel dizzy?", etc. The doctor takes your blood pressure and listens to your heart and lungs then, based on these initial observations, prescribes additional diagnostic testing BEFORE deciding on a plan of treatments. The beginning of the diagnostic process begins with questions so we have developed and validated several versions of a diagnostic instrument from which one may be selected based on the patient's initial responses and initial screening. Similar to the doctor selecting the need for either an MRI or a CAT scan or further blood analysis, multiple customizable diagnostic instruments are available that provide additional insight into the unseen and rarely discussed values, beliefs, and shared assumptions that infect organizations, preventing superior performance or inhibiting change. Trained diagnostic mentors select the instrument that will provide the deepest insight into what is happening within the organization. The trick is to ask the right questions. The Performance Triangle diagnostic instrument contains multiple questions designed to provide insight into the "right" questions for each of the elements of the Performance Triangle model which is repeated as a reminder in Figure 10.1.

People

We know that people perform at their highest potential by winning their "inner game" and overcoming the self-doubt, fear, bias, limiting concepts or assumptions that distort perceptions, decisions, behaviors, actions and stress that interfere with, and diminish, performance.[8,9] Awareness about what is going on around them, choice to choose the best solution, and trust in others help people to focus attention on tasks and problems. Reaching a state of flow, the state where performance and creativity are at a peak, must be a primary objective at all levels of an agile, people-centric, organization.[10] Questions applicable for the people dimensions are the following.

- **Focus** – Are people allowed to focus attention and energy on tasks? Are interferences preventing people from focusing their abilities to complete tasks?
- **Awareness** – Are people aware of forces that influence actions and decisions?
- **Trust** – Do people trust co-workers and management to be treated fairly and with respect? Is management credible?
- **Choice** – Are people allowed the freedom to use their own creative ability to solve problems, respond to customers, or be innovative?

Systems

In the PTM, "systems" represent more than just the computer-driven information technology-driven systems. Systems consist of the institutional framework with rules, routines, and tools that set the stage for rigorous and disciplined leadership. Technology-based information systems accumulate, store, process, and provide access to information and facilitate immediate feedback. Human systems in the form of rules, routines, and guidelines of many types provide frameworks that give technology structure and relevance. To support collaboration among people, systems make information available to assist people to find purpose, support the decision-making process, and set boundaries balancing entrepreneurship with efficiency. The diagnostic questions for systems are:

- **Information** – Do decision-makers at all levels have access to timely and relevant information to know what is going on inside and outside the organization to make informed decisions?
- **Strategy** – Do leaders and followers clearly understand the rules of the game and what is needed to achieve strategic and operational objectives?
- **Implementation** – Do decision-makers throughout the organization clearly understand what actions are needed to be successful?
- **Beliefs** – Do decision-makers throughout the organization have a shared ambition to support organizational objectives?
- **Boundaries** – Do decision-makers throughout the organization have a firm understanding of the boundaries of or limits to their decisions or authority?

Leadership

Effective leaders in agile, people-centric, organizations interact with individuals on a personal level, relate to others to facilitate meaningful collaboration, and establish a supportive work environment based on trust.[11] Successful leadership varies by organization and situation. A leadership style that is successful in one organization may not necessarily be effective if applied in a different organization or situation. However, the need for effective communication skills and interaction with followers is a recurring theme in the literature.[12,13,14] It becomes essential for effective leaders in an agile organization to develop effective communication and interaction skills that are natural and unique to the leader and organization. Ultimately, what is important is that the individuals in the organization adopt a shared vision, collaborate in a culture of trust, and engage with multiple personalities, while leaders champion creativity and experimentation. The Performance Triangle diagnostic instrument asks the following questions related to leadership.

- **Sense making** – Do leaders have the capability to sense changes in internal and external environments and interpret meaning?

- **Strategy conversion** – Do leaders have an understanding of why the organization has established strategic goals, and are goals founded on lessons from the past?
- **Performance conversion** – Do leaders have a clear understanding of whether the organization is on track, what needs to be done to remain on track, and what needs to be done to achieve superior performance?
- **Contribution dialogue** – Do leaders have a clear understanding of what they can do to contribute toward moving the organization forward? Do leaders clearly understand their role?
- **Risk dialogue** – Do leaders have a clear understanding of the potential risks and the level of risk that the organization can tolerate?

Culture

The culture of the organization creates a shared context, enables or inhibits knowledge exchange, and defines the invisible boundaries of collaboration. A vibrant culture establishes a shared context as the common ground with a shared agenda, language, mental models, purpose, and relationships.[15] A shared context describes a shared mindset and the behavior of individuals based on shared norms, beliefs, values, and assumptions. The organizational culture becomes the invisible force that, like gravity, shapes all interactions within the universe in which the organization exists.

Organizational culture either enables knowledge sharing or is a barrier to sharing even simple pieces of information.[4] Similar to a virus infecting a living organism, organizational traits like autocratic leadership styles, silos, and lack of trust and respect throughout the organization effectively block knowledge sharing. An unseen or unnoticed virus makes the culture an organizational bottleneck that constrains the amount and quality of knowledge sharing, limiting the creativity of people and the ability to act, and disrupting flow. Knowledge that is not shared, exchanged, and transferred has no value to an organization. The challenge for any executive is to create a culture that facilitates people working together on tasks that add value to the organization. Effective collaboration requires a shared problem and commitment with people working together with shared ways of doing things. The questions to give insight into organizational culture are the following.

- **Understanding** – Do people share an understanding of where the organization is and where it is going or attempting to go?
- **Intent** – Do people share a common intent of how to move the organization forward to meet goals and objectives?
- **Agenda** – Do people share a common agenda on what needs to be done to move the organization toward meeting goals and objectives?
- **Aspirations** – Do people share a common sense of purpose to meet goals and objectives?
- **Norms** – Do people share a common set of norms of behavior needed to get ahead within the organization?

Collaboration, Purpose, and Relationships

A high-energy work environment produces intense collaboration, a high sense of purpose and trusting relationships. These features have a stabilizing effect on organizations known as resilience or "robustness."[16,17] Organizations reach higher levels of resilience through collaboration,[18] purpose, and relationships.[19] The diagnostic questions targeting the sides of the Performance Triangle Model are as follows.

- **Relationships** – Do co-workers and management have and maintain healthy, trusting, relationships?
- **Purpose** – Do people share a common higher purpose for the organization and organizational objectives?
- **Collaboration** – Do people collaborate effectively by sharing knowledge to achieve common goals and objectives?

Does this work, and can I believe the results?

In 2014 my colleagues and I had an opportunity to use our diagnostic instrument with a client that was a mid-size city in the Southeast United States with 1,162 participants. This large sample provided enough raw data for us to subject the model and the instrument to independent statistical testing for validity and reliability. To the best of my knowledge no other methodology has been subjected to independent testing. Raw data from our diagnostic instrument with 55 questions were sent to an independent PhD in statistics at a university in Germany with an instruction to "do your thing" and test to see if the answers to the questions fit the model and provide information that is reliable and valid.

The Sample

The sample consisted of employees of a mid-sized city government in the Southeastern United States. A series of highly publicized scandals in the city resulted in the recommendation by a select committee of citizens for a survey of the culture and morale of all city employees. The Performance Triangle diagnostic instrument was selected after a comparison with multiple "morale surveys" promoted by multiple consultants because the model provided greater depth and insight into the organization as a system and a general recognition that significant change was needed. 1,162 employees participated out of a total employee population of 2,400 (48.4% participation rate). Participants were asked to identify the department in which they worked and whether they were a top executive (department or assistant department head), supervisor (anyone below department head with supervisory responsibility), or employee (anyone with no supervisory responsibility). Figure 10.2 titled "Distribution of Sample Participants" shows the distribution of all participants horizontally by management level and vertically by department. Departments with fewer than ten employees were grouped into "Other" to protect the confidentiality of individual respondents.

Figure 10.2 – Distribution of Sample Participants

	Total	Electric Utility	Finance	Police	Airport	Community Dvpt.	Parks & Recreation	Information Technology	Water Utility	The Lakeland Center	Fire	Public Works	Other
Executives	38	8	2	2	1	1	2	1	1	2	2	2	14
Supervisors	421	86	15	39	5	17	74	17	47	21	29	50	20
Employees	703	162	23	94	6	34	103	37	75	12	47	65	45
Total	1162	256	40	135	12	52	179	55	123	35	78	117	79

Results of statistical analysis

The results of the independent statistical analysis indicated that the diagnostic instrument had a good fit with the model and generated results with high levels of validity and reliability for both the detailed elements and the summary levels of the Performance Triangle. Anyone interested in exploring the details of this analysis is invited to read "Organizational agility – Testing, Validity, and Reliability of a Diagnostic Instrument" which was published in the *Journal of Organizational Psychology* by myself and our research team.[20] The important point of the study is that the results from the diagnostic instrument have validity and reliability at levels high enough to be confident that the results can be used to generate actionable knowledge. Executives can take actions based on the diagnostic results with a high degree of confidence that they are targeting behaviors and beliefs that are meaningful.

What did the results say? ... A case study

After careful analysis of the data gathered from the employees of the city, we conducted a one-day workshop with the top executives from each department. This group included the city manager, police chief, fire chief, and finance director, and their assistant or deputies in each department. This was a highly politicized situation that had metastasized over several years into an extremely sensitive and emotional issue throughout the city. The situation began several years prior with the revelation that several members of the police department had been having inappropriate interactions while on duty. The resulting investigation spread to other departments to expose similar behaviors throughout the various departments within the city operations. A committee of highly respected citizens was formed to evaluate the findings and make recommendations on what should be done. All meetings of the citizen's committee were open to the public, very well attended, and widely publicized in the local media. At the end of approximately nine months of public meetings, the citizen's committee recommended that the city perform a "morale survey" to gain insight into the underlying beliefs and values that would allow public servants to rationalize that such behavior was acceptable. After evaluating several proposals, the city selected our diagnostic instrument because it offered to provide deeper insight and direction than other survey instruments. In addition to the one-day workshop with the city leadership teams, we conducted a three-hour televised presentation of the results to the elected city commissioners. Inserting data for the various dimensions and elements into a variety of visual aids, it is possible to recognize how the diagnostic approach can help focus attention on what matters to senior leaders. The following visual aids were part of the presentation to the city commission.

Interpreting the data

In order to fully understand the following visual aids, it is important to understand where the numbers came from and what they mean. All the raw data were converted to a 100-point scale, like the Celsius temperature scale, to help people to more easily interpret the results. The numbers shown represent the average of the responses from that particular sample. Higher numbers mean that the strength of the underlying perception is high while low numbers indicate weakness like hot and cold. The diagnostic instrument was initially developed with data from 102 organizations and has since been used with over 200 clients representing a wide range of industries and business sizes, nonprofits, for-profit companies, and governmental entities (see Figure 10.3). Consequently, we are able to establish benchmarks that vary from industry to industry so that our city is being compared to other governmental entities rather than banks (for example).

Figure 10.3 – Demographics of Diagnostic Instrument Development

Organizations	N=102
Participants per Organization	1-5 (48); 6-19 (24); 20-99 (27); 100-999 (2); > 1,000 (1)
Time Period	2006 through 2015
Industries	Financial Services (13); Technology (17); Pharmaceuticals & Chemicals (7); Telecom & Communications (6); Logistics & Infrastructure (9); Natural Resources & Energy (4); Manufacturing (7); Retail (7); Professional Services (16); Public Services (5); Education (5); Healthcare (2); Tourism & Media (4)
Organization size (number of employees)	1-99 (21); 100-999 (21); 1,000-9,999 (20); > 10,000 (29)
Life cycle growth stage (Greiner Model)	Creativity/Start-up (13); Direction (15); Delegation (39); Coordination/Collaboration (35)
Region (of origin)	Europe (67); US/Canada (12); Middle East/Africa (6); United Kingdon (6); Asia (6); Latin America (2); Australia/New Zealand (3)
Ownership	Public shareholders (62); Private/family (24); Public services (9); Foundations/NGO (7)
Scope of Operations	Global (33); International (17); Regional (25); Local (27)

So, as you consider the following visual aids, numbers above 75 mean a strong or good perception, while 65 or below represents weak or poor perceptions as compared to similar governmental entities. Results between 66 and 74 indicate no particular leaning one way or another. It is important to remember that these are benchmarks established after evaluating the results from other governmental organizations in our population.

You should also notice a small square in the upper right of many of the boxes. This is important because the square indicates whether the average of the responses resulted from a wide range of responses or a narrow range. The darkest shading is a strongly held belief with little variation while lighter shading indicates that the belief varies widely among the group.

What you should be asking yourself as we explore the various visual aids is "If I were the boss, is this information that I could work with?" and "Now that I know this, what action should I take?"

The Performance Triangle Diagnostic Results

Beginning at the topmost, summary, level (see Figure 10.4) we can see the average of results from all 1,162 people which tells us a few important things about the underlying beliefs and possible organizational interferences that exist. We will explore the underlying perceptions within the various subgroups of the city organization further on, but this is the starting point.

Notice the 81 for success. This score indicates that the people in the organization have a clear vision of what needs to be done to be successful and the small square indicates that this perception of success is widely held with little variation. Moving around the Performance Triangle, culture, leadership, and systems are all between 66 and 74 indicating no particular leaning in any direction, which is common since the numbers represent the average of such a large group.

Looking at the connectors; purpose and collaboration are both in the mid-range but a 79 for relationships was a surprise given what was known about the events leading up to our engagement. However, notice that the small squares on relationships and purpose indicate a wide variety of perceptions. The wide range of the input for relationships indicates that some feel as if they have terrific and healthy relationships while others feel that it is a toxic environment. A similar interpretation applies to purpose where the input ranged from, we do not have a clue to we are highly committed to a higher purpose. Looking at dimensions that drive people performance, growth, innovation, and creativity, these are all below 64. These results indicate that the majority of these 1,162 people do not feel that they have opportunities to grow either personally or professionally and lack opportunities to use their talents to be innovative and creative. The small box in growth indicates that this is a strongly held belief with little variation.

Figure 10.4 – Summary of Top-Level Results

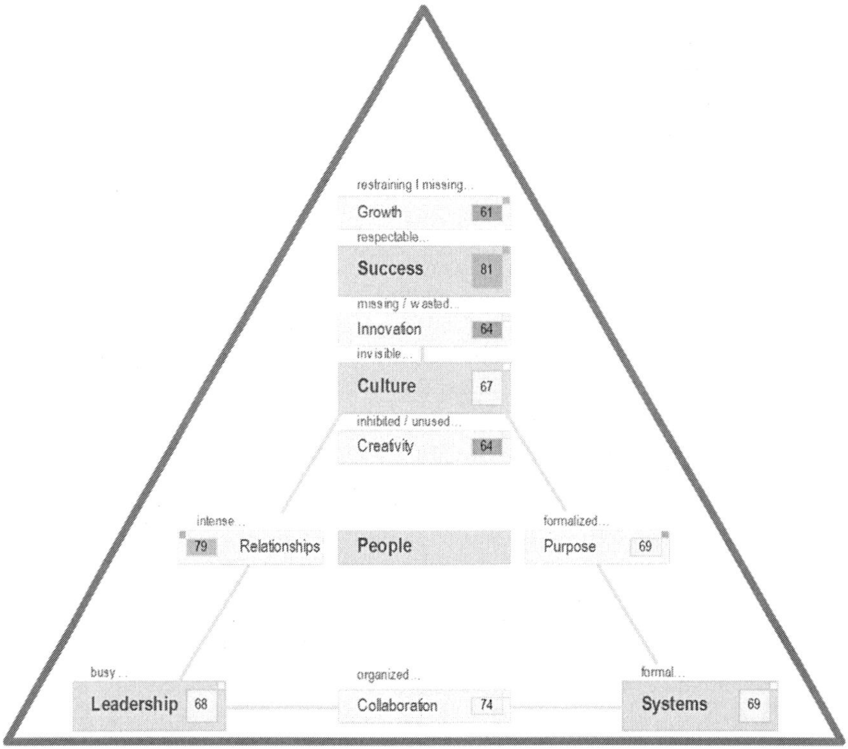

At this point, you should be thinking: "Wow! there are some real areas to work on and investigate more" followed closely by "What does my department look like?" if you were one of the department heads. Let us dig a little deeper. Remember that the objective is to provide insight into questions that stimulate more questions and introspective thinking to help managers understand some of those unseen and rarely discussed shared beliefs and assumptions. Our objective is NOT to TELL managers that their organization has problems but rather to present them with hard data that lead the managers to come to their own conclusions that help to generate their own corrective actions.

Success

With a score of 81 for success and a dark corner, the vast majority of these people believe that they know what is needed to be successful and they have the tools to do it. But let us drill down a little deeper.

Figure 10.5 – Measures of Success by Department

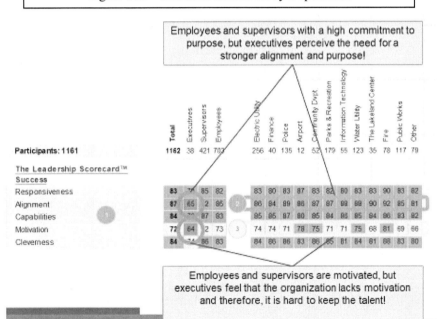

What we see in the deeper dive into measures of success in Figure 10.5. When we separate out the perceptions of the various department heads and the rest of the employees, there is a definite disconnect. We see that the executives believe that their people are not aligned in that they share common goals and beliefs on how to achieve those goals and that employees under their command are not motivated. The results for supervisors and employees indicate that people believe that they do share common goals and that they are already motivated to do their jobs well. Scanning across the various departments, employees' perceptions are fairly uniform and widespread across all of the city's operations.

Now put yourself in the position of the executives. How would you treat employees who you believe are not aligned to work toward common goals and are not motivated? The classically trained manager would work hard to force employees into alignment and motivate employees to give more and to go above and beyond the basic job description. The manager typically conducts meetings with pep talks, issues various "call to action" memos, establishes numerical goals including "stretch" goals, and more. Now put yourself in the position of the employees who work closely with their immediate workgroup where they routinely agree on common goals and then work collaboratively and diligently to achieve those objectives. How would the constant pressure from above to "do more" be perceived? How would the constant barrage of emails or pressure to achieve goals be perceived by a group of people who already feel as if they are highly motivated and going above and beyond? If you are like most people, the response goes something like this: "Oohh, not again. What more do they want from us?" Many times, the result is the exact opposite of what the manager intended as people say to themselves, "What the heck, no matter what I do, it is not enough" and morale along with intrinsic motivation declines. We have seen this situation in many organizations including the city in this case study. In this case, when presented with the data, the executives agreed that alignment and motivation were strengths, not weaknesses, which should be praised, celebrated, and leveraged for the benefit of the citizens of the city. Over the next year, several department heads introduced activities to identify and recognize individuals for their extraordinary efforts and shared these recognitions with the citizenry so that public perception was significantly enhanced.

"If you tell people where to go, but not how to get there, you'll be amazed at the results." **– Gen. George S. Patton**

The Angles of the Triangle: Systems, Leadership, and Culture

Let us look at the angles of the Performance Triangle: systems, leadership, and culture. The data in Figure 10.6 offer insight into what the executives, supervisors, and employees perceive as strengths and weaknesses among these dimensions that help to support a balanced and stable organization needed for superior performance.

The aggregate average of all 1,162 people (#1) does not tell us much since it is in the mid-range.... neither good nor bad. However, a deeper look at the details in Figure 10.6 exposes both strengths to be leveraged and weaknesses to be worked on.

> Figure 10.6 – Culture, Systems, and Leadership by Department

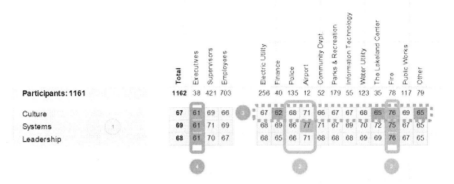

Participants: 1161	Total	Executives	Supervisors	Employees	Electric Utility	Finance	Police	Airport	Community Dept	Parks & Recreation	Information Technology	Water Utility	The Lakeland Center	Fire	Public Works	Other
	1162	38	421	703	256	40	135	12	52	179	55	123	35	78	117	79
Culture	67	61	69	66	67	62	68	71	66	67	67	68	65	76	69	65
Systems	69	61	71	69	68	69	66	77	71	67	69	70	72	75	67	65
Leadership	68	61	70	67	68	65	66	71	68	68	68	69	69	76	67	65

The natural tendency of most humans is to look for the bad or weaknesses. Let us start with the good in this case. We see that the fire department's rank and file employee perceptions in square #2 are all above 75. In our workshop with the executives, it became quickly apparent why this is the condition. The fire department is, in many ways, a quasi-military organization in which the immediate threat of danger creates a brotherhood where everyone looks out for each other. Every person must know his/her role, what systems are available for any situation, and what boundaries he or she must operate within. The fire chief and his immediate staff were clearly part of this brotherhood and had built an efficient, open, organization that encouraged individuals to be assertive when they needed to be. Looking more closely at the other square #2, we see a similar although not as strong perception among the rank and file. Since the police department had experienced a series of scandals over the previous couple of years, mid-range results in the police department were not a surprise. Actions that were initiated as a result of the realizations that came partially from this inquiry led to a significant reorganization within the department and the emergence of multiple communication channels that promoted productive dialogue as opposed to discussion and a significant turnaround over the next two years. Since operating an airport is also inherently dangerous, we see a similar pattern that is supported by high scores for systems in airport operations.

This would make sense since if the systems including processes and procedures break down, a disaster becomes likely.

In circle #3, which encompasses the culture of employees for all departments, the scores indicate pockets of opportunity. For the departments with low scores, the department heads were surprised with the negative sentiment. In our one-day workshop, department heads received the detailed results for their specific command which prompted questions upon questions as the leaders tried to reconcile the results with questions for understanding, intent, agenda, aspirations, and norms within the context of their organization and the people within it. As with all the senior departmental leaders, the search for understanding to answer the questions led to more questions followed by a lot of dialogue along the lines of "maybe this…. is going on" or "how can this be?" then "what can we do about it?" The thought process became virtually identical for all the executives as they dove into the details and related the data to what they knew about their organization and the people in it.

Now we come to grouping #4. What we see here again is a significant disconnect between the perceptions of the senior leaders and the rest of the organization. Given the long-running, very public, and highly critical local media environment, the low scores for all three dimensions for the executives were not much of a surprise. This should be, and quickly was, recognized as a significant virus that was infecting the senior ranks of the city leadership. Remember that while all questions dealt with the same construct, the questions given to the executives asked them to assess the operations and people under their command, and the questions given to the supervisors and employees on the same topic asked them to assess their immediate work group. Running down the list, these 38 leaders felt that within their organizations there is little uniformity or a weakly held understanding on what is to be done or what is needed to get there (culture); necessary information is not relevant or timely and people do not know what to do with it when they get information (systems); people do not sense what is going on around them, and they don't really understand their place in the overall operations and what they need to do to contribute to making the city better. Again, consider how these perceptions of subordinates would influence the behavior and management style of these senior leaders. As the department heads dove deeper into the results from their specific department, there were many comments along the lines of "I had a feeling, but this confirms it" or "I had no idea that people felt this way." By asking probing questions during individual meetings with senior department leadership groups, they arrived at their own conclusions that resulted in a laundry list of actions to either leverage the strengths to benefit the department and the services provided or address the viruses to make improvements.

"Today's problems come from yesterday's 'solutions'." – **Peter Senge**

The Sides of the Triangle: Purpose, Collaboration, and Relationships

Now, look at the sides of the Performance Triangle in Figure 10.7 to gain insight into how people perceive the strengths of their relationships and their ability to collaborate, and share a common higher purpose. These attributes give an organization resilience which means that it can absorb a shock or disruption without falling apart, become dysfunctional, and ineffective. In this case, two years of scandals combined with withering criticism from the local media and public outrage and anger at the entire leadership and management team of the city put resilience to a strong test. Resilient organizations typically exhibit a lot of high scores mixed in with some in the mid-range.

Figure 10.7 – Sides of the Triangle by Department

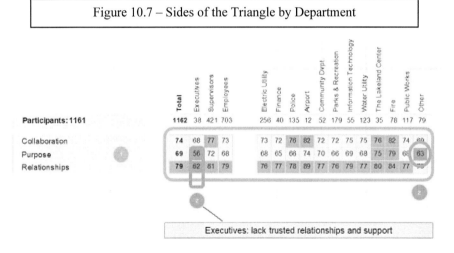

Executives: lack trusted relationships and support

What we see in the data in Figure 10.7 is a lot of high and mid-range scores with a few low score squares. This was a very positive sign which indicates that the city's operations are able to absorb shock and continue providing necessary and essential services to the citizens of the city. Not surprisingly, given the scandals and media pressure applied to the senior leadership, the executives have a negative view of their organizations. The media attention combined with a public records law which makes every meeting, email, text message, and phone conversation available for public scrutiny made the senior leadership team "gun shy" when dealing with anyone in their own organization or outsiders. The low scores for purpose and relationships were entirely understandable under the circumstances. However, during our discussion of this data at the one-day workshop, the executives were pleasantly surprised to find that their perceptions were not shared by the people under their command. This was a positive realization that enabled the department heads to formulate corrective action plans with a reasonable expectation that they would be well received or at least given a chance to succeed. In fact, while there were some significant changes to the management team, initiatives in virtually every department over the following two years brought about positive change that raised the service level of city operations as well as the image among citizens, and yes, even some of the media. The city had taken a series of gut punches and emerged stronger than ever, and the unseen reasons for this are readily visible by looking at the sides of the Performance Triangle … purpose, relationships, and collaboration, which were all strong.

The Center of the Triangle: Engaging People

Think back all the way to Chapter Seven where I explained how people provide the energy that powers the Performance Triangle dynamic system. Superior performance is achieved by creating an environment where people trust each other and can focus their creative energy on the things that matter and are needed to get things done. Figure 10.8 shows what the center of the triangle looked like with the results of all 1,162 people averaged.

I suspect your first response is "WOW… that is a LOT of low scores" followed by "we have a LOT of work to do." You would be right. What we see in the perceptions of these 1,162 people is that they are not aware of what is going on, they are not able to focus their energy on their tasks due to management interferences, they do not have freedom of choice to determine the best way to do their jobs, and they are not given opportunities to use their creative talents to make things better. If you look closely, you will notice the small dark square in the focus box. This indicates that the perception of management interfering with employees' ability to focus on their jobs is a tightly held belief. A whole lot of them feel the same way.

Figure 10.8 – The Center of the Triangle – People

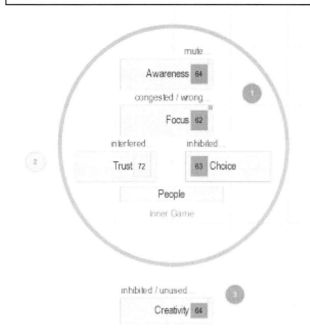

On the positive side, the department heads observed that there is a relatively high level of trust compared to the other elements. This is a good thing that can be built on and leveraged when initiatives designed to move all those low scores to the mid-range or high range are implemented. Let us dig a little deeper to see what we can learn from Figure 10.9. There may be more to this story that will help to provide insight on both weaknesses and strengths that can be leveraged to make improvements.

Figure 10.9 – The Center of the Triangle – People by Department

	Total	Executives	Supervisors	Employees		Electric Utility	Finance	Police	Airport	Community Dept	Parks & Recreation	Information Technology	Water Utility	The Lakeland Center	Fire	Public Works	Other
Participants: 1161	1162	38	421	703		256	40	135	12	52	179	55	123	35	78	117	79
People																	
Focus	62	72	63	62		58	65	60	67	69	60	52	62	64	68	61	63
Awareness	64	65	65	64		62	65	60	72	66	64	62	61	66	71	64	64
Trust	72	81	74	70		71	67	71	79	73	71	74	69	68	80	73	72
Choice	63	77	66	60		64	60	60	67	61	62	64	63	65	68	64	62
Creativity	64	72	68	61		66	61	61	66	68	64	65	64	60	71	63	63

Yes, there are a LOT of low scores across the board particularly among the employees (notice group #2). This view of the people elements of the Performance Triangle confirms that there is a high level of trust throughout the organization. The mid-range scores in #1 indicate that the senior leaders trust their subordinates and that subordinates trust the people in their work groups. Referring to earlier chapters, you should recall that trust is the single most powerful force either for or against knowledge sharing and change. Despite all the stress that the city operations were subjected to in the prior two years, the level of trust remained high throughout the city from top to bottom. This is an important strength that paid dividends in the subsequent year as the employees were involved in multiple changes that impacted operations at all levels, improving the service and image of the city operations.

Notice the high scores in #3 and the other relatively high scores for the perception of the executives for their commands. Here again, we see a disconnect but, in this case, it is the reverse of the prior views. The executive leaders seem to think that everything is great, and they are doing a great job creating an environment that enables their people to maximize their abilities. Clearly, the 1,123 people who work for the 38 department heads feel very differently. In our workshop with the department heads, this visual aid was received with a variety of responses from gasps to head banging. The initial emotional responses were quickly followed with "what in the world is going on?" The low scores in focus for both supervisors and employees got particular attention. "What are we doing to interfere with people being able to focus on their work?" was heard throughout the room. Multiple department chiefs included "focus groups" with supervisors on their laundry list of things to be done because of the diagnostic to gain insight in management interferences. During the following year, many departments conducted focus groups to invite honest feedback, and several leaders adopted more of a "management by wandering around" approach to gain an appreciation for how their management was having a negative effect on the mass of the people. Subsequently, many processes were changed or modified and improved dialogue (as opposed to discussion) between leadership and employees resulted in improved performance in many, if not most departments. We did not TELL the leaders what the problem was. We helped to interpret the data, and THEY realized the problem and developed their own plans of action.

The Leadership Scorecard

There are many other visual aids that we can, and do, use with clients to help them visualize the dynamic unseen and rarely discussed perceptions that permeate their organizations. In the case of this city, the many disconnects between what the 38 senior leaders perceived and the perceptions of the people under their command prompted us to present the Leadership Scorecard for consideration. As with everything else in the PTM, you will notice questions that represent the construct under evaluation. The Leadership Scorecard shown in Figure 10.10 only summarizes the responses of these 38 departments heads.

The first thing that jumps out on the Leadership Scorecard is all the high scores for the elements necessary for success (group #1) and understanding (group #2). These results indicate that the leadership team feels as if they have a clear understanding of what is needed to be successful and a shared understanding of what needs to be done. However, the low scores for agenda, aspirations, and norms (group #3) suggest that there is disagreement on HOW to get things done. Within this leadership team there is a lack of a shared agenda, widely differing views on the overarching purpose that drives their organization, and norms of behavior that are flexible or subject to interpretation. The groupings in #4 for systems and leadership are topics of deep dialogue and introspection. If you scan down the questions, you should ask yourself how effective this management team will be if they, for example, feel that the information systems and processes are weak and do not necessarily provide the information needed to make timely and effective decisions. Similarly, the leadership team indicates that

Figure 10.10 – The Leadership Scorecard
(38 executives only)

they are not strong on the elements that make up effective leadership. Given the scandals and negative media coverage along with the intense pressure from the citizenry over the prior two years, this is not necessarily a surprise. However, diagnostics from healthy leadership teams typically contain many boxes with high scores.

Now, observe grouping #5. Having performed several hundred diagnostics with organizations worldwide, it is possible to gain meaning from groupings or patterns within the data. What this pattern suggests is that we, the leadership team, believe that we have adequate rules and boundaries, and they are appropriate. However, there is not a clear understanding on the risks the organization is willing to take and that the norms of behavior are flexible. Taken as a whole, this grouping says that the leadership team has rules and knows what they are, but it is ok to bend the rules to advance or further your career or gain some advantage over a rival. In our presentation to the city commissioners, this interpretation was greeted with a powerful emotional response because it helped to explain some of the events from the preceding two years. It should be no surprise that in the year following our diagnostic process there were significant changes in the makeup of the leadership team including a new city manager who demonstrated a more communicative and collaborative management style than his predecessor. Among the changes implemented by the new city manager was a process of changing discussions to dialogue to help everyone involved gain insight into the real dynamics of the city operations. This was highly successful over the next six years.

"Never tell people how to do things. Tell them what to do and they will surprise you with their ingenuity." – **Gen. George S. Patton**

So, what have we learned?

Clearly, developing the dynamic capabilities of an agile organization is a complex task. The Performance Triangle Model offers a way to visualize some of the key elements that continuously interact to either promote or inhibit superior performance. All executives and business owners seek a superior performance and ways to gain a competitive advantage over their rivals. However, through time, unseen, unspoken, and rarely discussed interferences creep into the organization that prevent it from reaching its full potential. Executives need a tool that provides insight into those unseen viruses in order to be able to take focused corrective action. The diagnostic instrument is designed to provide numerically and statistically validated data of the strength of the many elements within the

Performance Triangle Model. Armed with this tool along with interpretation of the data from trained diagnostic mentors, executives may be able to target unseen viruses within their organizations for elimination.

Unlike the evolution of animal species, business executives do not have eons to bring about meaningful change. A few quarters or years (at best) are about as much time as the modern executive gets to demonstrate improvement. There is rarely time to try this approach or that approach and hope that something works. Investors are rarely that patient. The key is to build an organization that has the dynamic capabilities illustrated in the Performance Triangle Model imbedded into the DNA of the organization. In this way, the vast amount of tacit knowledge that exists in the organization can be harnessed and focused on finding and implementing innovative ways to meet any challenge. The ability of organizations to quickly adapt to and change with disruptions can be a competitive advantage and help executives develop the ambidextrous thinking needed to apply the strategies outlined by the Delta Model. We do not know what the future will bring so developing the dynamic capabilities needed to sense and then implement changes quickly is essential for virtually every business in the VUCA 21st century. The Performance Triangle Model and the associated diagnostic instrument offer a roadmap to help executives root out unseen viruses and design an agile organization built for the modern world.

Thinking Exercises

1. Refer to Figures 10.5 and 10.6. How do you think the discrepancy between what the senior executives perceive and what the people in the rest of the company perceive influences the management style of the executives and managers?
2. Refer to Figure 10.7. How effective do you think this organization is in harnessing the energy and tacit knowledge of the employees? Are the capabilities of the people being used effectively? Explain your reasoning.
3. Refer to Figures 10.8 and 10.9. In your own words, describe the perceptions of the people in this organization. How does the disconnect between the executives and the rest of the people affect performance and strategies? Explain your reasoning.
4. In your opinion, does this organization have the dynamic capabilities needed to be able to adapt and change rapidly in a VUCA world? Explain your reasoning.

5.   Using the organization that you work for or one that you know well, evaluate the strength of the various dimensions of the Performance Triangle as you perceive them. Are they complementary or do they interfere with performance? Explain your reasoning. What would you do differently if you had the authority to change anything?

Suggested Reading

Kotter, J. *Leading Change*. Boston, MA: Harvard University Press, 1996.

Michel, L. *The Performance Triangle: Diagnostic Mentoring to Manage Organizations and People for Superior Performance in Turbulent Times*. London, UK: LID Publishing Ltd., 2013.

Michel, L. *Management Design: Managing People and Organizations in Turbulent Times*. London, UK: LID Publishing Ltd., 2015.

Michel, L. *People-centric Management: How Managers use Four Levers to Bring Out Greatness of Others*. London, UK: LID Publishing Ltd., 2020.

Nold, H., & L. Michel. "Organizational Culture: A Systems Approach". In *21st Century Approaches to Management and Accounting Research*. London, UK: Intech, 2021. ISBN 978-1-83968-571-2.

NOTES

Chapter 1

1. See, David Russell Shilling, "Knowledge Doubling Every 12 Months, Soon to be Every 12 Hours", *Industry Tap*, April 19, 2013, http://www.industrytap.com/knowledge-doubling-every-12-months-soon-to-be-every-12-hours/3950.
2. Data compiled from two sources, Canalys.com Ltd. 2006-2007 and IDC.
3. See, Charles Arthur, "The History of Smartphones: Timeline", *The Guardian*, January 12, 2012, https://www.theguardian.com/technology/2012/jan/24/smartphones-timeline.
4. See, E. Schein, *Organizational Culture and Leadership* (San Francisco: Jossey-Bass, 1985), or any of several subsequent editions.
5. See, H. Nold & A. Hagelthorn, "Investigating Business and National Culture during Due-Diligence and its Impact on Multi-National Ventures," *Organizational Cultures: An International Journal* 16, no. 2 (2016): 1-19, http://ijmoc.cgpublisher.com/product/pub.258/prod.90, where 90% of the study participants responded that they recognized culture as a critical success factor in both the due diligence and implementation phases of a merger or acquisition yet fewer than 10% initiated actions specifically targeting cultural differences in either phase.
6. See, M. L. Marks, "The Merger Syndrome: The Human Side of Corporate Combinations," *Journal of Buyouts and Acquisitions* (January/February 1988): 18-23.
7. See, M. R. Czinkota, *Global Business* (Fort Worth, TX: Harcourt College, 1994).
8. See, J. Badrtalei & D. L. Bates, "Effect of Organizational Cultures on Mergers and Acquisitions: The Case of DaimlerChrysler," *International Journal of Management* 24, no. 2 (2007): 303-318.
9. See, D. R. Cooper & P. S. Schindler, *Business Research Methods*, rev. ed. (Boston, MA: Irwin, 2002).
10. W. Scott, "Developments in Organization Theory, 1960-1980: Trends in theoretical models, the existence of organizations, rational system explanations, natural system explanations, the characteristics of organizations, rational system explanations, natural system explanations, the diversity of organizations, rational system explanations, natural system explanations, future directions, notes references," *The American Behavioral Scientist (pre-1986)* 24, no. 3 (1981): 407-418.

11. W. Scott & G. Davis, *Organizations and Organizing: Rational, Natural, and Open System Perspectives* (Upper Saddle River, NJ: Pearson Prentice Hall, 2003).

12. D. Katz & R. Kahn, *The Social Psychology of Organizations* (Hoboken, NJ: John Wiley & Sons, Inc., 1978).

Chapter 2

1. T. Phillips, ed., *Roots of Strategy: The 5 Greatest Military Classics of All Time* (Harrisburg, PA: Stackpole Books, 1985). This book contains a clear and concise explanation of Sun Tzu's "The Art of War" along with other great military strategists all of which have philosophies that can be applied to modern business.
   The briefs contained in Chapter Two were compiled from the following sources.

2. J. Barney & W. Hesterly, *Strategic Management and Competitive Advantage: Concepts and Cases*, 4th ed. (Upper Saddle River, NJ: Pearson Prentice Hall, 2012).

3. F. David & F. David, *Strategic Management: Concept and Cases: A Competitive Advantage Approach*, 15th ed. (Upper Saddle River, NJ: Pearson Prentice Hall, 2015).

4. G. Dess, G. McNamara, & A. Eisner, *Strategic Management: Text and Cases*, 8th ed. (New York, NY: McGraw Hill, 2016).

5. H. Mintzberg, J. Lampel, J. Quinn, & S. Ghoshal, *The Strategy Process: Concepts, Contexts, Cases* (Upper Saddle River, NJ: Prentice Hall, 2003).

6. T. Wheelen & J. D. Hunger, *Strategic Management and Business Policy: Toward Global Sustainability* (Upper Saddle River, NJ: Pearson Prentice Hall, 2012).

7. M. Porter, *Competitive Advantage: Creating a Sustaining Superior Performance* (New York, NY: Free Press, 1985).

8. C. K. Prahalad & G. Hamel, (1990). "The Core Competence of the Corporation," *Harvard Business Review* (May-June, 1990): 79-91.

9. Ben Dobbin, "Kodak engineer had revolutionary idea: the first digital camera", *Seattle Post-Intelligencer*, September 8, 2005, retrieved on 2019-04-19, https://www.seattlepi.com/business/article/Kodak-engineer-had-revolutionary-idea-the-first-1182624.php.

10. I. Nonaka & H. Takeuchi, *The Knowledge-creating Company: How Japanese Companies Create the Dynamics of Innovation* (New York: Oxford University Press, 1995).

Chapter 3

1. I. Nonaka & H. Takeuchi, *The Knowledge-creating Company: How Japanese Companies Create the Dynamics of Innovation* (New York: Oxford University Press, 1995).

2. P. Drucker, "The New Productivity Challenge," *Harvard Business Review* (November-December 1991): 69-79.

3. P. Drucker, *Post-Capitalist Society* (Oxford, UK: Butterworth Heinemann, 1993).

4. For a clear and easily understood discussion of the conversion of data to knowledge see, T. Davenport & L. Prusak, *Working Knowledge: How Organizations Manage What They Know* (Boston, MA: Harvard Business School Press, 1998).

5. Ibid., page 5.

6. Ibid.

7. C. Argyris & D. Schön, *Organizational Learning* (Reading, MA: Addison-Wesley, 1978).

8. See, T. Phillips, ed., *Roots of Strategy: The 5 Greatest Military Classics of All Time* (Harrisburg, PA: Stackpole Books, 1985), or any of the many books that explore *The Art of War* for an in-depth description of the nine situations, each of which apply to the business world in some form if you use just a little imagination. Sun Tzu's descriptions: (1) When a chieftain is fighting in his own territory, it is dispersive ground; (2) When he has penetrated into hostile territory, but to no great distance, it is facile ground; (3) Ground whose possession imparts great advantage to either side, is contentious ground; (4) Ground which has liberty of movement on each side is open ground; (5) Ground which forms the key to three contiguous states... so that he who occupies it first has most of the Empire at his command; (6) When an army has penetrated into the heart of a hostile country, leaving a number of fortified cities in its rear, it is serious ground; (7) Mountains, forests, rugged steps, marshes and fens – all country that is hard to traverse: this is difficult ground; (8) Ground which is reached through narrow gorges, and from which we can only withdraw by tortuous paths, so that a small number of the enemy would suffice to crush a large body of our men: this is hemmed-in ground; (9) Ground on which we can only be saved from destruction by fighting without delay, is desperate ground.

9. M. Polanyi, *The Tacit Dimension* (London, UK: Routledge and Kegan Paul, 1966).

10. See, P. Robinson, dir., *Field of Dreams* (Universal Pictures, 1989).

11. Before the battle of Antietam unfolded, General George McClellan (Commander of the Army of the Potomac, North) received a copy of General Robert E. Lee's (commander of the Confederate Army of Northern Virginia, South) battle orders to his commanders that had been found wrapped around three cigars, yet decided to ignore this vital information leading to the bloodiest day in American military history. In the years since December 7, 1941, information has come to light that there was a wealth of information gathered by US intelligence agencies prior to the fateful surprise attack by Japan at Pearl Harbor that, if correctly interpreted, would have warned US military commanders of the impending attack and allowed the preparation of effective defenses.

12. M. Rennie, "Accounting for Knowledge Assets: Do we Need a New Financial Statement?" *International Journal of Technology Management* 18, no. 6 (1999): 648-659.

13. A. Hax & D. Wilde, *The Delta Project: Discovering New Sources of Profitability in a Networked Economy* (New York, NY: Palgrave, 2001).
14. A. Hax, *The Delta Model: Reinventing your Business Strategy* (New York, NY: Springer, 2010).
15. C. O'Reilly & M. Tushman, *Lead and Disrupt: How to Solve the Innovator's Dilemma* (Stanford, CA: Stanford University Press, 2016).
16. R. Agarwal & M. Gort, "The Evolution of Markets and Entry, Exit, and Survival of Firms," *Review of Economics and Statistics* 78 (1996): 489-498.
17. C. Stubbart & M. Knight, "The Case of the Disappearing Firms: Empirical Evidence and Implications," *Journal of Organizational Behavior* 27 (2006): 79-100.
18. R. Foster & S. Kaplan, *Creative Destruction* (New York, NY: Currency, 2001).
19. W. Bennis, cited in C. Kemp Jr., *Wisdom Honor and Hope: The Inner Path to True Greatness* (Franklin, TN: Wisdom Company, 2000): 207.
20. I. Nonaka, "A Dynamic Theory of Organizational Knowledge Creation," *Organization Science* 5, no. 1 (1994): 14-37.
21. I. Nonaka & N. Konno, "The Concept of 'Ba': Building a Foundation for Knowledge Creation," *California Management Review* 40, no. 3 (1998): 40-54.
22. G. Von Krogh, I. Ichijo, & I. Nonaka, *Enabling Knowledge Creation: How to Unlock the Mystery of Tacit Knowledge and Release the Power of Innovation* (New York: Oxford University Press, 2000).
23. R. Sabherwal, & I. Becarra-Fernandez, "An Empirical Study of the Effect of Knowledge Management Processes at Individual, Group, and Organizational Levels," *Decision Science* 34, no. 2 (2003): 225-261.
24. H. K. Mohajan, "Sharing Tacit Knowledge in Organizations: A Review," *American Journal of Computer Science and Engineering* 3, no. 2 (2016): 6-19. Retrieved from https://www.researchgate.net/publication/314062797.

Chapter 4

1. A. De Geus, "Planning and Learning," *Harvard Business Review* 66 (March/April 1988): 70-74.
2. P. Senge, *The Fifth Discipline: The Art and Practice of the Learning Organization* (New York, NY: Doubleday, 1990).
3. I. Nonaka, "A Dynamic Theory of Organizational Knowledge Creation," *Organization Science* 5, no. 1 (1994): 14-37.
4. I. Nonaka & N. Konno, "The Concept of "Ba": Building a Foundation for Knowledge Creation", *California Management Review* 40, no. 3 (1998): 40-54.
5. I. Nonaka & H. Takeuchi, *The Knowledge-creating Company: How Japanese Companies Create the Dynamics of Innovation* (New York, NY: Oxford University Press, 1995).
6. I. Nonaka & R. Toyama, "The Knowledge-creating Theory Revisited: Knowledge Creation as a Synthesizing Process," *Knowledge Management Research and Practice* 1, no. 1 (2003): 2-10.

7. I. Nonaka & R. Toyama, "The Theory of the Knowledge-creating Firm: Subjectivity, Objectivity and Synthesis," *Industrial and Corporate Change* 14, no. 3 (2005): 419-436.

8. I. Nonaka, R. Toyama, & P. Byosière, "A Theory of Organizational Knowledge Creation: Understanding the Dynamic Process of Creating Knowledge," in *Handbook of Organizational Learning and Knowledge,* eds. M. Dierkes, A. Antal, J. Child, and I. Nonaka (New York, NT: Oxford University Press, 2001).

9. I. Nonaka, R. Toyama, & A. Nagata, "A Firm as a Knowledge-creating Entity: A New Perspective on the Theory of the Firm," *Industrial and Corporate Change* 9, no. 1 (2000): 1-20.

10. I. Nonaka & G. von Krogh, "Tacit Knowledge and Knowledge Conversion: Controversy and Advancement in Organizational Knowledge Creation Theory," *Organization Science* 20, no. 3 (2009): 635-643.

11. H. Nold, "Using Knowledge Processes to Improve Performance and Promote Change: Continuous Loop Model and Cultural Enablers," *International Journal of Knowledge, Culture, and Change in Organizations: Annual Review* 12 (2013): 53-70.

12. D. Bumblauskas, H. Nold, P. Bumblauskas, & A. Igou, "Big Data Analytics: Transforming Data to Action," *Business Process Management Journal* 23, no. 3 (2017): 703-720.

13. A. Bharadwaj, "A Resource-based Perspective on Information Technology Capability and Firm Performance: An Empirical Investigation," *MIS Quarterly* 24, no. 1 (2000): 169-196.

14. I. Becarra-Fernandez, A. Gonzalez, & R. Sabherwal, *Knowledge Management: Challenges, Solutions and Technologies* (Upper Saddle River, NJ: Prentice Hall, 2004).

15. R. Sabherwal & I. Becarra-Fernandez, (2003). "An Empirical Study of the Effect of Knowledge Management Processes at Individual, Group, and Organizational Levels," *Decision Science* 34, no. 2 (2003): 225-261.

16. H. Nold, (2011). "Merging Knowledge Creation Theory with the Six Sigma Model for Improving Organizations: The Continuous Loop Model," *International Journal of Management* 28, no. 3 (2011): 469-477.

Chapter 5

1. L. Michel, *The Performance Triangle: Diagnostic Mentoring to Manage Organizations and People for Superior Performance in Turbulent Times* (London, UK: LID Publishing Ltd., 2013).

2. H. Nold, J. Anzengruber, M. Woelfle, & L. Michel, "Organizational Agility – Testing, Validity, and Reliability of a Diagnostic Instrument," *Journal of Organizational Psychology* 18, no. 3 (2018): 104-117.

3. H. Nold & L. Michel, "The Performance Triangle: A Model for Corporate Agility," *Leadership and Organizational Development Journal* 37, no. 3 (2016): 341-356, DOI: http://dx.doi.org/10.1108/LODJ-07-2014-0123.

4. E. Schein, *Organizational Culture and Leadership* (San Francisco: Jossey-Bass, 1985).

Edgar Schein is a former professor at the MIT Sloan School of Management and one of the most influential researchers and authors in the field of organizational development in many areas, including career development, group process consultation, and organizational culture. *Organizational Culture and Leadership* (1985) and its several subsequent revisions, as well as Schein's many other books and research papers, are fundamental sources in the field of organizational culture.

5.   G. Hofstede, B. Neuijen, D. Ohayv, & G. Sanders, "Measuring Organizational Cultures: A Qualitative and Quantitative Study across Twenty Cases," *Administrative Science Quarterly* 35 (1990): 286-316.

Geert Hofstede is a Dutch social psychologist, former IBM employee, and Professor Emeritus of Organizational Anthropology and International Management at Maastricht University in the Netherlands. He is primarily known for his pioneering research on cross-cultural groups and organizations. Hofstede's most famous work was in developing cultural dimension theory. Cultural dimension theory describes national cultures along six dimensions: Power Distance, Individualism, Uncertainty avoidance, Masculinity, Long Term Orientation, and Indulgence vs. restraint. He is known for his books *Culture's Consequences* and *Cultures and Organizations: Software of the Mind*, co-authored with his son Gert Jan Hofstede. The latter book deals with organizational culture, which is a different structure from national culture, but also has measurable dimensions, and the same research methodology is used for both.

6.   N. Ashkansay, C. Wilderom, & M. Peterson, *Organizational Culture and Climate*, 2nd ed. (Thousand Oaks, CA; Sage Publications, Inc., 2011).

7.   H. Nold & A. Hagelthorn, "Investigating Business and National Culture during Due-Diligence and its Impact on Multi-National Ventures," *Organizational Cultures: An International Journal* 16, no. 2 (2016): 1-19, http://ijmoc.cgpublisher.com/product/pub.258/prod.90.

8.   J. Hollmann, A. de Moura Carpes, & T. Beuron, "The DaimlerChrystler Merger: A Cultural Mismatch?" *Universidada Federal de Santa Maria – Brazil* 3, no. 3 (2010): 431-440, https://periodicos.ufsm.br/reaufsm/article/viewFile/2506/1536.

9.   R. Grube, "Der post-merger-integrationsprozess der DaimlerChrysler AG," in *Handbuch Mergers & Acquisitions Management*, ed. W. Wirtz, 757-783 (Wiesbaden, Germany: Springer-Verlag, 2006).

10. S. Finkelstein, *The DaimlerChrysler Merger* (Dartmouth University, Tuck School of Business, 2002).

11. The Association to Advance Collegiate Schools of Business, also known as AACSB International, is an American professional organization and arguably one of the most sought-after accreditations for business schools worldwide. The AACSB was founded in 1916 to provide accreditation to schools of business. It was formerly known as the American Association of Collegiate Schools of Business and as the International Association for Management Education. Not all members of the association are accredited, and the AACSB does not accredit

for-profit schools. In 2016 the AACSB lost recognition by the Council for Higher Education Accreditation.

12. L. Ilieş & D. Metz, "The Link between Organizational Culture and Organizational Performance – a Literature Review," *Managerial Challenges of the Contemporary Society* 10, no. 1 (2017): 35-40. Retrieved from https://search-ebscohost-com.contentproxy.phoenix.edu/login.aspx?direct =true&db=bth&AN=128134886&site=ehost-live&scope=site.

13. S. Sirikrai, *Measurement of Organizational Culture: A Literature Review*, 2006, www.jba.tbs.tu.ac.th/files/Jba109/Article/JBA109Sajee.pdf

14. J. Taylor, "Organizational Culture and the Paradox of Performance Management," *Public Performance and Management Review* 38, no. 1 (2014): 7-22, https://doi-org.contentproxy.phoenix.edu/10.2753/PMR1530-9576380101.

15. H. Nold, "Linking Knowledge Processes with Firm Performance: Organizational Culture," *Journal of Intellectual Capital* 13, no. 1 (2012): 16-38, https://doi.org/10.1108/14691931211196196. (2013 Outstanding Paper Award, Emerald Literati Network).

16. T. B. Whalen, "Utilizing the Social Transaction Theory of Social Ontology to Understand Organizational Culture Change," *Journal of Business and Economics Research (Online)* 12, no. 1 (2014): 37-n/a. Retrieved from https://search-proquest-com.contentproxy.phoenix.edu/ docview/1477975247?accountid=35812.

17. D. Walonick, "General Systems Theory" (essay) 1993, https://statpac.org/walonick/systems-theory.htm.

18. D. McNeill & Freiberger *Fuzzy Logic* (New York, NY: Simon & Schuster, 1993).

19. A. Kuhn, *The Logic of Social Systems* (San Francisco, CA: Jossey-Bass, 1974).

Chapter 6

1. L. Michel, *The Performance Triangle: Diagnostic Mentoring to Manage Organizations and People for Superior Performance in Turbulent Times* (London, UK: LID Publishing Ltd., 2013).

2. H. Nold & L. Michel, "The Performance Triangle: A Model for Corporate Agility," *Leadership and Organizational Development Journal* 37, no. 3 (2016): 341-356, DOI: http://dx.doi.org/10.1108/LODJ-07-2014-0123.

3. For the third time since 2008, the Agility Insights team of Lukas Michel, Guido Bosbach, and Herb Nold conducted a survey on the design of management with the same structure, questions and content. The 2017/18 survey included 220 companies across many sectors, many sizes, and many types of companies from around the globe. Participants were senior executives who responded to a standardized online survey with 33 questions on agile capabilities and demographic information of their organizations.

Half of the questions relate to the maturity of the agile concepts and their application in the design of their organizations and management. Maturity levels are reported as scores with 0 as lowest maturity and 100 as highest maturity. Scores below 62 indicate low maturity, while scores between 62 and

68 indicate medium maturity, and scores above 68 indicate high maturity. Organizations with high scores are already fairly advanced in implementing agile management concepts relative to other, similar organizations. The second half of the questions reviewed the external and internal contexts that determine much of the agile design.

This report offers insights from the 2017/18 survey and compares the results with our surveys from 2008 and 2013. For participants in previous studies, this report adds comparative information to their individual organizations.

In particular, we looked at the standards, maturity levels, capability profiles, patterns, models, decision options, and paths of organizations with attributes of agile designs in the organization and management design. The 2017/18 survey can be downloaded in its entirety at https://agilityinsights.net/en/resources/global-study.

4.   H. Nold, J. Anzengruber, M. Woelfle, & L. Michel, "Organizational Agility – Testing, Validity, and Reliability of a Diagnostic Instrument," *Journal of Organizational Psychology* 18, no. 3 (2018): 104-117.

5.   T. Ohno, *Toyota Production System: Beyond Large Scale Production* (Portland, OR: Productivity, Inc., 1988).

6.   A. P. Sloan, *My Years with General Motors* (Garden City, NY: Doubleday, 1964).

7.   International Organization of Motor Vehicle Manufacturers (OICA). World Ranking of Manufacturers, 2017, http://www.oica.net/wp-content/uploads/World-Ranking-of-Manufacturers-1.pdf.

8.   T. Howerton, "Most Big Companies are Dying, While Some Have Found the Fountain of Youth," Forbes Blog, 2017, https://www.forbes.com/sites/terryhowerton/2017/04/18/most-big-companies-are-dying-while-some-have-found-the-fountain-of-youth/#492dfa6a17aa.

Chapter 7

1.   L. Michel, *The Performance Triangle: Diagnostic Mentoring to Manage Organizations and People for Superior Performance in Turbulent Times* (London, UK: LID Publishing Ltd., 2013).

2.   H. Nold & L. Michel, "The Performance Triangle: A Model for Corporate Agility," *Leadership and Organizational Development Journal* 37, no. 3 (2016): 341-356, DOI: http://dx.doi.org/10.1108/LODJ-07-2014-0123.

3.   Fredrick Winslow Taylor (1856-1915) was an American mechanical engineer who sought to improve industrial efficiency. He was one of the first management consultants. Taylor was one of the intellectual leaders of the Efficiency Movement, and his ideas, broadly conceived, were highly influential in the early industrial era (1890s-1920s). Taylor summed up his efficiency techniques in his book *The Principles of Scientific Management* (1901) which the Fellows of the Academy of Management voted as the most influential management book of the twentieth century in 2001. His pioneering work in applying engineering principles to the work done on the factory floor was

instrumental in the creation and development of the branch of engineering that is now known as industrial engineering. Taylor made his name, and was most proud of his work, in scientific management; however, he made his fortune patenting steel-process improvements. Taylor was also an athlete who competed nationally in tennis.

4. P. Senge & J. Sterman, "Systems Thinking and Organizational Learning: Acting Locally and Thinking Globally in the Organization of the Future," *European Journal of Operational Research* 59, no. 1 (1992): 137-150, DOI: 10.1016/0377-2217(92)90011-W.

5. M. Weber, *Economy and Society* (Oakland, CA: University of California Press, 1987).

6. Maximilian Weber (1864-1920) was a German sociologist, philosopher, jurist, and political economist. His ideas profoundly influenced social theory and social research, and he is often credited, with Émile Durkheim and Karl Marx, as being among the three founders of sociology. Weber's main intellectual concern was understanding the processes of rationalization, secularization, and "disenchantment" that he associated with the rise of capitalism in the modern world. He saw these as the result of a new way of thinking about the world. Weber is best known for his thesis combining economic sociology and the sociology of religion, elaborated in his book *The Protestant Ethic and the Spirit of Capitalism*, in which he proposed that Protestantism was one of the major philosophies associated with the rise in the Western world of market-driven capitalism and the rational-legal nation-state. He argued that it was the basic teachings of Protestantism that justified and boosted capitalism. Thus, it can be said that the spirit of capitalism is inherent to Protestant religious values. Weber emphasized the importance of cultural influences embedded in religion as a means for understanding the beginnings of capitalism. Weber was also the first to categorize social authority into distinct forms, which he labelled as charismatic, traditional, and rational-legal. His analysis of bureaucracy emphasized that modern institutions are increasingly based on rational-legal authority. Weber also made a variety of other contributions in economic history, as well as economic theory and methodology. After the First World War, Max Weber was among the founders of the liberal German Democratic Party. He also ran unsuccessfully for a seat in parliament and served as advisor to the committee that drafted the ill-fated democratic Weimar Constitution of 1919. *Wirtschaft und Gesellschaft* (*Economy and Society*) was published in 1922 by Weber's wife after he contracting Spanish flu and died of pneumonia in 1920, aged 56.

7. R. Likert, *New Patterns of Management* (New York, NY: McGraw-Hill, 1961).

8. T. Waters & D. Waters, *Weber's Rationalism and Modern Society* (New York, NY: Palgrave Macmillan, 2015).

9. Mayo, E. *The Social Problems of an Industrial Civilization* (London: Routledge & Kegan Paul, [1949] 1975).

10. George Elton Mayo (1880-1949) was an Australian born psychologist, industrial researcher, and organizational theorist. Mayo was formally trained at the University of Adelaide in Australia, acquiring a Bachelor of Arts Degree,

graduating with First Class Honors, and majoring in philosophy and psychology, and was later awarded an honorary Master of Arts Degree from the University of Queensland. While in Queensland, Mayo served on the University's war committee and pioneered research into the psychoanalytic treatment of shellshock. As a psychologist Mayo often helped soldiers returning from World War I to recover from the stresses of war and with a Brisbane physician, pioneered the psychoanalytic treatment of shellshock and conducted psycho-pathological tests on what we today know as post-traumatic stress syndrome (PTSD). He was a lecturer in psychology and mental philosophy at the University of Queensland between 1911 and 1922, when he sailed to the United States. In 1926 he was appointed to the Harvard Business School as a professor of industrial research. In Philadelphia he conducted research at a textile plant to develop a method to reduce the very high rate of turnover in the plant known as the Hawthorne Studies. Mayo's association with the Hawthorne studies as well as his research and work in Australia led to his enjoying a public acclaim granted to few social scientists of his day. Mayo has been credited with making significant contributions to several disciplines, including business management, industrial sociology, philosophy, and social psychology. His research in industry had a significant impact on industrial and organizational psychology. Mayo is widely credited for having established the scientific study of what today is called organizational behavior where he gave close attention to the human, social, and political problems of industrial civilization.

Mayo's work helped to lay the foundation for the human relations movement in the second half of the 20th century. He emphasized that alongside the formal organization of an industrial workplace there exists an informal organizational structure as well. Mayo recognized the inherent inadequacies of existing scientific management approaches in industrial organizations and underlined the importance of relationships among people who work for such organizations. His ideas on group relations were advanced in his 1933 book *The Human Problems of an Industrialized Civilization*, which was based partly on his Hawthorne research.

11. A. H. Maslow, "A Theory of Human Motivation," *Psychological Review* 50, no. 4 (1943): 370-96.

12. A. H. Maslow, *Motivation and Personality* (New York: Harper and Row, 1954).

13. F. Herzberg, B. Mausner, & B. Snyderman, *The Motivation to Work*, 2nd ed. (New York: John Wiley, 1959), ISBN 0471373893.

14. F. Herzberg, "The Motivation-Hygiene Concept and Problems of Manpower," *Personnel Administration* 27 (January-February 1964): 3-7.

15. V. Hattangadi, "Theory X and Theory Y," *International Journal of Recent Research Aspects* 2 (December 2015): 20-21.

16. E. Fischer, "Motivation and Leadership in Social Work Management: A Review of Theories and Related Studies," *Administration in Social Work* (2009): 356.

17. C. Carson, "A Historical View of Douglas McGregor's Theory Y," *Journal of Management Decision* 43, no. 3 (2018): 450-460,

doi:10.1108/00251740510589814.

18. P. Drucker, *The Practice of Management* (New York, NY: Harper, 1954).

19. C. Mio, A. Venturelli, & R. Leopizzi, (2015). "Management by Objectives and Corporate Social Responsibility Disclosure: First Results from Italy," *Accounting and Auditing Accountability Journal* 28, no. 3 (2015): 325-364, doi:10.1108/AAAJ-09-2013-1480.

20. R. Kaplan & D. Norton, *The Balanced Scorecard: Translating Strategy into Action* (Boston MA: Harvard Business School Press, 1996), ISBN 978-0-87584-651-4.

21. H. Nold, "Linking Knowledge Processes with Firm Performance: Organizational Culture," *Journal of Intellectual Capital* 13, no. 1 (2012): 16-38, https://doi.org/10.1108/14691931211196196 (2013 Outstanding Paper Award, Emerald Literati Network).

22. H. Nold, "Using Knowledge Processes to Improve Performance and Promote Change: Continuous Loop Model and Cultural Enablers," *International Journal of Knowledge, Culture, and Change in Organizations: Annual Review* 12 (2013): 53-70 (International Award for Excellence, Best Paper for 2012, Common Ground Publishing).

Chapter 8

1. L. Michel, *The Performance Triangle: Diagnostic Mentoring to Manage Organizations and People for Superior Performance in Turbulent Times* (London, UK: LID Publishing Ltd., 2013).

2. H. Nold & L. Michel, "The Performance Triangle: A Model for Corporate Agility," *Leadership and Organizational Development Journal* 37, no. 3 (2016): 341-356, DOI: http://dx.doi.org/10.1108/LODJ-07-2014-0123.

3. C. Argyris and D. Schön, (1974) *Theory in Practice: Increasing Professional Effectiveness* (San Francisco: Jossey-Bass, 1974).

4. R. Simons, *Levers of Organizational Design: How Managers use Accountability Systems for Greater Performance and Commitment* (Cambridge, MA: Harvard Business School Press, 2005).

5. K. Bijlsma-Frankema & A. Costa, "Consequences and Antecedents of Managerial and Employee Legitimacy Interpretations of Control: A Natural Open Systems Approach," in *Organizational Control,* eds. S. Sitkin, L. Cardinal, & K. Bijlsma-Frankema, 2010 (S. 396-433).

6. G. Klein, *Streetlight and Shadows* (Cambridge, MA: MIT, 2009).

7. R. Kaplan & D. Norton, *The Balanced Scorecard: Translating Strategy into Action* (Boston, MA: Harvard Business School Press, 1996).

8. A. Neely, C. Adams, & M. Kennerley, *The Performance Prism: The Scorecard for Measuring and Managing Business Success* (London: Pearson Education I Financial Times Prentice Hall, 2002).

9. A. Hax & D. Wilde II, *The Delta Model, Discovering New Sources of Profitability in a Networked Economy* (New York, NY: Palgrave, 2001).

10. J. Pfeffer & R. Sutton, *Hard facts, Dangerous Half-truths, and Total Nonsense: Profiting from Evidenced-based Management* (Boston, MA: Harvard Business School Press, 2006).
11. E. Williams III, *Civil War Trivia* (Nashville, TN: Premium Press America, 2008).
12. M. Van Alstyne, "Create Colleagues, not Competitors," *Harvard Business Review* (September 2005): S. 24.
13. G. Miller, "The Magic Number Seven, Plus or Minus Two," *The Psychology Review* 36, no. 2 (1956): 81-97.
14. J. Pfeffer, "Six Dangerous Myths About Pay," *Harvard Business Review* (May-June 1998): 109-119.
15. H. Nold, "Linking Knowledge Processes with Firm Performance: Organizational Culture," *Journal of Intellectual Capital* 13, no. 1 (2012): 16-38, https://doi.org/10.1108/14691931211196196 (2013 Outstanding Paper Award, Emerald Literati Network).
16. H. Nold, "Using Knowledge Processes to Improve Performance and Promote Change: Continuous Loop Model and Cultural Enablers," *International Journal of Knowledge, Culture, and Change in Organizations: Annual Review* 12 (2013): 53-70 (International Award for Excellence, Best Paper for 2012, Common Ground Publishing).
17. L. Michel, "Enable Tomorrow's Decisions," *Perspectives on Performance* (January 2008): 14-16.
18. I., Nonaka & H. Takeuchi, *The Knowledge-creating Company: How Japanese Companies Create the Dynamics of Innovation* (New York: Oxford University Press, 1995).
19. I. Nonaka & N. Konno, "The Concept of 'Ba': Building a Foundation for Knowledge Creation," *California Management Review* 40, no. 3 (1998): 40-54.
20. E. Schein, *Organizational Culture and Leadership,* 4th ed. (San Francisco, CA: Jossey-Bass, 2010).
21. J. P. Kotter & J. L. Heskett, *Corporate Culture and Performance* (New York, NY: Free Press, 1992).

Chapter 9

1. L. Michel, *The Performance Triangle: Diagnostic Mentoring to Manage Organizations and People for Superior Performance in Turbulent Times* (London, UK: LID Publishing Ltd., 2013).
2. H. Nold & L. Michel, "The Performance Triangle: A Model for Corporate Agility," *Leadership and Organizational Development Journal* 37, no. 3 (2016): 341-356, DOI: http://dx.doi.org/10.1108/LODJ-07-2014-0123.
3. C. Argyris and D. Schön, *Theory in Practice: Increasing Professional Effectiveness* (San Francisco: Jossey-Bass, 1974).
4. J. Habermas, *Morality and Communicative Action* (Suhrkamp-Verlag, Frankfurt, 1988).

5. W. Kahn, "Psychological conditions of personal engagement and disengagement at work," *The Academy of Management Journal* 33, no. 4 (1990): 692-724.
6. K. Weick, *Making Sense of the Organization* (Hoboken, NJ: Wiley-Blackwell Press, 2000), ISBN: 978-0-631-22319-1.
7. F. Herzberg, "Workers' Needs: The Same Around the World," *Industry Week*, September 21, 1987.
8. E. Schein, *Organizational Culture and Leadership,* 4th ed. (San Francisco, CA: Jossey-Bass, 2010).
9. G. Miller, *Managerial Dilemmas: The Political Economy of Hierarchy* (Cambridge, UK: Cambridge University Press, 1992).
10. B. Frey & M. Osterloh, *Successful Management by Motivation: Balancing Intrinsic and Extrinsic Incentives* (New York, NY: Springer, 2002).
11. E. Deci & R. Ryan, "The "What" and the "Why" of Global Pursuits: Human Needs and the Self-determination of Behavior," *Psychological Inquiry* 11 (2000): 227-268.
12. R. Baumeister & M. Leary, "The need to Belong: Desire for Interpersonal Attachments as a Fundamental Human Motivation," *Psychological Bulletin* 117 (1995): 497-529.
13. J. Conger & R. Kanungo, "The Empowerment Process: Integrating Theory and Practice," *Academy of Management Review* 13, no. 3 (1988): 471-482.
14. G. Spreitzer, K. Sutcliff, J. Dutton, S. Soneshein, & A. Grant, "A Socially Embedded Model of Thriving at Work," *Organization Science* 16, no. 5 (2005): 537-549.
15. H. Nold, (2013) "Using Knowledge Processes to Improve Performance and Promote Change: Continuous Loop Model and Cultural Enablers," *International Journal of Knowledge, Culture, and Change in Organizations: Annual Review* 12 (2013): 53-70 (International Award for Excellence, Best Paper for 2012, Common Ground Publishing).
16. https://www.greatplacetowork.com/our-methodology.
17. H. Nold, "Linking Knowledge Processes with Firm Performance: Organizational Culture," *Journal of Intellectual Capital* 13, no. 1 (2012): 16-38, https://doi.org/10.1108/14691931211196196 (2013 Outstanding Paper Award, Emerald Literati Network).

Chapter 10

1. E. Schein, *Organizational Culture and Leadership*, 4th ed. (San Francisco, CA: Jossey-Bass, 2010).
2. I. Nonaka and H. Takeuchi, *The Knowledge-creating company: How Japanese Companies Create the Dynamics of Innovation* (Oxford University Press, New York, NY, 1995).
3. https://www.greatplacetowork.com/our-methodology.
4. H. Nold, "Linking Knowledge processes with Firm Performance: Organizational Culture," *Journal of Intellectual Capital* 13, no. 1 (2012): 16-38, https://doi.org/10.1108/14691931211196196

(2013 Outstanding Paper Award, Emerald Literati Network).

5. H. Nold, "Using Knowledge Processes to Improve Performance and Promote Change: Continuous Loop Model and Cultural Enablers," *International Journal of Knowledge, Culture, and Change in Organizations: Annual Review* 12 (2013): 53-70 (International Award for Excellence, Best Paper for 2012, Common Ground Publishing).

6. L. Michel, *The Performance Triangle: Diagnostic Mentoring to Manage Organizations and People for Superior Performance in Turbulent Times* (London, UK: LID Publishing Ltd., 2013).

7. H. Nold & L. Michel, (2016). "The Performance Triangle: A Model for Corporate Agility," *Leadership and Organizational Development Journal* 37, no. 3 (2016): 341-356, DOI: http://dx.doi.org/10.1108/LODJ-07-2014-0123.

8. T. Gallwey, *The Inner Game of Work: Focus, Learning, Pleasure, and Mobility in the Workplace* (New York, NY: Random House, 2000).

9. J. Whitmore & T. Gallwey, "What is the Inner Game? John Whitmore and Tim Gallwey in Conversation," *Coaching at Work Limited* 5 (2010): 36-37.

10. M. Csikszentmihalyi, "Finding Flow," *Psychology Today* 30 (1997): 46-48.

11. B. LaRue, P. Childs, & K. Larson, *Leading Organizations from the Inside Out: Unleashing the Collaborative Genius of Action-learning Teams* (Hoboken, NJ: John Wiley & Sons, 2006).

12. L. Haneberg, "Training for Agility," *T+D* 65, no. 9 (2011): 50-55.

13. M. Hugos, *Business Agility, Sustainable Prosperity in a Relentlessly Competitive World* (Upper Saddle River, NJ: John-Wiley, 2009).

14. D. Ulrich & N. Smallwood, *Why the Bottom Line isn't: How to Build Value Through People and Organization* (Upper Saddle River, NJ: John Wiley & Sons, 2003).

15. G. von Krogh, K. Ichijo, & I. Nonaka, *Enabling Knowledge Creation, How to Unlock the Mystery of Tacit Knowledge and Release the Power of Innovation* (Oxford, UK: Oxford University Press, 2000).

16. E. Beinhocker, "Robust Adaptive Strategies," *Sloan Management Review* 40, no. 3 (1999): 95-106.

17. D. Deevy, *Creating the Resilient Organization* (Englewood Cliffs, NJ: Prentice Hall, 1995).

18. Y. Doz & O. Baburoglu, "From Competition to Collaboration: The Emergence and Evolution of R&D Cooperatives," in *Cooperative Strategy: Economics, Business and Organizational Issues,* eds. D. Faulkner & M. de Rond (173-192) (New York, NY: Oxford University Press, 2000).

19. M. Alpaslan & I. Mitroff, "Bounded Morality: The Relationship Between Ethical Orientation and Crisis Management, Before and After 9/11," in *Current Topics in Management*, eds. M. Rahim, K. Mackenzie & R. Golembiewski (13-43) (Stanford, CT: JAI Press, 2004).

20. H. Nold, J. Anzengruber, M. Woelfle, & L. Michel, "Organizational Agility – Testing, Validity, and Reliability of a Diagnostic Instrument," *Journal of Organizational Psychology* 18, no. 3 (2018): 104-117.